06/10

Blazing Saddles

The Cruel & Unusual
History of the
Tour de France

Matt Rendell

VELO press

Contents

Prologue, or 'The Sporting Bumblebee'

1 July 1903, 3 a.m. One summer morning in the middle of the night, a random selection of homburgs, berets, tam-o'-shanters, deerstalkers, drainpipes, plus-fours, long shorts and short ones gathered outside a bar south of Paris, appropriately named 'The Alarm Clock'. Swaddled in extra clothes against the cold, and with every available pocket, pouch and opening stuffed with food, tools and spare parts, the riders set off along the rubble corridors that passed for roads, fighting more for survival than speed – victory to the last man standing.

As well as inner tubes twisted into figures-of-eight across their shoulders in anticipation of the collarbone breaks many would suffer during the ordeal, the riders wore long sleeves, knee-length socks, and moustaches modelled on the handlebars beneath them. What rules there were stated the obvious: article five read 'Bicycles of all types will be admitted, provided they are propelled solely by muscular force.' The most important rule wasn't written down at all: it was that the organisers could make any rule change they liked, at any time, and impose it on the racers.

A century on much has changed, but plenty of the old Tour remains. For the humblest water-carriers, it's still all about survival, although the stars can amass enormous fortunes. And, for everyone concerned, it's still about speed – although these days, that also means steroids, growth hormone, blood transfusions, EPO, the occasional bribe, not to mention endless, inconclusive investigations through the courts or in the media. In short, the Tour is a typical manifestation of contemporary sport, with all its chemical, judicial and extra-sporting paraphernalia. Perhaps not typical: the Tour de France has no permanent infrastructure or fixed installations, other than France itself. Perhaps it was the very gauntness of this skeletal structure that allowed it to take everything the twentieth century could throw at it, and emerge intact, like a miraculous oak tree or outhouse untouched by a blitz that has razed the surrounding city to the ground.

A whiff of the apocalypse has always hung over the Tour. The 1904 edition was so blighted by cheating that its founder Henri Desgrange announced it would be 'the last Tour'. Much the same was said in 1967, 1998 and 2006 – not, strictly speaking, the first Tour to see its winner test positive in an anti-doping test (Pedro Delgado had that honour, or dishonour – or didn't have it, depending on your point of view – in 1988). In 2006, for once, there was no confusion over the illegality of the product concerned – which was a break with tradition, because confusion and illegality have been woven into the fabric of the Tour. Frame builders, component manufacturers and the riders themselves have always dreamed of weightlessness, so it's hardly surprising some of the latter have tended to dispense with the excess baggage of a conscience. In 1904, a rider named Chevalier – his forename has been lost – finished third in stage one after using a method of performance-enhancement with no equal even today: a car. The following year, it was estimated that 125 kilos of tin-tacks had been strewn across the roads: the favoured rider made the early break, and his followers booby-trapped the road ahead of his pursuers. And to think it took British intelligence half a century to fit James Bond's Aston Martin with a nail dispenser. In 1906, Maurice Carrère, Henri Gauban and Gaston Tuvache availed themselves of a passing train. However dastardly our contemporaries may be, they can't even approach such epic standards of dishonesty. The closest that pantomime prince of performance enhancement Richard Virenque ever came was to ask a TV helicopter pilot to fly behind him during a time-trial and carry him along with the downdraught. Small beer, you might say, if the bottles of cold beer lined up beside the road during a stage held in oppressive heat hadn't achieved their dastardly

Bernard Gaulthier grabs a malted barley, hops and yeast
sports rehydration package during the 1950 Tour de France.

goal in 1935: a truce to imbibe them allowed Julien Moineau – whose associates were responsible for the ale – to ride away and reach Bordeaux fifteen minutes ahead of the peloton. Lance Armstrong would never have fallen for it.

Most sports seem to work, in part, by demanding a set of obviously contradictory skills – footballers run using one set of super-developed thigh muscles, and kick the ball using a different and opposing set; boxing requires perfectly calibrated blows and razor-sharp reactions, delivered by a brain that's taking a pummelling. The cyclist has to school his heart in steady-state output over hours and hours, yet races are decided by sudden, darting accelerations. The rare physiques that can stand up to such wildly conflicting demands are centaur-like: a Tour de France winner must be capable of time-trialling, climbing and sprinting, and also be lucid, calculating and unflappable. A fair few, we may be forgiven for supposing, have also had to be doped, not just to the nines, but halfway to the roaring forties.

These days, there are still inoffensive shoves from team cars and extended drafts behind them, but the glass of brandy against the cold is a thing of the past. Modern performance enhancement means mobile hospitals, blood transfusions and genetically engineered copies of human hormones – procedures that can fool anti-doping tests and cost small fortunes. 'The drugs were for my dog/mother-in-law', 'I'm the chimeric brother of an unborn twin', 'Don't treat me like a criminal by asking for a DNA test to prove my innocence': the surreal poetry of the Tour has no end. In the old days, the accomplices were practical jokers, and the cheating was obvious. Today, they're mad scientists, raving doctors, two-faced team staff, lawyers with no concept of right and wrong, authorities like headless chickens, and riders with forked tongues. They're part of a long tradition, whose longevity runs against all reasonable expectation. Every known theory would suggest the Tour, like the bumblebee, should never get off the ground. But the French have a saying that could have been invented for the Tour: 'Theory's all very well, but it can't stop things existing'. A lesser event would never have survived.

Paradoxically, this longest of sporting events, with so much time for terrible losses of form and miraculous recoveries, can also be one of the most predictable. Why, then, despite its interminable length, its sometimes unbearable tedium, and the scandals that accompany the race year after year, does the French public love the Tour? And – despite the famous *Daily Mirror* headline in 1974, when the Tour visited England for the first time: 'Can forty million Frenchmen be wrong?' – not just the French?

Doubtless, if doping and traffic jams were all there is to it, there'd be no Tour de France. Going back to 1903, and those entrants who looked more like nineteenth-century Arctic explorers than today's elite athletes, what was it all about? And what does the Tour hand down, year by year, like a shock wave? Does the answer lie in history? After all, when the Tour was created, France was reeling from years of dislocating forces. Between 1789 and 1914, it staggered through the Revolutionary Terror, two empires, a monarchy, two short-lived republics, a third that stood on the edge of the precipice for years, the siege of Paris, defeat in the 1870 Franco-Prussian War and the loss of Alsace-Lorraine, the Paris Commune and the 'week of blood' that followed it, and then the Dreyfus affair, which revealed the depth of racist bigotry in an otherwise civilised country. Over barricades or in government-backed intrigues, Frenchmen had been killing Frenchmen for more than a century. In 1903, the wounds were still wide open.

Given all this, is it too much to suspect that the protective circle the Tour drew around France provided a metaphor for keeping the nation whole? In the 1920s and 1930s, the Tour soothed more anxious souls than the Maginot Line ever would. Ancient history, some will say – although the hand-crafted, modern racing bike, like the hand-crafted mechanical watch, betrays our sense of nostalgia for an age that has passed.

Yet the Tour isn't backward looking. Its physical demands may drive body and mind to breaking point, but these days they do so on technology imported from Formula One and the aerospace industry, and timed to the thousandth of a second. More than a century ago, Géo Lefèvre complained he couldn't catch the racers, even on an express train. What would he say of today's riders, with their superhero physiques, and the science-fiction monitoring of their blood chemistry? Would he see them as paragons of the modern era – or as scapegoats? Lefèvre's boss, Henri Desgrange, that vigorous, self-obsessed titan who bestrode the race until his death in 1940, saw the perfect Tour as a race in which only one rider finished. Insanity! If the mad Marquis with the pornographic imagination had never existed, the word for taking pleasure from the infliction of pain and mental suffering on others would be 'desgrangism.' No wonder the Tour developed a tradition of recourse to illicit forms of assistance. And no wonder, even today (in common with almost every other major sporting event), we're as likely to find the results in police enquiries, court cases, journalistic accounts and confessional biographies as in the sports pages. The curious entertainment of the chase (it could almost be called a bloodsport) as lawyers and riders answer the indefensible with the risible, and the authorities attack the hornets' nest with a fly-swatter, keeps the Tour in our minds and hearts for the other eleven months of the year.

But to see the Tour as the subject of sporting and legal proceedings is only part of the picture. The sheer spectacle of the race just can't be ignored. Best seen first-hand, there's no better vantage point than a desolate mountainside, surrounded by bands of crazy, beer-fuelled Dutch in hysterical orange wigs, groups of zany, beer-fuelled Basques in hilarious orange wigs, and clutches of wacky, beer-fuelled Texans in uproarious orange wigs. An hour before the riders arrive, the scene before the Eurotrashed onlookers morphs into a hallucinogenic vision as a surreal flotilla drifts into view: infinite columns of madcap variations on gaudy, motorised coffee-pots, gigantic wine gums on wheels, and towering cuddly toys with lunatic grins copulating with high-pitched, panting go-carts. Along its length of two hundred vehicles or more, this creeping slug of marketing artifice oozes an odd secretion that reeks – that's it! – of boiled sweets and miniature cheeses, and drives otherwise civilised adults into a frenzy of desire for the giveaway key rings and biros that will never work spewing out of its pores. What an impression the publicity caravan would make on any passing Martian curious about that miracle, the human brain!

Then, a long, tense silence, several false alarms, and suddenly – blink and you've missed them – the giants of the road. First, the riders who are really racing, followed, in drips and drabs over the next half-hour, by the sick, the injured, and the hangers-on. Then, just as suddenly, the show's over, folks! Prepare for the mother of all tailbacks – twenty hours to get off the mountain, and all in the name of a good time. Huh? you think: they must be joking. But they're not: it really is a good time, the best of times, and you'll never forget it. You, at the side of the road; them, inches away, rib-cages housing hearts and lungs that beat and bellow at such a pitch, you could be in the engine-room of a transatlantic liner. Extraordinary machines. Extraordinary men. And, years later, guaranteed, you'll remember the day you saw the Tour de France. You'll have that glow, even if you break down the component parts of your Tour de France experience, put them back together again, and get nothing more than empty hours, aching legs, and the buzz of a distant bumblebee, catching the breeze in impossible flight.

Alternatively, you can stay at home and enjoy the razor-sharp action pictures generated by ever more sophisticated television cameras carried by squadrons of helicopters and motorbikes. Can any sporting event compare? Except that, at every point, the sublime peaks and the gutter troughs coincide: for all the brilliant photography, you might as well be watching shapes in the fog. The mental gymnastics involved in never knowing whether to believe our eyes might just be driving us all insane. But the Tour, and the world, were ever thus. As the French also say, the more things change, the more they stay the same.

The Tour means wheeling and dealing, and always has done. Overall, and in every sense, the positives outweigh the negatives – although instead of 'positives', pending completion of the appeals procedure, we should probably say 'non-negatives'. The Tour de France may have to be careful with its language, but rumours of its demise have been greatly exaggerated. It has always been as much about the world it exists in as about sport, and it has always attracted, in Desgrange's famous phrase 'blind passions and filthy suspicions', which may be why, in spite of – because of – its extravagant panoply of faults, the Tour has always made a cruel and unusually good story, and always will.

It's not about the bike – Pascal Poisson gets a lift in the 1982 Tour.

1906: René Pottier, not only the fastest man in a Easter bonnet, but also the Tour's first great climber.

Le Grand Départ

1903 The First Annual Congress of Hardy Crotches

If the first Tour de France had gone according to plan, it would never have survived. Three weeks is bad enough: a race lasting thirty-five days would have driven the public to despair. And if it had started, as planned, on 1 June 1903, it wouldn't have coincided with the annual July holidays introduced thirty-three years later by France's first Socialist government. However, only fifteen riders had entered by 21 April, so the organisers postponed the race until 1 July, cut it to nineteen days, halved the entry fee from twenty to ten francs, and offered the riders five francs a day expenses. By 30 June, there were seventy-eight entries – and the race was on.

When the Tour de France was first devised as a publicity stunt to revive the failing *L'Auto* newspaper, cycling was still in its infancy. There were bike races, but no racing bikes: gears, the free-wheel and drop handlebars all belonged to the future. And once you've agreed to propel an iron bedstead 2,428 kilometres around France, day and night, through sun, rain and dust, with no mechanical assistance, perhaps doubting it's even physically possible, what do you wear? The race rules were silent on the matter, cycling shorts were yet to be invented, and the chamois insert hadn't migrated to the mainstream from the shadow-world of Victorian pornography. Chafing was inevitable. Whatever else the Tour was – and it would become many things – it was also an undeclared congress of Europe's hardiest scrota.

Maurice Garin, at five foot three, a pocket-sized Charles Bronson look alike with a handlebar moustache, might have had the hardest-wearing crotch of all. His choice of under-garments remains a mystery, but outwardly he took on the supreme athletic test in a white blazer with long black trousers tucked into woollen socks. Topped with a flat cap, he resembled a mad Yorkshire barber.

'**Garin and Pagie, whom I'd seen eating quickly at Moulins before disappearing into the night, beat me to Lyon. They were on simple bicycles; I was on an express train.**'

Géo Lefèvre, journalist, *L'Auto*

At 15.16, Wednesday 1 July 1903, Georges Abran fires his starting pistol and unleashes the first Tour de France.

Cigarette and all, Maurice Garin looks more circus performer than modern athlete.

Stage one was a 467-kilometre odyssey from Paris to Lyon. Garin, the favourite, won it. Géo Lefèvre, covering the race for the organisers, missed the stage finish because the cyclists were faster than the trains of the day: 'Garin and Pagie,' he wrote, 'whom I'd seen eating quickly at Moulins before disappearing into the night, beat me to Lyon. They were on simple bicycles; I was on an express train.' The only rival capable of making a race of it was the magnificently named Hyppolite Aucouturier. But after riding the remains of the night, the whole of the following day, and into the darkness again, he had unbearable stomach pains and abandoned. It ruined any suspense about who was going to win – the race was Garin's – but hundreds of thousands came out to watch regardless. This led Aucouturier to re-enter, although this time he was only allowed to compete for stage wins, not overall victory.

'I struggled and wept,
I was thirsty and tired ...
Your race is the hardest
imaginable ... You have
revolutionised cycling,
and the Tour de France
will mark an important
date in the history
of racing.'

Maurice Garin

In the small hours of 5 July, the thirty-five remaining General Classification (GC) contenders left Lyon for Marseille, with eleven others only interested in stage wins. The stage, and the next one, from Marseille to Toulouse, would be Aucouturier's. But by then it was too late: the Tour belonged to Garin, from start to finish.

Henri Desgrange, *L'Auto*'s editor, whipped up interest where there was little. From the first, he mythologised his race with shameless overstatement: 'The steepest mountains,' he wrote, 'the coldest and blackest nights, the sharpest and most violent winds, constant and unjust setbacks, the most difficult routes, never-ending slopes and roads that go on and on – nothing,' he wrote, 'has been able to break the spirit and willpower of these men.' Desgrange duly spent the better part of the next four decades trying.

Thanks to this crazed rhetoric, so many spectators turned out to see the riders that Garin asked to be allowed to enter the Parc des Princes in a car: 'I don't want to kill myself in an overenthusiastic crowd...' The danger proved the first Tour de France had been an unqualified success.

1903 — 2,428 km

	Podium	Nationality	Time	Av speed
1st	Maurice Garin	France	94h 33m 0s	25.68kph
2nd	Lucien Pothier	France	+2h 59m 21s	
3rd	Fernand Augereau	France	+4h 29m 34s	

1904 The Last Tour

Pills, bribes and roadside sabotage are as central to the Tour as sprint finishes and skin loss. EPO and blood transfusions might add a few percentage points, but the ultimate in artificial performance enhancement was already in use in 1904, the year Le Tour discovered... *la voiture*. Not to mention blackmail, and the performance-diminishing powers of a thorough beating. Local riders made early attacks so their accomplices could booby-trap the road behind them with nails. Mercifully, the landmine wasn't commonly available until the First World War.

Like cheating, improvisation – rules made up on the spot, with no real means of communicating them to the riders – is also in the Tour's DNA. They nearly undid the Tour in only its second year. The man who, in 1903, won the first stage, took the race lead and kept it all the way to Paris, did so again in 1904. But this time, Maurice Garin's victory only lasted until November, when the judges of the French cycling federation met and, with a wave of their pen, wrote Garin, his brother César, and their rivals Lucien Pothier and Hippolyte Aucouturier – the top four – out of the results sheet.

The early Tours drew on orienteering's considerable mystique by peppering the route with checkpoints. The last car collected the time-lists, and the rest-day between each stage was spent collating them. This was sport as a bland form of accountancy, but it was the only way of knowing what was going on. However, the accountants soon had their revenge. At least two riders, it transpired, had worked their heavy bikes into handy wormholes in the space-time continuum, popping back into earthly form a good way up the road. Either that, or they'd taken a lift.

By Fontainebleau, only fifty kilometres into stage one, Lucien Pothier had crashed and damaged his bike. Another rider, known only as Chevalier of Moulins – his Christian name is forgotten – had already lost thirty minutes. But ninety kilometres further on, as if by magic, Chevalier reached the next checkpoint with Garin and the leading group. Thirty kilometres further on – abracadabra! – Pothier joined them. Then, after 311 kilometres of racing, on a steep hill near Varennes-sur-Allier, Garin – or the 'wild boar' as Desgrange had labelled him – attacked. Only Pothier was able to cling to his wheel. Garin crossed the finish line at Lyon twenty-three seconds ahead of Pothier and twenty minutes later, Chevalier took third place.

Garin, his brother César, and Lucien Pothier negotiate a motor-car, a horse and cart, a railway line – and the danger of flying laundry.

Henri Desgrange, the witchfinder general of the Tour, confronted them. Pothier admitted drafting behind the car of his team manager and was fined 500 francs. Chevalier's case was more extreme. Other riders would get a lift by taking drugs: he got a lift by taking a lift. Desgrange disqualified him on the spot. What Desgrange didn't know was that Garin had been blackmailing *L'Auto*'s Géo Lefèvre into giving him food from an official vehicle by threatening to abandon the race. His time would come.

> **'The Tour de France is over and its second edition, I fear, will also be its last.'**
>
> Henri Desgrange

Stage two was even worse: south-east of Saint-Étienne, on the way up the Col de la République, a crowd of men blocked the road. A local rider named Antoine Fauré threaded his way through them as Maurice Garin and Giovanni Gerbi were beaten with sticks. Desgrange fired a shot into the air from his car, and the crowd drew back. Gerbi had a broken finger and could no longer hold his handlebars. He soon abandoned.

At the Café du Murier in Saint-Antoine, just outside Marseille, Desgrange had arranged one of the over-elaborations that made the early Tours so difficult to follow. According to Desgrange's plan, the riders should have been stopped outside the café and handed a card stamped with their arrival time. Then, they would have had sixty minutes to get into the Larcheveque Velodrome in Marseille. There, the race was to resume with the final kilometre around the track.

But everyone was tired, and the velodrome wasn't prepared for the finish, so Desgrange stood a kilometre upstream of the Café du Murier with a megaphone, announcing to the riders that the finish would now take place at Saint-Antoine. Jean-Baptiste Dortignacq sprinted for a banner stretched across the road and celebrated the stage win, ahead of Pothier, Aucouturier and César Garin. Aucouturier was declared the winner: it was simple mistaken identity.

Late in the same stage, a rider named Ferdinand Payan was disqualified for drafting behind an accomplice. But two days later Payan was back in the Tour, this time at the head of a crowd of several thousand hometown supporters intent on stopping the race. Garin took a punch to the face and a blow to the leg. Pothier's left arm was injured. Aucouturier waded into the fray and delivered some punches of his own. Again, only shots fired in the air from the *L'Auto* car stopped the brawling.

And so it continued, day after day. Aucouturier was given four stage wins, and Lucien Pothier ate steadily into Garin's lead, reducing it to three minutes, twenty-eight seconds before running out of Tour. On 24 July, Maurice Garin's 100 per cent record in the Tour was intact – although Desgrange wrote, pessimistically, 'The Tour de France is over and its second edition, I fear, will also be its last.' On 2 December, the results were revised, and cycling's accountants achieved what miles, mountains and men with big sticks couldn't. With a flourish of the pen they deprived Garin of his victory. Despite an official warning that suggested wrongdoing on his part, too, Henri Cornet, fifth in the original classification, was awarded the Tour.

> '**The riders named below are suspended:**
> **Chevalier – for life.**
> **Pothier – for life.**
> **Garin – for two years.**'
> Official Communiqué of the French cycling federation, 2 December 1904.

1904			2,397 km
Podium	Nationality	Time	Av speed
1st Henri Cornet	France	96h 5m 56s	24.94kph
2nd Jean-Baptiste Dortignacq	France	+2h 16m 14s	
3rd Aloïs Catteau	Belgium	+9h 2m 18s	

1905-6
Myths of Mountains

After the scandals of 1904, Desgrange decided a little calculated mythologising would distract the public from the cheating. The mountains were the obvious place to start; in particular, the 1,178-metre Ballon d'Alsace, included in the route for the first time. Desgrange strangely forgot that the 1903 and 1904 Tours de France had tackled the 1,161-metre Col de la République. The Ballon was just seventeen metres higher, but Desgrange worked himself up to a rhetorical peak of his own about it.

He started by doubting, overdramatically, that it could be climbed by bike. Then, when the riders got over it, Desgrange couldn't and raved, 'the ascent of the Ballon d'Alsace... was one of the most thrilling sights I've ever witnessed, and confirms – after many others – my opinion that man's courage knows no limits and a highly trained athlete can aspire to remarkable performances.' In subsequent versions of events, the Ballon d'Alsace became – wrongly – the first mountain in Tour history.

Desgrange also changed the rules to allow pacers on the first and last stages. This must have pleased Lucien Pothier, now suspended for life for using an illegal pacer on stage one a year earlier. There was another change: the results were decided by points, not timings. In the age before electronic systems removed the margin of error of hand-timing, the organisers wanted to avoid a close finish. As Géo Lefèvre wrote: 'A fifth of a second gained at Bordeaux might have represented a bicycle length and two or three places, and another fifth of a second at Nantes might have represented one place and the width of a tyre... *L'Auto* has created a points system that combined the finish position and the amount of time that separated each rider from the one who finished immediately ahead of him.' It seemed a good idea at the time, but as Lefèvre later recalled, 'The labours of Hercules were nothing compared with the calculations, and errors made at night often had to be corrected in the morning.'

> '**Suffering, Trousselier, is the full unfurling of the will. Prove you're a man.**'
>
> Henri Desgrange

When the race finally got under way, nails ruined it from start to finish. On stage one alone, every rider punctured at least once, thanks to nails; Jean-Baptiste Dortignacq, who eventually finished third overall, punctured fifteen times on the stage. The following day, after the leading group had completed that first ascent of the Ballon d'Alsace, the chasers hit another carpet of nails. Later in the stage, between Lunéville and Épinal, yet more nails brought the first man over the Ballon, the whippet René Pottier, to a halt. He had no more spare tyres, but Hyppolite Aucouturier caught up with him and gave him a spare. Justice was done when Aucouturier won the stage.

Pottier abandoned on stage three after a fall, before the Tour entered the Alps. There, Aucouturier was master. He and Dortignacq took three stages each, but this Tour belonged to a slight, straight-backed showman named Louis Trousselier. Aged barely twenty-four, Trousselier played to the crowd with fairground leaps in and out of the saddle. He'd won Paris-Roubaix earlier in the year, and abandoned Bordeaux-Paris when he was in the first three. Desgrange praised him for a season so successful, it was 'unprecedented in our sport'. But Desgranges always attached a barb to his praise: it wasn't enough to win, he intoned: 'Suffering, Trousselier, is the full unfurling of the will. Prove you're a man.'

Trousselier did so by collecting five stage wins and the GC. His victory celebrations were deflated when military police met him in Paris and dragged him off to the nearest barracks. He'd won stage three at Grenoble on the day he had been due to start his military service, and there was no escape, even for the winner of the Tour de France. The night after his victory, in a defiant act of self-sabotage, Trousselier is said to have gambled away his winnings in their entirety.

Yet, despite that other self-sabotage, the scoring system, Desgrange's diversionary tactics worked. After the race, he wrote in *L'Auto*, 'Last year we saw the contenders ready to come to blows at any moment, agitated onlookers bombard them with threats, scandals erupt beneath their feet and the race submerged in the filthiest of reputations. This year everything unfolded admirably': to the pathologically distracted, perhaps it had.

The 1905 Tour also sowed the seeds for the first excursion into the Pyrenees. On the final stage, the riders reached Bordeaux two hours outside the race schedule. Desgrange was livid. His response was to threaten to send them into the mountains the following year: 'Everything has its consequences, and in all probability they have laid the basis for a supplementary stage in the 1906 Tour de France – a stage which will climb into the Pyrenees in the way stage two took them into the Vosges and stage four into the Alps.'

1905   3,021 km

	Podium	Nationality	Points	Av speed (kph)
1st	Louis Trousselier	France	35 pts (110h 26m 58s)	27.48
2nd	Hyppolite Aucouturier	France	61 pts	
3rd	Jean-Baptiste Dortignacq	France	64 pts	

1906

The Tour was evolving fast. Between 1904 and 1906, it almost doubled in length from 2,428 to 4,637 km. It finally became a loop around the whole of France – with detours through Germany, Spain and Italy, to boot. But some things never change. Stage two of the 1906 Tour de France was waved off at 12.15 in the morning of 6 July. 100 metres up the road, Charles Faroux of *L'Auto* saw a rider in a red and blue shirt at the side of the road:

'What's up, Aucouturier?'

'Nails.'

Within two kilometres, many riders had used up their spare tyres, and faced the ninety-kilometre ride to the first checkpoint at Cambrai on naked rims. The Tour's worst nightmare was starting all over again. On the Douai-Nancy stage every rider punctured except a diminutive track star brought up in Argentina called Lucien Petit-Breton.

As if the nails weren't bad enough, there was René Pottier to contend with. In 1905, Pottier tamed the Ballon d'Alsace in a flat cap. This year, he wore something resembling a milk-maid's bonnet. It did the trick. He jigged up the Ballon, then sauntered the remaining 220 kilometres to victory at Dijon by forty-eight minutes. Add that to the quarter of an hour advantage he gained at Grenoble and the twenty-six minutes he won by at Nice, and Pottier resembles a time traveller, a full-colour, tightly focused athlete from the future – and he looked like a modern cyclist, undersized, no bulk filling out the fibre – against the brawny, black and white tradesmen of the past. Pottier's intense gaze and quick smile shielded an identity easily hurt,

> **'At the foot of the climb, Pottier bolted, as if the bell had sounded the final lap of a track race. He hadn't reached the first hairpin before the group was torn apart.'**
>
> *L'Auto* describes the ascent of the Ballon d'Alsace

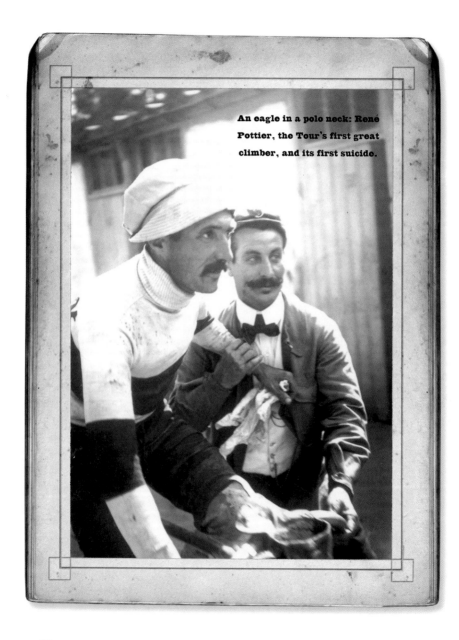

An eagle in a polo neck: René Pottier, the Tour's first great climber, and its first suicide.

making the first great climber the template of those to come: Gaul, Ocaña, Pantani.

Having built up his lead, he had to defend it. Fortunately for him, the race was better policed

> 'Hills, more hills, nothing but hills. I thought it would never end.'
>
> René Pottier

this year. Pottier quipped, 'If I'd wanted to cheat, it wouldn't have been easy.' Perhaps he was right not to try: Maurice Carrère, Henri Gauban and Gaston Tuvache covered part of the stage to Dijon by train, but they were found out and ejected. For Pottier, the final stages to Paris seemed interminable. Afterwards, he told *L'Auto*, 'Nothing was harder than Brest-Caen, which started in an icy night and continued in a day of terrible heat. 400 kilometres of climbing roads: hills, more hills, nothing but hills. I thought it would never end.'

But it did, although only fourteen of the ninety-six starters finished. René Pottier had won five of the thirteen stages, including four consecutive stages. It had been a gruelling Tour, but Pottier seemed to find real life even harder. On 25 January 1907, he committed suicide. A Peugeot mechanic found his body hanging from the hook where his bike usually hung. No one knows the truth about a suicide, although Pottier's brother said René was unhappy in love. He was survived by a widow and an orphan. A few weeks later, Henri Desgrange, patron of the Tour, erected a stele in his memory at the top of the Ballon d'Alsace. It's still there.

1906   4,546 km

	Podium	Nationality	Points	Av speed (kph)
1st	René Pottier	France	31 pts (189h 34m 0s)	23.98
2nd	Georges Passerieu	France	39 pts	
3rd	Louis Trousselier	France	59 pts	

1907-8 Argie-Bargie

When Émile Georget punctured near a checkpoint on stage nine of the 1907 Tour, he might have taken things calmly. He'd won five of the first eight stages, and he was running away with the Tour. Instead, he panicked. To reach the checkpoint and mechanical help, he begged a machine from a passing independent entrant named Pierre Privat, and gave it back just before the checkpoint. When the misdemeanour came to light, Georget was fined 550 francs. Then, like footballers brandishing imaginary red cards at the ref, the Alcyon team protested that the punishment was too light and abandoned, taking the 1905 winner Trousselier with them. Desgrange then relegated Georget to last place in the stage – which effectively cost him the race. That left Petit-Breton, an Argentine track specialist with no support leading the world's greatest bike race.

The Tour may be 'de France', but it hasn't always smiled on the French. The first to win two Tours – before the second was scrubbed out by the French cycling federation – was the Italian-born Maurice Garin. The second was the Buenos Aires-raised Lucien Petit-Breton. Born Lucien Mazan in Plessé, north of Nantes, in 1883, Petit-Breton's career started in Argentina, his home since he was six. He won his first bike in a lottery aged sixteen. Within two years he held national track titles in South America, and by 1902, he had returned to France and the golden age of the velodromes. Until the First World War, the road to riches in cycling

**The boss: Henri Desgrange, with aviator's goggles and
great coat, gets scrutineering.**

wasn't the road, but the track, and Petit-Breton made good money: second in the twenty-four hour Bol d'Or in 1903, he was first a year later, and broke the world hour record in 1905.

He won the third Paris–Tours in 1906, and the first ever Milan–San Remo in 1907; in 1905, he had astonished by finishing the Tour de France fifth overall. In 1906, he was fourth. But by stage five of the 1907 Tour, between Lyon and Grenoble, his bid for victory seemed to be over. The Col de la Porte was supposed to decide the Tour, and as Émile Georget, on a Peugeot bike with a revolutionary freewheel, accelerated towards his third stage win, Petit-Breton was the first to lose contact. He finished the stage tenth, nearly twenty-eight minutes after Georget. But thanks to the points system, which counted only the order to the finish, the time didn't matter.

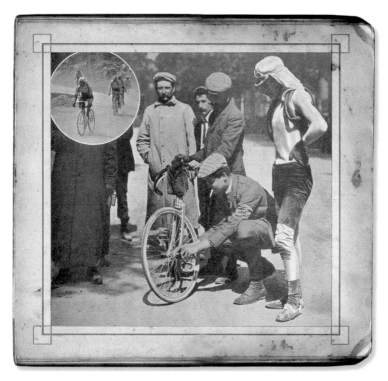

**The moment the Tour was lost: Émile Georget's illegal bike change
is discovered.**

Like his watchmaker father, Petit-Breton was meticulous, keeping
his bike in perfect condition. He was regular as clockwork, too: in
1907, he finished first in two stages, second in four and third in four
more. But Petit-Breton's father disapproved of cycling, and his son
abandoned the family name. Some say he was known as 'El Breton'
in Argentina; in France he was nicknamed 'the Argentine', but
assumed the name Breton, which he changed to Petit-Breton because
there was another cyclist named Breton. He passed on Petit-Breton
to his own son.

No competition in sight for Peugeot teammates Petit-Breton and Garrigou.

1907   4,488 km

Podium		Nationality	Points	Av speed (kph)
1st	Lucien Petit-Breton	France	47 pts (158h 45m 5s)	28.27
2nd	Gustave Garrigou	France	66 pts	
3rd	Emile Georget	France	74 pts	

1908

A year later, in perhaps the most boring Tour in history, his team, Peugeot, won all fourteen stages, leading in the rain with François Faber, in the heat with Jean-Baptiste Dortignacq and in the mountains with Gustave Garrigou. Petit-Breton was always in close attendance. These were Lance Armstrong tactics, ninety years before their time – except that Peugeot took the first four places in the overall classification, and Petit-Breton finished outside the first four in a stage only once. The final stage, by the way, was held using cars to pace the riders. The twenty-one-year-old François Faber won it at the Parc des Princes, two bike lengths ahead of his teammate Petit-Breton, whose dominance had been total, and stultifying.

'It has been said I owe my greatest victories to drugs. Allow me to contest these absurd rumours. Do you seriously think a man, however strong, could survive such treatment for 28 days? Lucien Petit-Breton

1908   4,488 km

Podium		Nationality	Points	Av speed (kph)
1st	Lucien Petit-Breton	France	36 pts (156h 53m 29s)	28.6058
2nd	François Faber	Luxembourg	68 pts	
3rd	Georges Passerieu	France	75 pts	

1909 Giant Haystacks

The innocent organising of a bicycle race brought upon
France the might of two sleeping giants: Luxembourg
and Belgium. Its place at the head of the peloton
(a word used for the first time in cycling during the
1909 Tour) was quickly taken by a Luxembourg-born
giant now resident in Colombes, in the outskirts
of Paris: François Faber. Faber was cycling's Giant
Haystacks, a Jonah Lomu on wheels, weighing over
ninety kilos, and looking more like a wrestler or
weight lifter than a cyclist. But his six-litre lungs were
a cyclist's lungs, and, in any case, if he was freakish,
so were the weather conditions, and the stout
Luxembourger was the best equipped to survive.

Winter 1909 took place in July. From the morning of stage two, the
main obstacle was the weather. Faber, hardened by manual labour
along the Seine, was impervious to the cold: his less sturdy rivals
succumbed. After stage three, Faber recalled seeing 'Garrigou and
Van Houwaert frozen to the core, Lapize bent over himself with
cold, and Trousselier with a nose that outshone the headlamps of the
official cars.' Faber's front wheel sank eight inches into roads that
turned to mulch in the wet. Filthy and frozen, he approached the
Ballon d'Alsace alone: 'It disappeared into the murk and, as I reached
it, snow was blanketing the summit.' He is said to have ridden alone
for 254 kilometres that day; the gale blew him off his bike twice, and
he was attacked by a horse. But he still finished thirty-three minutes
before the second-placed rider, Gustave Garrigou – the same
advantage he had gained over Octave Lapize, who finished second

In Paris, François
Faber and his colossal
bouquet tower over
the mortal world.

the day before. But his astonishing superiority never made the record books: the classification was still based on points.

Between Lyon and Grenoble, Faber decided not to attack until Saint-Laurent-du-Pont. Paul Duboc, Gustave Garrigou and Cyrille Van Houwaert tried to follow, but each ran into problems: in Faber's account, 'Duboc slipped in the mud and had to give up. Garrigou stopped at the entrance to the tunnels. Van Houwaert, dropped back after a mistake, but only after a heroic struggle on roads that felt like black soap.'

Faber's weight, balance and luck won him the Tour. On the way into Nice, the moment he attacked, his sole challenger, Garrigou, punctured and had to stop. Faber rode off alone to his fifth consecutive stage win, an unprecedented achievement in the Tour's short history.

As magnificent as Faber was in victory, others matched him in the scale of their defeat. On the final stage, won by Jean Alavoine, his brother Henri Alavoine wrecked his bike in a crash and carried it ten kilometres. There were worse performances: Georges Goffin of Liège, an April Fool's Day child, started the 1909 Tour, but dropped out on stage one. Two years later, he started again, and abandoned, again, on stage one. In 1922, he went back for one final attempt – and again abandoned before the end of stage one. Goffin's natural successor was the first Japanese rider to enter the Tour. Kisso Kawamuro kissed the 1926 Tour goodbye during stage one, and repeated the feat a year later.

1909 — 4,488 km

	Podium	Nationality	Points		Av speed (kph)
1st	François Faber	Luxembourg	37 pts	(157h 1m. 22s)	28.60
2nd	Gustave Garrigou	France	57 pts		
3rd	Jean Alavoine	France	66 pts		

1910 Over the Top

The Tour wouldn't be the Tour without a family-size dollop of criminal negligence in the planning. In 1910, it led to Desgrange's threatened stage through the towering Pyrenees. Shortly after *L'Auto* had published its intent to usher the riders over the great Pyrenean cols, a letter arrived disabusing them of their illusions: 'You are clearly unaware that the passes you speak of don't exist. There's something over the Tourmalet, but nothing over the Aubisque beyond the simple trail used by woodcutters to drag blocks of timber down the mountain to the timberyards with oxen.'

The roads over the Pyrenees didn't even belong to the national road network: they were 'thermal routes', private roads serving the spas at Eaux-Bonnes, Argelès-Gazost, Luz-Saint-Sauveur, Barèges and Luchon. So *L'Auto* cobbled together 1,500 francs, the French highways authority matched it, and a team of engineers did what they could in a month to make the route passable. The stage went ahead anyway. Little wonder that Octave Lapize, the eventual winner, hissed 'Vous êtes des assassins' - 'Murderers!' at the officials as he passed them on the Aubisque.

As a description of the Col du Tourmalet, 'quite feasible, even for an average cyclist' isn't entirely full and open. As a report of a near-death experience, it's stoic to the point of insanity. Telling the tale forty years later, *L'Auto* journalist Alphonse Steinès recalled, 'It was a terrifying experience... Even today, aged eighty-six, I'm suffering the consequences.' A month before the race, Steinès reconnoitred the stage, including ten kilometres covered in four metres of snow.

Striding out of the dawn and into the Pyrenees, Octave Lapize brews up one of the great Tour insults: 'Murderers!'

He headed into the darkness, until, he said, 'I was lost and alone in the frozen desert. I didn't want to die on a hostile, unknown mountain at an altitude of 2,255 metres.' Teams of guides from Barèges and Sainte-Marie-de-Campan headed into the mountains, but they couldn't find him. Steinès made it over the 1,750-metre Aubisque, spent the night with miners, then descended to Eaux Bonnes. There, he was told a Mercedes had slipped off the mountain four days earlier, killing the driver and four passengers. A pertinent point for a risk assessment of anything other than the Tour de France, and no part of his account to Henri Desgrange: 'I gave him a brief – very brief – account of my journey through the Pyrenees, and assured him everything was fine, and the Tourmalet was very good, and quite feasible, even for an average cyclist.'

Octave Lapize was rather more than the average cyclist. The winner of Paris–Roubaix in 1909, 1910 and 1911, and of Paris–Brussels in 1911, 1912 and 1913, Lapize's Tour career was all-or-nothing. He started six and finished one – and the one he finished, he won, despite the efforts of his Alcyon teammate François Faber. On stage two from Roubaix to Metz, Faber gained seventeen minutes on Lapize. He added to his advantage by winning stage four, subtracted from it when Lapize won stage five, then added to it again when he won stage seven, at Nîmes. But just before the stage finish, a collision with a dog left him seriously injured at the foot of the Pyrenees, where the gaunt Lapize made him suffer for his size. The first leg of the ordeal, between Perpignan and Luchon, over the Col de Port, the Portet d'Aspet and the Portet des Ares, saw Lapize finish first some twenty-two minutes ahead of the third-placed Faber. The second leg, between Luchon and Bayonne, over the Peyresourde, Aspin, Tourmalet and Aubisque saw Lapize, first again, finish ten minutes ahead of Faber, again third. Even then, only a cruel series of punctures on the final stage from Caen to Paris prevented Faber's last gasp attack from winning the Tour.

The Tour's Pyrenean excursion meant that of the hundred and ten riders that left Paris, only forty-one returned. It was forty too many for Desgrange: 'far too many riders made it back to Paris, and the numbers discarded en route are too small... The Tour de France presents itself as a gruelling trial: we must justify this by placing new obstacles before our men.'

1910   4,737 km

Podium		Nationality	Points	Av speed (kph)
1st	Octave Lapize	France	63 pts (163h 52m 38s)	28.91
2nd	François Faber	Luxembourg	67 pts	
3rd	Gustave Garrigou	France	86 pts	

1911 Domestique Bliss

'Doesn't the bike,' Henri Desgrange eulogised, 'represent the first successful attempt in human history to defy the laws of gravity?' It was the preamble, not to an appreciation of those seasoned bike makers the Wright brothers, but to more deranged Desgrangism: the first ascent of the towering Galibier. 'Are these men not winged, who today climbed to heights where even eagles don't go, and crossed Europe's highest summits? They rose so high they seemed to dominate the world!' Elbrus aside, Desgrange's raving took the Tour to new heights, and the riders had no choice but to follow. Octave Lapize's 'Vous êtes des assassins' – 'Murderers!' – on the Tourmalet in 1910 became Gustave Garrigou's 'Vous êtes des bandits' – 'Thugs!' on the Galibier a year later. But the climbs were here to stay.

The first to top the Galibier was Émile Georget, the man who lost the 1907 Tour. He half-pedalled, half-pushed his bike up a path of rutted mud, between five-foot snowdrifts. Behind him, Gustave Garrigou took his fourth third place in a row. He'd be third twice more, and second twice, too: that was how Garrigou rode – he was a team player who had finally earned his chance. He had finished second in the 1907 Tour and fourth in 1908 to his teammate Petit-Breton, second again in 1909 to his teammate Faber and third to another teammate Lapize in 1910. Grabbing his chance with both hands, Garrigou had built an early lead of sixteen points by the morning of stage seven. But after all that effort, he nearly blew it.

Six-foot snowdrifts in July and roads with eight-inch ruts can't stop Gustave Garrigou.

Between Nice and Marseille, Paul Duboc reduced it to fifteen, then to thirteen between Marseille and Perpignan, and to ten by winning the first Pyrenean stage from Perpignan to Luchon. Then, near the town of Argelès the following day, Duboc collapsed at the roadside, poisoned. Garrigou gained three hours on the stage, taking second place on the stage and consolidating his lead.

Except that Garrigou's second place soon became a first, when the putative stage winner, Maurice Brocco, was disqualified, guilty of unsportsmanlike behaviour, according to Desgrange. Time lost early in the race had robbed Brocco of any chance of winning the Tour, so he had begun selling himself as a pacer to the highest bidder. Between Perpignan and Luchon, Brocco had piloted his Alcyon teammate François Faber to the lead group. 'C'est un domestique' – 'He's like a domestic servant' – Desgrange raged, using the word for the first time.

Seeking to appease Desgrange, Brocco showed his mettle and powered away to win the stage by thirty-four minutes. But Desgrange was far from molified. Concluding that Brocco had callously been riding within himself on earlier stages, the race director cancelled his stage win and expelled him from the Tour.

After Garrigou had won the Brest–Cherbourg stage, the race approached Duboc's hometown of Rouen. Fearing 1904-style reprisals, Garrigou got away with his life by shaving off his conspicuous moustache, changing his jersey and taking the number off his bike. It won him the Tour, too.

1911				5,343 km
Podium		Nationality	Points	Av speed (kph)
1st	Gustave Garrigou	France	63 pts (163h 52m 38s)	27.32
2nd	Paul Duboc	France	61 pts	
3rd	Émile Georget	France	84 pts	

1912-14 Belgium attacks!

In 1912, France's negligible neighbour Belgium got the Tour between its teeth and, like a tiny, yapping terrier, refused to let go: the Tour title remained in Belgium until 1923. It was all Alcyon's fault for naming an all-French team to support its leader Gustave Garrigou. At the last minute, Alcyon's Belgian branch asked if Odile Defraye could be included for publicity purposes. Defraye made his contribution to international diplomacy by outsprinting Garrigou to win stage two. At the end of stage three, he outsprinted him again – although this time he finished second behind Eugène Christophe.

Christophe's stage win was the first of three consecutive victories, over the Ballon d'Alsace, into the Alps and across the Galibier. In his report from stage five, Desgrange praised Christophe who, he said, had 'put his nose on the handlebar at the stage start, and not lifted it for three hundred and sixty-six kilometres', only dropping 'that parasite' Alavoine, 'whom he'd been sucking along in his wake', on the ascent of the Galibier. But wheelsuckers were not Desgrange's only concern, to his eyes there was an altogether more revolutionary threat to the Tour: the freewheel. 'Over three hundred and seventy-nine kilometres the riders applied pressure to the pedals for scarcely half the distance. The rest was covered freewheeling. Behind the man setting the pace, all our strapping fellows lounged as if on a sofa; sucked along, they covered enormous distances without any fatigue. The presence of men like Everaerts and Deloffre, Huret and Engel, for example, clearly indicates the ease

Eugène Christophe and the Galibier: two giants of the early Tours.

with which they rode the stage.' 'Is there any remedy?' Desgrange seethed, 'Are our races seriously threatened with decadence by the freewheel? Will the Tour de France be undermined by this infernal invention? Where will it lead? I well know that as far as *L'Auto* is concerned, the 1913 regulations will authorise the race director to ban the freewheel in certain stages.'

1912   5,319 km

	Podium	Nationality	Points	Av speed (kph)
1st	Odile Defraye	Belgium	49pts (190h 30m 28s)	28.78
2nd	Eugène Christophe	France	108 pts	
3rd	Gustave Garrigou	France	140 pts	

The eyes have it: Lucien Petit-Breton in no mood to talk.

1913

The 1913 Tour saw two major rule changes. The experiment with a general classification based on points was declared a failure, and the Tour reverted to overall time as the measure of its men. Then, true to his word, Desgrange carried out his threat to ban freewheels on stage four of the following year's Tour. Riding on a fixed wheel left Odile Defraye, 1912's victor, so exhausted, that on stage six, halfway up the Tourmalet, he abandoned – despite the fact that he held the race lead. That left Christophe, who had finished the 1912 Tour second to Defraye, in the race lead – until a car drove into him and broke his fork in the most celebrated accident in Tour history (described in the 1919 chapter). Christophe, an expert engineer, was able to forge a new fork and carry on, despite the lost hours. When Marcel Buysse had a similar accident sixteen kilometres from

Cannes, but couldn't shape a replacement part himself, Desgrange carped: 'As a professional rider, you should know how to repair your bike.'

With Christophe gone, a dream was about to come true for the cycling equivalent of the Pop Idol winner. Belgium's Philippe Thys was a graduate of an ambitious series of races for young, independent riders, organised by Peugeot bikes and Wolber tyres. Thys had won the 1911 Circuit Français Peugeot, and two further stage races from Paris to Toulouse and from Paris to Turin. His prize, a place in the professional ranks, was his platform for victory in the 1913 and 1914 Tours. He rode away from the stricken Eugène Christophe to win the stage and the overall lead at Luchon.

However, his ride into Paris wasn't without incident. Marcel Buysse replaced him at the top of the general classification the following day and looked a likely winner until he broke a fork on the stage to Nice, and dropped out of contention. Then, on the penultimate stage from Longwy to Dunkirk, Thys fell and was knocked out. Dragged back into the action by his teammates, he was then penalised for accepting help to repair his bike. But, despite these misfortunes and Buysse's domination of the last two stages, Thys hung on to win.

> **'I've had enough. If I puncture, the peloton pelts off at top speed. But if one of my rivals crashes, no one wants to take the lead. It's me against everyone!'**
> Boo-hoo, Octave Lapize

1913   5,387 km

	Podium	Nationality	Time	Av speed (kph)
1st	Philippe Thys	Belgium	197h 54m 0s	27.22
2nd	Gustave Garrigou	France	+8m 37s	
3rd	Marcel Buysse	Belgium	+3h 30m 55s	

Le Grand Départ, 1914: 3 a.m. on the day Archduke Ferdinand will die.

1914

Thys lost little time asserting himself in 1914, his first stage victory to Le Havre was an ominous omen for his rivals. More ominously, for many of the 1914 peloton, the same day was marked by the assassination of an Austrian archduke in a remote Bosnian town called Sarajevo. As Europe prepared itself for war, Thys held the race lead from start to finish. On the penultimate stage, Thys made an unauthorised wheel change as he chased Faber's irresistible attack, an infringement that cost him a thirty-minute penalty, leaving Frenchman Henri Pélissier less than two minutes off his winning pace. The sanction added spice to the final stage, from Dunkirk to Paris. Anticipating a home victory, French fans along the route mobbed Pélissier, slapping him on the back in premature congratulation and ultimately preventing him from launching the

**With the outbreak of the First World War only weeks away,
a French soldier takes advantage of François Faber's slipstream.**

breakaway that might have won the Tour. Pélissier was first across
the line in Paris, but with Thys glued to his wheel, lost the Tour. Two
days later, Austria-Hungary declared war on Serbia. François Faber,
Lucien Petit-Breton and Octave Lapize were among the millions
who would perish as the conflict engulfed Europe.

1914   5,401 km

	Podium	Nationality	Time	Av speed (kph)
1st	Philippe Thys	Belgium	200h 28m 48s	26.94
2nd	Henri Pélissier	France	+1m 50s	
3rd	Jean Alavoine	France	+36m 53s	

No time to return the wave:
the peloton flashes past
spectators enjoying
France's first paid holidays
– a 1936 innovation.

From One War to the Next

1919 Baugé's Bright Idea

One year on from the Great War, the Tour de France had the faded hue of ancient undergarments beaten into colourlessness on a long succession of washboards. The post-war dearth meant there were cycling jerseys, but there was no dye, so the trade teams wore grey jerseys with embroidered shoulders to distinguish them. Then Alphonse Baugé, the team director whose riders had won the previous six Tours, had a bright idea. Halfway through the Tour, Baugé approached Henri Desgrange, the forbidding race director, and suggested dressing the race leader in a colourful shirt. Baugé used to dress his team staff in yellow to make them more visible to his riders. Since Desgrange's newspaper, *L'Auto*, was printed on yellow paper, it was the obvious choice. The yellow jersey was born.

Desgrange called Paris and ordered five yellow jerseys to be delivered to Marseille, but by the time they got there, Desgrange had gone, and it took them six days to catch him. Eventually, in front of the Café de l'Ascenseur in Grenoble, he presented the first yellow jersey to the prodigious Frenchman Eugène Christophe. Christophe quickly complained the spectators laughed at him: they said he looked like a canary. He didn't need this: he'd been leading the race for seven stages already. With five to go, the Tour was his to lose.

There could be no worthier winner. Christophe never said die: thick-skinned and swashbuckling, he won the 1910 Milan–San Remo suffering from exposure after a blizzard on the Turchino Pass.

It took him a year to recover his health. The war had taken his best years, but he had survived. His luck probably ended there: Eugène Christophe must have been the unluckiest sportsman left alive.

A cycling Sysiphus, Eugène Christophe had been condemned not to roll rocks up mountains, but to carry broken bikes down them. Second in the 1912 Tour de France, he had gone into the 1913 event the outstanding favourite, moving into the lead on stage six halfway up the 2,114-metre Tourmalet in the towering Pyrenees, when the reigning champion and race leader – Odile Defraye – abandoned the race in exhaustion. Christophe, who had broken away with the Tour's pre-war double champion Philippe Thys, was perfectly positioned to seize an unassailable lead – until a careless driver clipped him with a race vehicle, throwing Christophe across the road. He got up, unhurt – *he* was indestructible, more or less, but his front fork had been snapped in two. As Christophe

Outside the Café de l'Ascenseur in Grenoble, Eugène Christophe (fourth from left) looks none too pleased to be wearing the first yellow jersey.

'The fork is broken. It seems to me a mighty lyre whose broken strings sing his final misery.'
Henri Desgrange on Eugène Christophe's broken fork

stood over his ruined machine, Thys sped away alone towards the stage win and, eventually, overall victory. Another man would have abandoned there and then. Not Eugène Christophe, who wept, but picked up the pieces as he did so and set off on foot. Thirteen kilometres away, at Sainte-Marie-de-Campan, he found a forge. The race rules proscribed outside assistance, but Christophe was a skilled mechanic and forged a new fork from twenty-two millimetre steel. When the stem wouldn't enter the damaged head tube, he made another. As Christophe gripped the frame in one hand and a hammer in the other, he allowed a seven-year-old boy to man the bellows. For this assistance, the race marshall who policed the operation imposed a ten-minute time penalty. Then Christophe filled his pockets with bread and set off over two more mountains for the stage finish. Desgrange's stage report in *L'Auto* reads: 'As I telegraph you this, he is already two hours late and I have no news of him.' He arrived three hours, fifty minutes after Thys. Remarkably little, all things considered, but the Tour had gone.

So in 1919 Eugène Christophe took the race by the scruff of the neck. In the lead by the end of stage four, he showed no weakness until two thirds of the way through the Tour's penultimate stage. Chirpy as a canary, he was pounding through the border town of Valenciennes, when the greatest moment of sporting heartbreak in Tour history, deaths aside, occurred. On the only cobbled section of the stage, his fork snapped. Desgrange described the scene in *L'Auto*: 'The sky is gloomy and washed out. Huge, grubby clouds extend to the horizon. It is as if nature herself were grieving. In the outskirts of Valenciennes, Eugène Christophe stands on the pavement. He pushes his bicycle in front of him: the fork is broken. It seems to me a mighty lyre whose broken strings sing his final misery.'

This time, there was a forge within a kilometre, but the run and the repairs cost two hours all the same. Again, a Belgian profited from his misfortune: Firmin Lambot rode off the victory, shouting 'The old man's gone, the old man's gone!' But Lambot sportingly refused to accept the jersey at the start of the following stage until Christophe insisted. Despite his bad luck, Christophe still finished the 1920 Tour third, behind Lambot and Jean Alavoine.

It was the second time Christophe had lost the Tour de France with a broken fork. It wouldn't be the last. In 1922, he was in the top three, contending for overall victory, when yet another broken fork ended his hopes on the descent from the Galibier in the Alps.

Eugène Christophe was an honourable man. He couldn't bear the idea of doping, and swore that he'd never taken anything but mineral water throughout his career. Journalist Jacques Marchand recalls meeting him over dinner with another old Tour rider, Marcel Bidon, fifty years after their Tour heroics. Bidon confessed he used to drink a half-bottle of champagne before each stage. Christophe was astounded: 'Champagne? You drank champagne?', 'Yes... a little,' Bidot replied, honestly. Marchand goes on: 'And then, I swear, Eugène Christophe, furious, despite his eighty years or more, raised a threatening finger: 'So, you cheated, Marcel! You cheated! You had no right to drink champagne!'

Christophe never did win the Tour, but as the 'eternal second', he would be reincarnated in future Tours as René Vietto and Raymond Poulidor.

1919				5,560 km
Podium		Nationality	Time	Av speed (kph)
1st	Firmin Lambot	Belgium	231h 7m 15s	24.06
2nd	Jean Alavoine	France	+1h 42m 54s	
3rd	Eugène Christophe	France	+2h 26m 31s	

1920-2 **Tales of Torment**

Henri Desgrange had something on his mind. 'Some of our riders think nothing of doping,' he wrote in 1920. 'We cannot reproach strongly enough similar procedures, which run so counter to our idea of sport. The vigour of our condemnation is aimed less at the riders who drug themselves than at the managers, and above all certain doctors who don't hesitate before using such means. Those, like us, who would like our race to become magnificent will never accept such procedures.' Wise words, as true today as they were in the 1920s.

With these weighty matters occupying his thoughts, he should perhaps be forgiven for forgetting to order any yellow jerseys, which meant that the first one was awarded after stage nine, at Nice. Or perhaps this dereliction of duty was caused by Belgium's continuing domination: Belgians eventually took twelve of the fifteen stage wins, and filled eight of the top ten positions in the general classification.

The best among them was Philippe Thys, who waited just two stages before taking the race lead. Once he had it, wild horses couldn't drag it from his grip – although *L'Auto* considered the threat serious enough to merit the following disclaimer: 'Riders are invited, on all mountain routes, to redouble their caution, because numerous horses, mules, asses, bulls, cows, calves, goats, sheep and rams roam freely along the way.' Despite the meat available en route, Thys lost a stone during the Tour. Congratulating him, Desgrange wrote, 'France is not unaware that, without the war, the crack rider from Anderlecht would be celebrating not his third Tour, but his fifth or sixth.'

Jean Rossius, the stage winner at Perpignan, is interrogated by a
journalist with a long face but no pencil.

A handstand on a chair is one thing. A handstand on a chair after 400 km and sixteen hours in the saddle is something else. Jules Deloffre obliges.

1920   5,503 km

	Podium	Nationality	Time	Av speed (kph)
1st	Philippe Thys	Belgium	228h 36m 13s	24.07
2nd	Hector Heusghem	Belgium	+57m 21s	
3rd	Firmin Lambot	Belgium	+1h 39m 35s	

1921

Desgrange refined the Tour de France rules like a madman tweaking a garotte. In 1921, he gave the riders good news and bad news. The good news was that they'd be allowed to replace broken parts with spares. The bad news was that they'd have to carry the broken bits to the finish line, to be inspected. Léon Scieur had to carry a buckled wheel strapped to his back for 300 kilometres. The cogs cut deeply into his skin, scarring him for life. But he won the Tour de France.

1921   5,484 km

	Podium	Nationality	Time	Av speed (kph)
1st	Léon Scieur	Belgium	221h 50m 26s	24.72
2nd	Hector Heusghem	Belgium	+18m 36s	
3rd	Honoré Barthelemy	France	+2h 1m	

1922

A year later, Scieur abandoned with a broken fork; so did Christophe, who had to walk out of the mountains on foot for the second time in his career. Two riders won three stages in a row: Jean Alavoine and Philippe Thys. Alavoine claimed he'd suffered forty-six punctures, and lost his chain fifteen times. He didn't win. Thys

Twenty hours into the stage, tortured by saddle sores, Jacquinot stops for soup. He has lost the yellow jersey.

took five stage wins in all, but he didn't win either. Hector Heusghem had finished second overall twice before, in 1920 and 1921, and he took over the yellow jersey with three stages to go. But he didn't win either: he broke his frame the following day, changed bikes without permission, and was docked an hour. That left the 1919 champion, Firmin Lambot, in the lead – and he won.

1922				5,375 km
	Podium	Nationality	Time	Av speed (kph)
1st	Firmin Lambot	Belgium	222h 8m 6s	24.20
2nd	Jean Alavoine	France	+41m 15s	
3rd	Félix Seller	Belgium	+42m 2s	

1923-4
Chain Gang on Wheels

After a decade of abstinence, the Tour de France at last celebrated a French winner: Henri Pélissier, ably assisted by Ottavio Bottecchia, an Italian teammate who led the race for six stages. But Pélissier was a thorn in the flesh of Henri Desgrange. A unionist and organiser, he campaigned for better wages and complained at riders' working conditions. A year later, in 1924, he admitted defeat after two stages: 'In this form, Bottecchia is head and shoulders above the rest of us.' True to form, the Italian won the Tour. But Pélissier and his brother Francis stole the show. When they abandoned at Coutances on stage three, an outspoken special correspondent named Albert Londres, recently returned from a trip to the French penal colonies in Cayenne, chased them down to hear their side of the story.

Under the headline *'Les Forçats de la Route'*, or 'The Convicts of the Road', Londres' brilliant account of the Pélissiers' story was published in *Le Petit Parisien* on 27 June 1924. A counterblast to Desgrange's overblown rhetoric, it quite overshadowed the race.

Londres asked Henri Pélissier why the brothers had abandoned: 'This morning, at Cherbourg, the commissaire approached me and, without a word, lifted up my jersey. He was checking whether I had two jerseys. What would you say if I lifted your jacket to see if you were wearing a white shirt? I didn't like his manners, that's all.'

Londres: 'What could he have done if you'd had two jerseys?'

Pélissier: 'I could have fifteen of them, but I'm not allowed to start the stage with two and finish it with only one.'

Londres: 'Why?'

Pélissier: 'Those are the rules... I went to see Desgrange. "I can't throw my jersey onto the road, then?"'

Desgrange: 'No, you can't throw away your sponsor's material.'

Pélissier: 'It isn't my sponsor's, it's mine.'

Desgrange: 'I'm not discussing it on the road.'

Pélissier: 'If you're not discussing it on the road, I'm going back to bed.'

Which he did, taking his brother with him.

'You have no idea what the Tour de France consists of,' Henri told the journalist. 'It's a Calvary – except there are only fourteen

A French kiss unites Francis Pélissier, the kisser, and his brother Henri, a Tour winner at last.

Eyes full of dust, Ottavio Bottecchia finds a way through the crowd in 1924.

stations of the Cross. We have fifteen. We suffer on the road, but do you want to see how we cope? Look...'

He took a phial from his bag.

'Cocaine for the eyes and chloroform for the gums.'

'Liniment to warm your knees,' said Maurice Ville.

'And there are pills. Do you want to see pills?'

They took out three boxes each.

'Basically,' said Francis, 'we're on dynamite.'

Henri carried on:

'Haven't you seen us washing at the finish? It's worth paying to

'Beneath the mud, you're white as a sheet. You're drained by diarrhoea, your eyes roll in water. At night, in your room, instead of sleeping you twitch like someone with Saint Vitus Dance.' Henri Pélissier

'The day will come when they will put lead in our pockets because they'll say God made man too light.' Henri Pélissier

see it. Beneath the mud, you're white as a sheet. You're drained by diarrhoea, your eyes roll in water. At night, in your room, instead of sleeping you twitch like someone with Saint Vitus Dance. Look at our shoelaces: they're made of leather – and they still don't always hold, they break. And it's tanned hide, at least, I think it is. Imagine what happens to our skin. When we get off our bikes, we're hanging out of our shoes and britches, and nothing will stay on you.'

'And your toenails,' said Henri. 'I've lost six out of ten. They fall off, one by one, on each stage.'

Some say the Pélissiers preferred a strategic withdrawal than a Tour as lackeys for Bottecchia, who sang as he pedalled and wore the yellow jersey from start to finish.

1923   5,386 km

	Podium	Nationality	Time	Av speed (kph)
1st	Henri Pélissier	France	222h 15m 30s	24.23
2nd	Ottavio Bottechia	Italy	+30m 41s	
3rd	Romain Bellenger	France	+1h 4m 43s	

1924   5,425 km

	Podium	Nationality	Time	Av speed (kph)
1st	Ottavio Bottecchia	Italy	226h 18m 21s	23.97
2nd	Nicolas Frantz	Luxembourg	+35m 36s	
3rd	Lucien Buysse	Belgium	+1h 32m 13s	

1925 Living Dangerously

The two years of Ottavio Bottecchia's supremacy read like a spy thriller. One day during the 1924 Tour, he received a note threatening him for being anti-Fascist. Several times his tyres were slashed. Bottecchia was a known leftist and opponent of Mussolini, and may have been in real danger. Eighteen months after his second Tour win, he was found by the side of a road, covered with bruises, his skull fractured. His bicycle however, was undamaged and propped against a nearby tree. He was taken to a hospital but died soon afterwards. During the 1924 Tour, he also believed he was being stalked by a female fan. Henri Pélissier said he feared for Bottecchia's life '... if Bottecchia's wife ever finds out.'

Bottecchia was used to living dangerously. During the Great War, at a time when every major army had bicycle troops, Bottecchia was one of them. The French and Belgian forces are estimated to have used 150,000 bicycle troops, the British 100,000, the Germans and Turks about 125,000 each, and the US Expeditionary Force brought 29,000 bicycles. Some say the first casualty of the First World War was a squaddie on a bike sent over a hill on a reconnaissance mission, never to return. By the end of the War, more than 6,000 bicycle troops had been killed in combat and 8,000 seriously wounded. Tens of thousands more were taken prisoner: Bottecchia was one of them. Still, the war had taught him his talent, so after the armstice, he became a professional cyclist. In 1923, he became the first Italian to wear the yellow jersey, and his

Champion and soda: Bottecchia improvises high-pressure hygiene
in the age before the power-shower.

teammate, the victorious Henri Pélissier, told the press, 'Bottecchia will be my successor.' And so he was.

For the other riders, the threat came from Bottecchia himself. Nicholas Frantz said, 'It would be dangerous to follow Bottecchia on a climb. It would be suicide. His pace is so high, so relentless, it would suffocate another rider.' In 1924, he became the first to wear the yellow jersey from start to finish – a feat which would be repeated in 1928 by Nicholas Frantz and in 1935 by Romain Maes. In 1925, Bottecchia became the first to benefit from yet another of Desgrange's rule-changes.

> 'It would be dangerous to follow Bottecchia on a climb. It would be suicide. His pace is so high, so relentless, it would suffocate another rider.'
>
> Nicholas Frantz

Desgrange had railed against domestiques in 1911: now he admitted the domestique system to the Tour de France, after years of holding back the tide like King Canute. He introduced two categories of racing licence: 'Firstly, one allowing all riders indiscriminately to exchange or supply each other with food, small spare parts and light assistance in repairs; secondly, a licence applying only to the riders grouped into teams, permitting them to provide each other with very serious reciprocal aid which goes, for example, as far as waiting for a rider who has experienced a mishap and pacing him back to the leading group... within each group of twelve riders, the different members can work together in such a way as to finish all together, or to bring the marque they represent victory in the person of one or more of their members. Thus a greater or lesser number of the riders on a single team, if one of their number be distanced for whatever reason, may wait for him and pace him back to the peloton.' Desgrange continued: 'This is the *ésprit d'équipe* as authorised by the rules. They do not prohibit use of team tactics such as one or more members of a team leading out a sprint...'

**Bottecchia and Buysse arrive in Paris with every one of the
5,430 kilometres they have just covered etched into their faces**

In Bottecchia's case, the rules now allowed him to ride, Armstrong-style, hundreds of kilometres in the slipstream of his great domestique, the Belgian Lucien Buysse. The two immediate outcomes were overall victory, and the slowest Tour in history, at 24.78 kph – perhaps the result of tactical riding following the introduction of proper team-work.

1925   5,430 km

	Podium	Nationality	Time	Av speed (kph)
1st	Ottavio Bottecchia	Italy	219h 10m 18s	24.78
2nd	Lucien Buysse	Belgium	+54m 20s	
3rd	Bartolomeo Aimo	Italy	+56m 37s	

1926 The Fabulous Buysse Boys

There were enough fabulous Buysse boys (pronounce it 'Bursar') to form the first half of a formidable cycling team – so they did. The pick of the litter was Lucien, who homed in on victory in the Tour with the patience and inevitability of a heat-seeking tortoise: he finished eighth in 1923, third in 1924, and second in 1925 after shepherding home his leader Ottavio Bottecchia. But victory in the 1926 was a family affair: his youngest brother, Jules won stage one of the 1926 race, and took the yellow jersey for a couple of days. Add that he finished ninth overall, and that more or less summarises his cycling career. The rest was up to Lucien, who succeeded where his elder brother, Marcel, the winner of six stages in the 1913 Tour, had failed.

As hard luck stories go, Marcel Buysse's lurked just behind the tragi-comedy of Eugène Christophe. After finishing fourth in the 1912 Tour de France, Marcel Buysse was leading the 1913 Tour when a broken handlebar robbed him of his chances. Despite winning four of the six remaining stages, he could only claw his way back to third place overall. He never shone at the Tour again, although he did finish third in the 1919 Tour of Italy.

Now, Lucien and Jules aimed to right that distant wrong, and from the moment Jules won stage one, the brothers constructed victory like expert architects.

Lucien Buysse, with everything but fairy lights hanging off him.

On 20 June 1926, the Tour de France started outside Paris for the first time. Perhaps to forestall any surreptitious train journeys later on, the event began with a ceremonial assembly in the capital and the Tour de France special to Évian, where the 5,745-kilometre route – the longest in Tour history – began. Of the 126 who set off, just forty one would reach Paris. Too many for Desgrange, no doubt, but to any reasonable judge an indicator of just how tough the 1926 Tour was.

Unsure how the race would unfold, the riders set off slowly, to Desgrange's great annoyance. Only Jules Buysse disturbed the tedium by winning stage one, alone, by thirteen minutes and six seconds.

Fellow Belgian (and inveterate smoker) Gustave Van Slembrouck took the yellow jersey after the 433 kilometres and seventeen hours of torment that was stage three, and carried it to the Pyrenees, where Lucien Buysse rode off alone into a thunderstorm, and emerged two stages later with an overall lead of one hour, five minutes. Even the

Lucien Buysse rides through the storm on the Col d'Aubisque

relentless hyperbole of Henri Desgrange couldn't diminish the genuine tragedy behind Buysse's win: his daughter had died during the race, and only his brother's urging got him through.

It left Desgrange with quite a headache: no French rider won a stage, and *L'Auto*'s sales slumped for the first time since 1903. Cue more insane tinkering with the rules.

1926				5,745 km
	Podium	Nationality	Time	Av speed (kph)
1st	Lucien Buysse	Belgium	238h 44m 25s	24.06
2nd	Nicolas Frantz	Luxembourg	+1h 22m 25s	
3rd	Bartolomeo Aimo	Italy	+1h 22m 51s	

1927-8
Two Tours de Frantz

Still incensed at the slow stages that had started the 1926 Tour, instead of taking an anger management course, Henri Desgrange made eight of the sixteen flat stages into team time-trials. He wanted to force every rider to ride flat out for the entire stage – although the rules generously allowed individual riders the theoretical option of breaking away alone to obtain an even better time. In 1928, the legendary Australian rider Hubert Opperman called the new system 'a crime which should never have been perpetrated on the roads of France'.

Desgrange defended the new rules in *L'Auto*: 'Mass starts led to the scandal of riders who crawled along the road and ridiculed their profession. Something had to be done and, despite colleagues who are partisans of minimising effort and still haven't studied the new rules, the formula of staggered starts is an effective and definitive remedy to the torpor of the riders.'

He wanted a dynamic race that wouldn't be decided by the two Pyrenean stages. What he created was confusion that brought to mind the old points system of the pre-war years. Even armed with a stopwatch, pen and paper, spectators found the staggered starts undecipherable. And it was all for nothing: the race was won in the Pyrenees anyway.

Under the new rules teams mattered more than ever, and this Tour of three halves was dominated by Dilecta, then J.B. Louvet, and finally Alcyon. During the first week, in Dilecta's flagrant

Like a survivor from a cataclysmic mudslide, Adelin Benoît reached Bordeaux so early, the finish line hadn't been painted yet.

supremacy, Francis Pélissier won a stage and held the yellow jersey for five days. On the sixth day, he abandoned. On the ninth day, the rest of the team followed suit. Desgrange's barmy scheme had taken its first victims.

J.B. Louvet stepped into the vacuum, and five of their riders took stage wins in quick succession: Van Stembrouck, Decorte, Verhaegen, Geldhof and Hector Martin, who wore the yellow jersey down the Atlantic coast from Brest to Bayonne. But, with too many chiefs and not enough Indians, J.B. Louvet ran out of steam before the decisive Pyrenean stages. At the stage start in Bayonne, Luxembourg's

Nicolas Frantz lay seventeen minutes behind race leader Martin; at the stage finish in Luchon, Martin lay twenty-second overall, an hour and forty minutes adrift of the new leader, Frantz.

The following day, from Luchon to Perpignan, Frantz finished second. The day after that, he was third. Two days later, he won again between Toulon and Nice. It was a tactical success for Alcyon's eccentric new strategist, Ludovic Feuillet, who wore a pharmacist's gown, a white bandanna, pince-nez with John Lennon lenses and talked past a thick white cigarette butt in the corner of his mouth.

Four days from Paris, Frantz tightened his grip on the jersey at Metz, where he put the finishing touch on his dominance with a stage win. Second overall was Maurits Dewaele, an hour and forty-eight minutes back.

1927				5,320 km
	Podium	Nationality	Time	Av speed (kph)
1st	Nicolas Frantz	Luxembourg	198h 16m 42s	26.83
2nd	Maurits Dewaele	Belgium	+1h 48m 21s	
3rd	Julien Vervaecke	Belgium	+2h 25m 6s	

1928

In 1928, the start was brought forward to 17 June due to the Olympic Games in Amsterdam. Frantz came to the start wearing the yellow jersey, and never surrendered it. Desgrange complimented his fastidiousness: 'He has pushed the limits of preparation by bringing twenty-two pairs of shorts and twenty-two pairs of socks – one of each for each stage – because he doesn't want a hasty laundering to damage his skin and cause the boils that will affect some of his colleagues. I won't even go into the care he takes of his feet and his posterior...'

'He has pushed the limits of preparation by bringing twenty-two pairs of shorts and twenty-two pairs of socks... I won't even go into the care he takes of his feet and his posterior...'
Desgrange takes us into Frantz's suitcase, and beyond...

No such perfect preparation for the Australasian team, led by Hubert Opperman. Readers of *The Sporting Globe* had contributed £1,250 to pay for their participation, but the four-man team spent the five-week voyage in steerage, unlike the Australian Davis Cup

In the dark shirt, right, Nicolas Frantz has a lean and hungry look.

'**Let's not speak about the Australians, whose desire was admirable and whose courage was undimmed, but how could they compete against ten-man teams, without knowing a word of French?**'

Desgrange commiserates with Oppie and his friends

players, who went first class on the same ship. The four Australasians were supposed to join a contingent of top French riders for the Tour, but the Frenchmen never materialised, so they competed alone, four men who'd never been to Europe, riding one team time trial after another – fifteen of the twenty-two stages were team time trials – against much larger, race-hardened European teams. For once, Desgrange recognised that the Aussies had been let down, and showed some sympathy: 'Let's not speak about the Australians,' he wrote, 'whose desire was admirable and whose courage was undimmed, but how could they compete against ten-man teams, without knowing a word of French?'

Nicolas Frantz had a Eugène Christophe moment on the road to Charleville when his fork broke on a level-crossing, but he acquired a ladies' bike at a bike shop. The rules allowed the change, so Frantz was helped back into the race by three domestiques. The final podium of Alcyon teammates Frantz, Leducq and Dewaele accurately reflected Alcyon's supremacy.

1928   5,375 km

	Podium	Nationality	Time	Av speed (kph)
1st	Nicolas Frantz	Luxembourg	192h 48m 58s	27.88
2nd	André Leducq	France	+50m 7s	
3rd	Maurits Dewaele	Belgium	+56m 16s	

1929
Three Yellow Jerseys

Henri Desgrange was unbelievable. The team time trial, his 'definitive remedy' for slow stages was quietly dropped, but he reserved the right to reintroduce it without notice if the average speed for the 'flat' stages dropped below thirty kph. But, instead of reverting to the previous model, Desgrange ignored everything that had happened since 1925 and the introduction of teamwork. Suddenly, the Tour was a free-for-all again, with no assistence between teammates. The riders got away with no other Desgrangian innovations – feet to be nailed to pedals, for instance – but, by the end of the Tour, Desgrange was still dissatisfied, and decided to dispose of the whole set-up lock, stock and barrel.

At the end of stage seven, the timekeepers faced a delicate situation. At Bordeaux, Nicolas Frantz won stage seven in an exciting sprint finish. He, André Leducq and Victor Fontan had the same time in GC. Behind them, the race leader, Maurits Dewaele, had been held up by two punctures, and had undoubtedly lost the yellow jersey. Aimé Dossche, second overall, was in the chasing group but the line didn't come soon enough and he missed taking the race lead by a handful of seconds. That left three race leaders on the same time, with no race regulation in place to separate them: Article 39 stated baldly, 'The leader of the general classification wears the yellow jersey.' That evening, Desgrange wrote: 'Tomorrow, we'll have three yellow jerseys. Our national team is now in with a serious chance.'

**A gruelling climb for the riders, a leisurely ride on the
running boards for the press.**

Twenty-four hours later, Gaston Rebry ended the embarrass-
ment by taking over the yellow jersey, before relinquishing it to
Victor Fontan who seized the race lead in the first of the two
Pyrenean stages, with Dewaele and Frantz ten minutes behind him.
Then, the fork gremlins escaped and started to play havoc.

Nine kilometres from Luchon and the start of stage ten, the
headlamps of Desgrange's car picked out a rider at the side of the
road: 'Fontan's fork has just broken; he has lost first place in GC...A
cyclist watching from the side of the road offers him his bike, but
Fontan is in despair, and, at first, he refuses. Then he changes his mind,
climbs on the bike and sets off into the unknown, with his broken
bike on his shoulder. A good six kilometres later, he finds a garage...

'Atop the Col du Portet d'Aspet, he is thirty-six minutes behind
the leading group. At Saint-Girons, he's no more than thirty. Then the

drama: at Aulos, 151 kilometres from the stage start, on the banks of the Aston, Fontan abandons and his whole team follows him.'

This left Dewaele in the race lead, with Nicolas Frantz seventy seconds behind him. 'Dewaele tops the Col du Portet d'Aspet fifty-five seconds ahead of Frantz, but then, his troubles begin. His first puncture means he goes through Saint-Girons in the third group. After Saint-Girons, he has another puncture, and he doesn't regain the group before the top of the Col de Port. At Tarascon, his deficit is four minutes. At Ax-les-Thermes, he's eight minutes back... at l'Hospitalet, half way up the Col du Puymorens, he's still four minutes behind Benoît Fauré. However, on the chasing group, he's no more than forty seconds behind.

'That's the moment in which, at the same place, Frantz starts to suffer a series of problems. When he suffers his first puncture, the yellow jersey is back with Dewaele...'

Dewaele had finished second in 1927 and third in 1928. In Grenoble he was so ill that he could only take a few spoonfuls of sugar dissolved in water. To Desgrange, the sight of a sick man being shepherded to victory in the Tour de France by his teammates was too much – especially when he was set against all forms of third-party assistance. Feeling that he was losing control of the Tour to the all-powerful cycle manufacturers, Desgrange had had enough. Dewaele, an exemplary winner in spite of everything, had unwittingly sparked a revolution.

1929 — 5,253 km

Podium		Nationality	Time	Av speed (kph)
1st	Maurits Dewaele	Belgium	186h 39m 16s	28.14
2nd	Giuseppe Pancera	Italy	+44m 23s	
3rd	Joseph Demuysère	Belgium	+57m 10s	

1930-1934
Four for France

In footballing terms, it's like the FA Cup refusing admission to Chelsea, Arsenal and the other London teams and insisting on a combined 'Greater London' entry to compete against a 'Merseyside' selection and a 'Greater Manchester' team. The very idea is lunacy – grist for the mill of a risk-taker like Desgrange. Driven to distraction by the feuding and poaching between Alcyon, Automoto, Peugeot and La Française, Desgrange invited the forty leading riders to take part in five eight-man teams in the national colours of Belgium, France, Germany, Italy and Spain, and added sixty *touristes-routiers* organised into regional teams. Instead of branded machines, the riders were obliged to use anonymous yellow bikes, and the whole enterprise was funded by a publicity caravan that preceded the race through the countryside. If Desgrange was mad, he had method, too – he had a shrewd idea that the new rules would favour the French. They did, and his new Tour de France enjoyed unimaginable success.

Desgrange's timing was impeccable: France had stable-loads of champions in waiting. In *L'Auto* in 1927, Charles Ravaud had written: 'Antonin Magne, most notably, is, with André Leducq, the confirmation that the Tour de France can engender Frenchmen whose muscles aren't immobile. Anonin Magne is a champion of

The moment the Tour was won: André Leducq recovers, Antonin Magne pushes, after Leducq's second fall on the Télégraphe.

the future. Be patient. The day will come when Antonin Magne, like André Leducq, will demand that his name figure alongside those of Pottier, Trousselier, Garrigou, Lapize, Petit-Breton, and Pélissier in the annals of the Tour de France.' André 'Dédé' Leducq, 'gueule d'amour, muscle d'acier' – muscles of steel and a face made for love – was the housewives' choice for the 1930 Tour. Leducq had won eight stages in previous Tours, and come fourth in 1927 and second in 1928. Supported by a brilliant French team dressed in patriotic blue, he caught the wave of patriotism that had been sweeping the nation since 1927, when Borotra, Brugnon, Cochet and Lacoste won the Davis Cup, which they then defended in the Roland Garros stadium in Paris. The Tour was dominated by the French team, with five of its eight riders in the top ten and the first French victor since 1923.

1930   4,818 km

	Podium	Nationality	Time	Av speed (kph)
1st	André Leducq	France	172h 12m 16s	27.98
2nd	Learco Guerra	Italy	+14m 13s	
3rd	Antonin Magne	France	+16m 2s	

1931

A year later, Antonin Magne made it two French victories in a row. Desgrange was sceptical: 'Antonin Magne is far from being a colossus like Frantz.' But Magne was stubborn, level-headed, unflappable, hard as nails. To Magne, preparation was everything: each May, he trained in the Pyrenees to reach Tour form. Thirty years later he was Raymond Poulidor's *directeur sportif*, and reproached him for his indiscipline: the work of preparing for the Tour, he said, was as intricate as a spider's web. During the 1931 Tour, between Nice and Gap, Magne had mechanical problems. When the peloton caught him, his closest rivals, Belgium's Joseph Demuysère and Italy's Antonio Pesenti, attacked. Magne might have lost the Tour then and there, had it not been for the old-timer Charles Pélissier, who led the chase with Magne on his wheel and limited his losses to a couple of minutes. Both men collapsed on the finish line at Gap – but the Tour was won.

1931   5,095 km

	Podium	Nationality	Time	Av speed (kph)
1st	Antonin Magne	France	177h 10m 3s	28.76
2nd	Joseph Demuysère	Belgium	+12m 56s	
3rd	Antonio Pesenti	Italy	+22m 51s	

Mind the gap. Charles Pélissier (right) has helped Magne (left) through his crisis to Gap. The Tour is won.

1932

In 1932, Dédé Leducq was back. On the punishing ride from Cannes to Nice, taking in the Col de Braus and Col de Castillon, he rode out an off-day with the help of his teammates. His teammate Georges Speicher even made the ultimate cycling sacrifice by handing his leader a wheel. Days later, Leducq, revitalised, disappeared into the snow and fog and emerged victorious at Aix-les-Bains. It was a decisive stage; his closest rivals, Germany's Kurt Stoepel and the Italian Francesco Camusso, lost more than thirteen minutes. Dédé's perfect knowledge of the route and excellent humour contributed to his composure. He hummed the melodies of Fredo Gardoni and Jean Cyrano and lent his name to toe-straps, watches, tyre patches and hair grease.

Pendant le TOUR, le " MIROIR DES SPORTS " PARAIT le MARDI et le SAMEDI

Le Numéro : 75 Centimes

Mardi 26 Juillet 1932. - N° 664

LE MIROIR
DES SPORTS

LE COUREUR DONT HENRI PELISSIER,
à Aix-les-Bains, disait : « Celui-là, c'est un costaud »,
André Leducq donc, atteint paisiblement, sagement, le som-
met du col du Galibier, au milieu d'une tourmente de
neige. Leducq est alors 14ᵉ, mais il comblera aisément son
retard et gagnera cette étape Grenoble-Aix, augmentant
ainsi son avance au classement général.

Photo d'un des envoyés spéciaux du « Miroir des Sports ».

'Gueule d'amour, muscle d'acier' – muscles of steel and a face made for
love. André 'Dédé' Leducq, the housewives' favourite

1932   4,520 km

	Podium	Nationality	Time	Av speed (kph)
1st	André Leducq	France	154h 12m 59s	29.31
2nd	Kurt Stoepel	Germany	+24m 3s	
3rd	Francesco Camusso	Italy	+26m 21s	

1933

Speicher, Leducq's sacrificial lamb in 1932, stormed to victory in 1933. He told *L'Auto*, 'Days before the Tour started, I was seriously ill. It was with some apprehension that I set off, and the first few stages were not good for me. I wasn't myself until Gap; I was just a touch of energy away from perfect form. Then, all at once, it came to me.' As the rest of France celebrated, Desgrange damned him with faint praise: 'I swear I'd find it hard to explain in detail why Speicher's victory doesn't give me the satisfaction earlier victories did... I'd like to see more imagination in his understanding of the race, a bit more of the initiative that makes true leaders. I'd like to see his intellectual faculties, if I may say so, reach the level of his muscular virtues, which are quite remarkable.'

1933   4,396 km

	Podium	Nationality	Time	Av speed (kph)
1st	Georges Speicher	France	147h 51m 37s	29.73
2nd	Learco Guerra	Italy	+4m 1s	
3rd	Giuseppe Martano	Italy	+5m 8s	
Mountains: Vicente Treuba		Spain		

Georges Speicher lurches down the Aubisque, fortified by a bottle of beer.

René Vietto has given his front wheel to Antonin Magne.

All he can do now is wait.

1934

A year later, Antonin Magne took his second Tour de France, with the assistance of a twenty-year-old climber who stole the show. René Vietto might have won the 1934 Tour de France if he hadn't got bitumen in his eyes on stage five and lost fifty-four minutes. Instead, Vietto's display of heroic – or abject – self-sacrifice went down in the canon of sporting anecdote. He had waltzed through the Alps to two stage wins; through the Pyrenees, he was staging a virtuoso performance when team duties cut his recital short. Between Perpignan and Ax-les-Thermes, he was forced to give up a wheel to his leader. Between Ax and Luchon, he actually had to turn round, ride back along the route and hand Magne his bike. The frustration was suffocating, both for Vietto and for the public watching from the roadside or following the race through the pages of *L'Auto*.

Without Vietto's twin acts of renunciation, Magne would certainly have lost the jersey. The question that no one could answer was whether Vietto would have been able to recover it? He thought so: 'My main problem,' he said later, 'was that I was so unlucky at the start of the Tour. Without the setbacks before Charleville and before Evian, I'd have had the yellow jersey at Cannes, I'd have become a "free man" and I'd have won the Tour de France.'

1934   4,370 km

	Podium	Nationality	Time	Av speed (kph)
1st	Antonin Magne	France	147h 13m 58s	29.72
2nd	Giuseppe Martano	Italy	+27m 31s	
3rd	Roger Lapébie	France	+52m 15s	
Mountains: René Vietto		France		

1935-9 Disraeli Gears

The Tour's Luddite tendencies meant a thirty-year wait before the derailleur got the nod. Paul de Vivie experimented with a two-speed mechanism as early as 1905, but not until the late 1930s was the derailleur de rigueur at the Tour. And it wasn't until 1967 that a top five album would be named after it: Cream's Eric Clapton was discussing bikes with drummer Ginger Baker, when their roady Mick Turner commented on the performance of 'those Disraeli gears'. Disraeli Gears reached number five in the UK chart, and number four in the US. Small beer: in 1937, 'those Disraeli gears' took Roger Lapébie to number one in France. Gino Bartali did even better, topping the charts in France and Italy – with Disraeli's help, of course.

In 1935, Romain Maes told *L'Auto*, 'If I ever have a son, he'll never be a cyclist. It's hard. Heck, it's hard!' The headline writer changed it to 'He'll never ride the Tour de France': cycling, for Desgrange, meant the Tour: he had interests to protect, and you can't have too much mythologising. At five foot three and ten and a half stone, Maes was a pocket-sized powerhouse. He won stage one and held the yellow jersey for the rest of the Tour, an incredible performance, accompanied, as usual, by sideshows that lurched from comedy to tragedy and back again. Italy's Raffaele Di Paco won the first time trial after hanging on to a car for a little extra speed. The Spaniard Francisco Cepeda could have done with a little less: on the descent from the Col du Galibier, he fell. Five days later, he died from his injuries: the first Tour rider to expire during the race, and sadly, not

Romain Maes takes the stage win at Cannes. Behind him, Francisco Cepeda, the Spanish climber, has fallen. He will never regain consciousness.

the last. Then, on stage seventeen, from Pau to Bordeaux, in overpowering heat, the riders found beer bottles lined up at the side the road, and declared a truce to sate their thirst. It was a well-designed ruse by Julien Moineau, who rode straight past the beer and reached Bordeaux fifteen minutes ahead of the peloton.

1935   4,062 km

	Podium	Nationality	Time	Av speed (kph)
1st	Romain Maes	Belgium	141h 23m 0s	28.7
2nd	Ambrogio Morelli	Italy	+17m 52s	
3rd	Félicien Vervaecke	Belgium	+24m 6s	

Mountains: Félicien Vervaecke   Belgium

1936

A year later, Henri Desgrange himself was at the centre of a health scare. At Charleville, on day two, he was taken ill, and rushed to hospital for a prostate operation. He was replaced as race director by his protégé Jacques Goddet, whose father Victor had been the financial comptroller of the Parisian velodromes at the Parc des Princes and the Vélodrome d'Hiver, and after 1900, of *L'Auto*. Goddet later became the Tour's great moderniser, but Desgrange needn't have worried: Goddet was his spiritual son, and observed, 'It's necessary to keep the Tour's inhuman side. Excess is necessary.' Goddet presided over another Tour dominated by a Belgian named Maes, but this time, it was Sylvère Maes, no relation. Antonin Magne did his best to resist, but he was cursed by bad luck. At St André les Alpes, the local postman threw a bottle of beer to a rider,

Truth in jest in 1937: Roger Lapébie really did give Sylvère Maes a cold shower, winning the Tour after attacking when the yellow jersey had punctured.

who dropped it. The bottle shattered in front of Magne, who lost minutes to the puncture. But Maes was supremely confident, and told *L'Auto*, 'I ordered a yellow jersey made of silk for the final stage when we were still in Perpignan. I was certain I'd win the Tour. I know the Pyrenees too well to be afraid of Magne beating me. I felt too strong to let that happen. I already felt like the winner.'

Magne had to make do with second place, which he took over at Pau, moving ahead of Belgium's Félicien Vervaecke, despite a five-minute penalty for accepting water from Victor Fontan. Vervaecke was penalised eleven minutes for accepting food from his wife – and for borrowing a bike fitted with a derailleur. Following Tour tradition, one year's crime was the next year's revolution: in 1937, Roger Lapébie used a derailleur to win the Tour.

1936 — 4,149 km

	Podium	Nationality	Time	Av speed (kph)
1st	Sylvère Maes	Belgium	142h 47m 32s	29.06
2nd	Antonin Magne	France	+26m 55s	
3rd	Félicien Vervaecke	Belgium	+27m 53s	
Mountains: Julio Berrendero		Spain		

1937

The 1937 Tour should have been Bartali's year; instead, it turned into an unsightly, nationalistic dogfight. Bartali was known as 'Ironman'. His impassive face remained expressionless, no matter the effort, and, at its centre, the boxer's nose, broken in a fall during a sprint in 1934, gave him the look of a slugger. He'd won his second Giro in the spring, and at the Tour he rode brilliantly over the Galibier and reached Grenoble eight and sixteen minutes ahead of Sylvère Maes and Roger Lapébie respectively. That gave him the race lead. But the next day, disaster struck! As Bartali descended from the Col de Laffrey, his teammate Jules Rossi fell crossing a bridge, forcing Bartali into the meltwater below. That was the end of the Italian challenge.

The Belgian threat ended in Bordeaux at the finish of stage sixteen. A series of incidents brought feelings to a head: in the Pyrenees, the handlebars of race leader Roger Lapébie were sabotaged and fell apart. Then he was accused of accepting unauthorised food from his brother Guy. Next, he was penalised ninety seconds' penalty for taking an illicit push, 'despite vehement protests'. Then, Sylvère Maes suffered a puncture, received illegal help from his teammates and from two individual countrymen, Gustaaf Deloor and Adolf Braeckeveldt, and was penalised in turn. Feelings overflowed at Bordeaux, where angry supporters of local hero Lapébie threw pepper into the faces of the Belgians. Before the next stage started, the Belgians withdrew and announced they would take part in no future Tours. One added, melodramatically, that they didn't want to be lynched in Paris.

1937				4,415 km
	Podium	Nationality	Time	Av speed (kph)
1st	Roger Lapébie	France	138h 58m 31s	31.77
2nd	Mario Vicini	Italy	+7m 16s	
3rd	Leo Amberg	Switzerland	+26m 13s	
Mountains: Félicien Vervaecke Belgium				

1938

In 1938, Gino Bartali was back, and this time, he made no mistake. Everyone was expecting his attack, but when it came, between Digne and Briançon, no one could do a thing about it. He crossed

**After winning the 1938 Tour, Gino Bartali is put through the ritual
humiliation of open male snogging before a crowd of thousands.**

the finish line five minutes, eighteen seconds ahead of his teammate Vicini, followed by Mathis Clemens. Between Belfort and
Strasbourg, Desgrange watched Bartali closely, and wrote
afterwards: 'I have never seen anything as wonderful as Bartali on
the Ballon d'Alsace.'

On the final stage, with the Tour in Bartali's bag, Magne and
Leducq attacked together. Both men had ridden their first Tour in
1927, both had finished nine Tours, both had won two of them. The
officials awarded the stage to them both in a dead heat.

1938   4,205 km

	Podium	Nationality	Time	Av speed (kph)
1st	Gino Bartali	Italy	148h 29m 12s	28.32
2nd	Félicien Vervaecke	Belgium	+18m 27s	
3rd	Victor Cosson	France	+29m 26s	
Mountains: Gino Bartali		Italy		

1939

Bartali didn't defend his title: in 1939, on the eve of war, there were no Germans, Italians or Spaniards among the seventy-nine starters. A French rider, André Bramard, had already been allocated his race number when he was called up and had to withdraw from the race.

Desgrange may have left the race, but his spirit lived on: always ready to spice up things with a daft rule change, and de-spice them

Into the Alps, and not a Frenchman in sight. Belgium's Edward Vissers leads, followed by Sylvère Maes of Belgium, capless, with Albert Ritserveldt, a Belgian, third.

later with a shame-faced reversion to the obvious, the organisers decided to disqualify the last-placed rider in the general classification each day. So they did between stages two and seven, dispatching the Luxembourger Jean Majerus, who had worn the yellow jersey for seven stages in 1938. When a fall put Amédée Fournier, the first yellow jersey of the 1939 Tour, in last place, the rule was hastily consigned to the scrapheap. It was soon joined by a number of famous names. 1935 champion Romain Maes won the first time-trial on day two, took the yellow jersey, but reached the Pyrenees exhausted and abandoned during the next time-trial to Pau, never to start another Tour. Then, between Pau and Toulouse, back pain forced Félicien Vervaecke, Bartali's vanquisher in the Pyrenees a year earlier, to abandon. He'd never ride another Tour either. By then René Vietto was in pole position, but he'd been hit by bronchitis in Royan and suffered through the Pyrenees.

Victories on successive days decided the Tour: over the gruelling Izoard, 1936 winner Sylvère Maes finished seventeen minutes ahead of Vietto. The following day, he won the Tour's first ever mountain time-trial by the massive margin of four minutes. The stage took the Tour over the Iseran for the first time, at 2,770 metres Europe's highest pass (the road had been completed just two years earlier). Maes won his second Tour by over half an hour, raising the average speed to 31.99 kph – speeding the Tour towards the looming conflict.

1939   4,224 km

	Podium	Nationality	Time	Av speed (kph)
1st	Sylvère Maes	Belgium	132h 3m 17s	31.99
2nd	René Vietto	France	+30m 38s	
3rd	Lucien Vlaemynck	Belgium	+32m 8s	
	Mountains: Sylvère Maes	Belgium		

Table manners are the first victim as the riders make for the trough during the scorching summer of 1947.

The
Golden Age

1947 A Marriage of Convenience

By August 1940, when Henri Desgrange and his joyous sporting sadism left this world, so much cruelty had been unleashed that his passing subtracted little from the sum of human suffering. In any case, his successor Jacques Goddet ensured the great man's legacy would be lasting. The reborn Tour de France, said Goddet, would send 'a message of joy and confidence... across the radiant landscape... a heroic adventure from which hatred is absent.'

Not entirely absent, though. Hatred may be too keen a word to describe Goddet's relationship with Félix Lévitan, the man appointed to oversee him by the Tour's new majority shareholders, but for the next four decades, the two men would bicker heroically across the Tour's radiant landscape. Like the mountain time-trial and the positive doping test, their rows were to become one of the great set pieces of the Tour de France.

After Desgrange's death and the German occupation of France, *L'Auto* was taken over by German directors. Jacques Goddet had to decide whether to scuttle his newspaper, or to continue to publish under the occupation. He chose the latter, knowing that to do so meant to print an obligatory column of triumphant German propaganda. After the war, this decision would cost him his newspaper. On the other hand, Goddet refused to organise the Tour de France. 'The Germans wanted to use popular celebrations to convince the French that life was normal under the Occupation,' he wrote. 'I refused.' This decision would keep him the Tour.

Air attack: on the Tourmalet, seconds separated L'Équipe's plane, on the way down, and René Vietto (leading), on the way up.

On *L'Auto*'s demise after the Second World War, Goddet created the newspaper *L'Équipe* in association with Émilien Amaury, the owner of the newspaper *Parisien Libéré*. Goddet continued to write: Jean Cocteau would describe him as 'The last of the troubadors, who sings the Tour like a *chanson de geste*.' But Amaury's trust had limits, and he sent an agent to assist Goddet, but also to keep him in check; his name was Félix Lévitan. Goddet and Lévitan were an odd couple. Lévitan had risen from lowly origins through hard work and driving ambition. Goddet regarded him as a parvenu. Goddet delegated responsibilities; Lévitan issued curt orders. Lévitan was a devoted husband all his life; Goddet had four wives and observed: 'I always wanted to marry the woman I loved at the moment I loved her.' Lévitan was prompt; Goddet was frequently late. The rows between them were legendary. Their uneasy collaboration ended only in 1986.

The 1947 Tour was a passionate affair. René Vietto's knees had survived three major wartime operations – that's one more than El Alamein – but they nearly perished three kilometres from the summit of the Tourmalet when *L'Équipe's* light aircraft brought back memories of aerial bombardment by crashing just ahead of him. Thanks to wins at Brussels and Digne, the yellow jersey spent most of the race on his back, but at the crucial moment, he was found wanting. In the antepenultimate stage, a 134 kilometre time-trial, he conceded six and a half minutes to the Italian Pierre Brambilla. The race was won – or would have been, had an oblique, down-at-heel rider from Brittany, 'tall as three apples', who wore a helmet of leather rolls over asymmetric, cabbage ears, not thought better. Jean Robic had few prospects to offer his prospective in-laws, but before the race, he reportedly told his new wife: 'I've got no dowry, but I'll bring you the first prize of the Tour de France.'

On stage fifteen, between Luchon and Pau, Robic had ridden 192 kilometres alone to win by nearly eleven minutes. All the same, by the final stage, Robic's marriage vow looked dangerously exposed: he started nearly three minutes behind the yellow jersey. Robic opened the hostilities on the steep Côte de Bonsecours, outside Rouen. Under Brambilla's impotent gaze, he was joined by Vietto's teammate Edouard Fachleitner, whose attacks on Robic only served to hasten Brambilla's collapse. So Robic reached Paris and victory in the 'Tour of Liberation' without ever having worn the yellow jersey.

1947   4,630 km

	Podium	Nationality	Time	Av speed (kph)
1st	Jean Robic	France	148h 11m 25s	31.24
2nd	Edouard Fachleitner	France	+3m 58s	
3rd	Pierre Brambilla	Italy	+10m 7s	
	Mountains: Pierre Brambilla	Italy		

1948 'V' for Vatican

There are people you want on your side. Lance
Armstrong had the two Georges – Hincapie and
W. Bush. Ivan Basso had Bjarne Riis and a dog called
Birillo. In a time and place of values more elevated,
but also rudimentary, Gino Bartali had Giovanni
Corrieri, a faithful domestique and enforcer who
was handy with his fists, and, even more faithful
and handier with a prayer mat, Pope Pious XII.

In September 1947, Catholic Action called an enormous rally at the
Vatican, where Pope Pious XII greeted them with a rousing speech:
'The opposing fronts in the religious and moral battleground are
becoming more and more clear. The time to be tested has come!
Look at your Gino Bartali, like you a Catholic Action member.
He has worn the sought-after yellow jersey many times. Enter this
championship of ideas.' Not sportswriter of the year stuff, but it was
the Pope.

Fortified by Roman apostolic support, Gino the Pious lost twenty-
one minutes, twenty seconds in twelve stages to a brilliant young
Frenchman called Louison Bobet. With heart-warming loyalty,
Bartali's team director, Alfredo Binda, admitted after the race: 'If I'd
managed Bobet, he'd have won the Tour.' The Italian press corps
thought Bobet already had won the Tour: when the race reached San
Remo, most of them abandoned the race and went home. But Bartali
had won at Lourdes, and prayed before the Virgin's shrine. He was
convinced divine assistance was at hand. Italy certainly needed it.

14 July 1948 was a rest day for the riders. In Italy, Domenico
Pallante, a slightly-built Sicilian packing a Smith and Wesson
decided it was time Palmiro Togliatti, the chairman of Italy's

Gino Bartali trails Louison Bobet on the Croix de Fer – but is it man against man, man against mountain, or man against mud?

powerful Communist Party, had a rest day, too – but he was going to make sure it was permanent. At 11.30 that morning, before he could be overpowered, Pallante fired four bullets into Togliatti's neck, spleen and close to his heart. He was rushed to hospital in critical condition. Thousands of leftists were quickly on the streets; by late afternoon, Italy was paralysed by a General Strike and some feared civil war was only hours away. That evening, the Italian President, Alcide De Gasperi, called Bartali at his hotel in Cannes. 'Gino, do you recognise me? It's Alcide De Gasperi. Everywhere's in chaos here. Do you think you can still win the Tour? It could make a difference, and not just for you.'

At 6 a.m. the following day, the Tour resumed. On the Col de la Croix de Fer, Bartali said to Bobet, 'You are a great fighter and a great champion', then rode away. By 3.30 p.m. Bartali was soaring over the Col d'Izoard, the highest and steepest climb of the day, more than eighteen minutes ahead of Bobet. He preserved his lead all the way to Briançon. Bartali now lay second overall, one minutes, six seconds behind the yellow jersey. Italy, instead of fighting in the streets, had gathered around its wirelesses in wonder.

The following day, newsflashes kept the nation informed of Bartali's progress. At 8.30 a.m., crossing the Col du Lauteret, he trailed Bobet by twenty seconds. On the Galibier, both riders attacked. Not an inch separated them as the wrestled over the next eighty kilometres, perfectly matched. At the summit of the Croix de Fer, Bartali had prised open a gap of just two seconds. Then, leaving Grenoble, Bobet cracked. On the Col de Porte, Bartali's lead was over six minutes. By the time he reached Aix-les-Bains, his lead over Bobet in the general classification was eight minutes, three seconds.

Italy was ecstatic. On Saturday 17 July, the Communist newspaper *L'Unità* called off the general strike. Over the page, it carried a dry account of the ultra-Catholic Bartali's victories. At hospital in Rome, Togliatti was stable, and awake, and asked his son for news of the Tour de France. Cycling had worked its healing power.

Fuelled by his profound religious faith, Bartali won a third consecutive stage from Aix to Lausanne; at Liège six days later, he won his seventh stage of the Tour and extended his overall lead to twenty-six minutes, sixteen seconds.

1948 — 4,922 km

	Podium	Nationality	Time	Av speed (kph)
1st	Gino Bartali	Italy	147h 10m 36s	33.44
2nd	Albéric 'Brik' Schotte	Belgium	+26m 16s	
3rd	Guy Lapébie	France	+28m 48s	
	Mountains: Gino Bartali	Italy		

1949 A Rare Bird

Middle age strikes suddenly, like nightfall in the tropics. As a thirty-four-year-old, Gino Bartali was on top of the world, winning the Tour by riding away alone on the Izoard. Less than a year later, the Izoard saw him humiliated by a younger man. In June 1949, Fausto Coppi won his third Tour of Italy with an unforgettable solo breakaway of 132 kilometres over the Col de Larche, the Col de Vars, the Izoard, the Mongenèvre, the ascent up to Sestriere and then the drop down to the village of Pinerolo. The old Bartali finished second, ten minutes after the new one, and the Italian selectors for the Tour suddenly had a problem.

Aquiline, sculpted, gaze shadowed by childlike timidity, Fausto Coppi embodied a new type of rider. To the Italian writer Curzio Malaparte, 'Bartali is for the orthodox, his talent is spiritual, the saints look after him. Coppi has no protection up there. Bartali has blood is his veins, Coppi has petrol.' He certainly seemed to have some petrel in him: ungainly on two feet, he spoke with great flaps of his huge hands. But when he took flight, soaring towards distant mountain summits, he became both sublime and unbeatable.

The problem was, no one had ever won the Giro, then gone to France and won the Tour. No one knew whether the double was physically possible. And even if it was, Coppi had never ridden the Tour. On the other hand, Bartali may have been the defending champion, but at thirty-five, taking him might have been a liability. Plus, the two men mistrusted each other. Coppi told Bartali: 'Gino, if we're on bikes, I can't get on with you.' Bartali told Coppi: 'You're

Cordial friends in civvies, the best of enemies in the saddle. Bartali and Coppi (left and right) await the outbreak of hostilities.

going to have to understand, I'll be at the Tour anyway. The Belgians have offered me a place in their team as captain.'

Faced with a change of nationality by one of its greatest athletes, Italy had to act. Alfredo Binda, a rider so crushingly dominant between the wars that in 1930 the Giro organisers had actually paid him to stay at home, was recruited to bring the two men together.

Early in the 1949 Tour, Coppi's emotional vulnerability made his selection look a mistake. On stage five, between Rouen and Saint Malo, a fall involving the yellow jersey, Jacques Marinelli, left Coppi unhurt but his bike unusable. The entire Italian team waited, and a teammate offered Coppi his bike, but the great man refused it: he wanted his own spare. The operation lost him eighteen minutes to Marinelli, and Coppi was close to abandoning. His teammates convinced him to carry on, at least to the stage finish.

Ferdi Kübler brandishes a bicycle pump at the passage of time. This
puncture on the Izoard lost him fifteen minutes to Coppi and Bartali.

A sporting genius. Lean, light, inexhaustible in the mountains and against the clock, Fausto Coppi redefines his sport.

Two days later, Coppi rode away with the ninety-two kilometre time-trial, regaining seven and a half minutes on Marinelli. He marked time through the Pyrenees and across southern France. Then, on Bartali's thirty-fifth birthday, the two greatest climbers in the sport attacked on the Izoard. At Briançon, Coppi allowed Bartali to take the stage victory and the yellow jersey. The following day, they attacked again. Plummeting down the slopes of the Petit Saint Bernard, Bartali punctured. Binda convinced Coppi to leave

> **'Bartali is for the orthodox, his talent is spiritual, the saints look after him. Coppi has no protection up there. Bartali has blood is his veins, Coppi has petrol.'**
>
> Italian writer Curzio Malaparte compares Italy's Tour champions

Bartali behind. He gained nearly five minutes on his teammate, and took the yellow jersey. Knowing that to fight Coppi for victory would destroy the Italian team, Bartali put himself at Coppi's service. On the penultimate stage, a 137-kilometre time-trial, Coppi and Bartali again finished first and second; Coppi increased his lead to nearly eleven minutes, and maintained it to Paris. He had won the Tour at his first attempt, and become the first to win the Tours of Italy and France in the same year.

In 1950, Coppi fell during the Tour of Italy and couldn't start the Tour. A year later, he was a stranger to himself and to the world around him, mourning the death of his brother Serse, who had died in a fall at the Tour of Piedmont on 29 June 1951, five days before the Tour began. On stage sixteen he suffered an emotional breakdown and almost finished outside the time limit, although he was sufficiently composed to win stage twenty, the great Alpine stage of the race, finishing at Briançon.

1949   4,808 km

	Podium	Nationality	Time	Av speed (kph)
1st	Fausto Coppi	Italy	149h 40m 49s	32.12
2nd	Gino Bartali	Italy	+10m 55s	
3rd	Jacques Marinelli	France	+25m 13s	
Mountains: Fausto Coppi		Italy		

1950-1 Special K

There had always been something distinctly Old Testament about the Tour, with Henri Desgrange as its jealous and vengeful God. In 1950, the Tour moved even further into Old Testament territory when French crowds, sick of the Italian dominance, turned stage eleven into a stoning. The Italians withdrew in protest – and handed the Tour to the Swiss.

In Coppi's absence, Italy adopted the curious but effective tactic of pursuing prime-number stages. With two, three and five already in the bag, Gino Sciardis spoiled the sequence by finishing only second in stage seven, and Fiorenzo Magni ruined it completely by winning stage eight. Then Gino Bartali rose majestically over the Pyrenees. On stage eleven, no doubt enraged by the prospect of more prime numbers falling to foreigners, French fans on the Tourmalet hurled insults at the Italians. On the Aspin, the insults turned to bottle tops and stones, and as the riders approached the finish line, the road before them was blocked. Bartali was brought down, which brought Robic down too, his fall and his wheel broken by the Italian. The race director, who carried himself softly but walked with a stick, arrived in the nick of time wielding his cane, and like a Jedi master, Jacques Goddet saved the day. It was a sign of the enlightenment of the age: between the Wars, the long arm of Desgrange used to use small arms. That's progress.

Incidentally, the main victim of the Italian withdrawal was Magni, who was wearing the

> '**Angular, gangly, dry and capricious... Kübler is sometimes suspected of artificiality: does he dope?**'
> Roland Barthes on Ferdi Kübler

'Surely the cyclists should have been acquiring, or re-acquiring,
the rudiments of their strenuous profession, rather than indulging
in these carnival antics.' Jacques Goddet, 1950.

yellow jersey at the time. It left the whimsical Swiss rider Ferdi
Kübler in the race lead, although he sportingly refused to wear the
jersey the following day. Even so, Kübler evoked mixed feelings,
even in his admirers. This is the French philosopher Roland Barthes:
'Angular, gangly, dry and capricious... Kübler is sometimes
suspected of artificiality: does he dope? A comedian of the tragic, he
only coughs and limps when he's being watched. He's also a Swiss-
German, which gives him the right, perhaps even the duty, to speak
comedy-French: "Ferdi, no luck." "Gém always on Ferdi's wheel."
"Ferdi no start."'

According to one, possibly apocryphal tale, Kübler once dropped
back to taunt the French rider Raphaël Géminiani: 'Ferdi attack
now, France ready?' Géminiani told him, Basil Fawlty-style, 'Ferdi

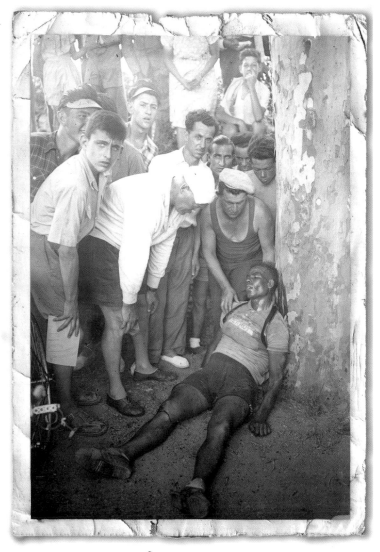

Sunstroke – or inebriation? Abdel-Kader Zaaf has taken cold wine for the southern heat – and paid the price!

shut up now or Ferdy get head knocked in.' In an interview after
the race, Kübler later admitted: 'According to my reputation, I was
good but inconsistent, something of a fantasist.' He went on, 'They
said I didn't have it in me to finish the Tour, and I wondered myself.
So it was an unlikely adventure...'

1950				4,784 km
Podium	**Nationality**	**Time**		**Av speed (kph)**
1st Ferdinand Kübler	Switzerland	145h 36m 46s		32.85
2nd Constant 'Stan' Ockers	Belgium	+9m 30s		
3rd Louison Bobet	France	+22m 19s		
Mountains: Louison Bobet	**France**			

1951

Kübler's Tour win was Switzerland's third major cycling triumph of
1950: Hugo Koblet had won the Tour of Italy and the Tour of
Switzerland. A year later, Kübler stayed away, but his compatriot
Hugo Koblet ensured the Tour de France had a Swiss protagonist.
French hopes surrounded
Louison Bobet, who had won
the one-day classic between
Milan and San Remo in the
spring, but on stage twelve from
Brive-la-Gaillarde to Agen,
Switzerland's man escaped alone

> **'His enormous talent,
> was matched only by
> the brevity of its
> duration.'**
> Bobet on Koblet

with 135 kilometres to ride and, incredibly, held off a chasing group
containing Coppi, Bobet, Bartali, Magni, Géminiani, Ockers and
Robic – the cream of world professional cycling at the time.
Intermittantly cooling his brow with a sponge from his shirt
pocket, Koblet had such a fluid, supple style that there was no

Showing the vanity of champions, Hugo Koblet always seems to have a comb poised.

impression of effort. After he crossed the finish line, he stopped, started his stopwatch, suavely ran a comb through his hair and waited for his pursuers to appear.

Koblet jumped into third place overall, and the French singer Jacques Grello, writing a column in *L'Équipe*, called him 'le pédaleur de charme' – something like 'Prince Charming on a bike.' The pantomime theme continued when the Cinderella-like Gilbert Bauvin missed a day in the yellow jersey thanks to an ugly sister of a time-keeping error. On the Aubisque three days later, Wim Van Est, the first Dutchman ever to lead the Tour, staged a hilarious silent movie parody by sliding into a deep ravine, and was only able to regain the roadside thanks to a tow rope made of all the Dutch team's spare tyres.

The following day, Koblet took over the race lead at Luchon after winning a two-man sprint against Fausto Coppi. The Swiss rider was in complete control; the Italian suffered an emotional breakdown two days later on stage sixteen and almost finished outside the time limit. Four days later, Coppi was sufficiently recovered to win the great Alpine stage of the race into Briançon, but it was too late to challenge Hugo Koblet.

Neither Kübler nor Koblet ever won another Tour. Kübler finished second in 1953; Koblet never finished again, and Louison Bobet's memories of him are mixed: 'Everyone found him inspirational. Women grabbed photographs with him. The fact is, never has anything so stunning been seen propelling a bicycle. Adroit and powerful, supple and smiling, relaxed and sovereign: this is how Hugo Koblet appeared to the crowds between 1950 and 1953. His enormous talent was matched only by the brevity of its duration.'

'He doesn't count. I'm the first human.'

Raphaël Géminiani explains his second place behind Hugo Koblet

1951			4,692 km
Podium	Nationality	Time	Av speed (kph)
1st Hugo Koblet	Switzerland	142h 20m 14s	32.96
2nd Raphaël Géminiani	France	+22m 0s	
3rd Lucien Lazarides	France	+24m 16s	
Mountains: Raphaël Géminiani France			

1952 The Greatest?

By 1952, Coppi was his old self. The only man to complete the Giro-Tour double came to France intending to repeat it. As early as stage five, Coppi showed his hand, breaking away on the road to Namur and finishing second, with his rivals languishing in his wake. Victory in the first time-trial put him third overall. Then, the Tour took its first excursion up to Alpe d'Huez. After an attack by Robic at the foot of the climb, Coppi rose out of the saddle and forged ahead. Pierre Chany described him as 'untroubled by the dead weight and useless muscles which make others look like mules staggering up the mountain passes.'

The next day, on the road to Sestriere, Coppi broke away on the Galibier and reached the bottom of the final climb alone. By the time he reached the stage finish, his lead in the overall classification was three seconds short of twenty minutes. In response, the organisers doubled the prize money for second place, creating a race within the race with Fausto Coppi, the undisputed Campionissimo, in a category of his own. From Sestriere to Monaco, he added four more minutes to his lead; in the Pyrenees, he extended it to twenty-seven with the stage win at Pau. He stretched it to over half an hour by winning on the Puy-de-Dôme. Raphaël Géminiani described the stage finish: 'With two kilometres to go, his eyes fixed, his mouth open, his hands on the tops of the bars, Coppi rose out of the saddle, his long legs and powerful thighs turning the pedals faster and faster, and started to sprint. I was ahead of him, engulfed in hooting cars, backfiring motorbikes and screaming fans. Young men

> **'Easily, necessarily, proudly, statistically, doggedly, decidedly, the greatest.'**
> Louison Bobet remembers Fausto Coppi

ran fifty-metre stretches beside me, shouting "Come on, Gém. Come on!" I tried, but someone was going even faster: Coppi. Like a bird, he flew past me...Three hundred yards from the line, he caught the stage leader, Nolten, and finished ten seconds ahead of him.'

Due to injuries and aging, Coppi never competed in another Tour. In December 1959, he joined a group of elite cyclists, including Raphaël Géminiani, on a trip to ride in Upper Volta (now Burkina Faso). On their return, both men fell ill. By chance, a doctor with experience in the tropics saw Géminiani, and diagnosed malaria; Gém, dosed to the eyeballs with quinine, instructed his brother to inform Coppi's carers of the diagnosis. They ignored the advice and, with no quinine to stave off the fever, Coppi died on 2 January 1960.

Eddy Merckx always said, 'I don't like to hear the words "Merckx was the greatest", knowing that Coppi lost five years to the war.' Tour historian Pierre Chany wrote that, incredibly, 'It is rigorously true that Fausto Coppi, once he had attacked the peloton, was never caught by his pursuers during the years from 1946 to 1954...' When the passage was brought to Merckx's attention, he commented, quietly: 'In that case, perhaps he really was better than me.'

1952   4,827 km

	Podium	Nationality	Time	Av speed (kph)
1st	Fausto Coppi	Italy	151h 57m 20s	31.77
2nd	Constant 'Stan' Ockers	Belgium	+28m 17s	
3rd	Bernardo Ruiz	Spain	+34m 38s	
	Mountains: Fausto Coppi	Italy		

1953-5 **Holey Trinity**

Cyclists' joke: Renowned Communist René Vietto
to Louison Bobet: 'Have you read Marx?' – 'Yes, it's the
narrow saddle.' A fine time-trialist, a great climber and
a formidable rouleur, Bobet was the complete cyclist in
every way, except one. If the chink in the armour of
Achilles exposed the Greek hero's heel, Bobet's Achilles'
heel was his crotch. Saddle sores blighted his career;
they forced him to abandon the 1953 Tour of Italy on
2 June, during the final stage. Even so, thirty-two days
later, Bobet started the Tour – despite all that was holey...

'La Paix', a French insurance company, was offering a 'Mishap
Trophy' and twenty thousand French francs to promote its personal
accident policies. An early claimant was Roger Hassenforder, a
twenty-three-year-old from Alsace. He had taken the race lead on
stage five by joining an eight-man breakaway, winning the stage, and
waiting nine minutes forty-three seconds for the peloton to cross
the line. After four days in the race lead, he lost the yellow jersey,
and then catapulted off the road on stage ten in the Pyrenees. A
photograph shows him holding a front wheel with all the clenched-
up rigor mortis of a dead spider: his Tour de France was over.

A day later, Jean Robic won between Cauterets and Luchon, and
gained a minute and a half on Bobet. It was enough to make him
race leader, and race favourite. The following day, he let twenty-four
riders get away. They gained over seven minutes, and Robic's race
lead came to a premature end. To celebrate, he put lead in his bottle
to improve his descending speed, went down the Col du Fauredon
like a lead balloon, touched a wheel and went over the edge. It was
a magnificent mishap, and the Trophy was his. Meanwhile, Louison

His wheel clenched like the limbs of a dead spider, Roger Hassenforder awaits a replacement. It comes too late – and he's eliminated.

Bobet was biding his time, until, on stage eighteen, he flew over the Izoard between Gap to Briançon, won the stage by over five minutes, and took the yellow jersey. Then he demolished all-comers with a heavyweight time-trial two days later. After a six year drought, the Tour de France had been won by a Frenchman again.

1953				4,476 km
Podium	**Nationality**	**Time**		**Av speed (kph)**
1st Louison Bobet	France	129h 23m 25s		34.59
2nd Jean Malléjac	France	+14m 18s		
3rd Giancarlo Astrua	Italy	+15m 2s		
Mountains: Jesús Loroño	Spain			
Green jersey: Fritz Schaer	Switzerland			

1954

A year later, at Caen, Robic's major mishap was a collision with a finish-line photographer. It forced him to abandon. Hugo Koblet did even better: in the Pyrenees, he managed two nasty falls. At Toulouse, he abandoned the race, and ended his sporting career. Louison Bobet, meanwhile, was in flower early this year. Victory in stage two followed by second place in the team time-trial gave him the yellow jersey. From then on, however, he saved himself for a moment of passion on the Izoard, allowing Gilbert Bauvin to build a four-minute lead, with the help of a disorganised, comedic Spanish climber named Federico Bahamontes, whose nonsensical flourishes could have cost the sensible Bobet the race. On the first day in the Alps, Bahamontes' irresistible ascent of the Col de Romeyère rode him into race legend – or rather the ice cream he stopped to enjoy at the summit while waiting for the others to catch up did. As Jesús Loroño, his teammate, put it: 'He's a very good climber, but completely mad.' In Jacques Goddet's distinguished estimation, with an iota of tactical sense, Bahamontes could have won the Tour.

As it was, Bobet flew like a champagne cork over the Izoard – again – and took two and a half minutes out of Kübler, the runner-up, in the final time-trial. It was formulaic more than spine-tingling, but it was victory, and that's what counts.

1954				4,865.4 km
	Podium	Nationality	Time	Av speed (kph)
1st	Louison Bobet	France	140h 6m 5s	34.73
2nd	Ferdinand Kübler	Switzerland	+15m 49s	
3rd	Fritz Schaer	Switzerland	+21m 46s	
Mountains: F. Bahamontes		Spain		
Green jersey: Ferdi Kübler		Switzerland		

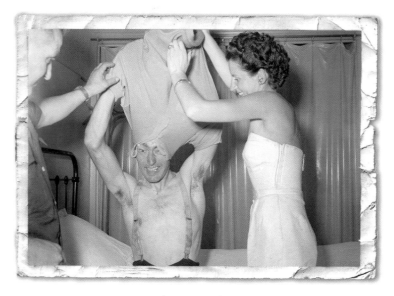

Louison Bobet bucks the 'No Women' rule: his wife, Christiane, divests him of the yellow jersey, and shows the world her husband's secret weapon: braces.

1955

In 1955, the action began in the Alps, where Charly Gaul, a twenty-two-year-old Luxembourgian, annihilated the field over the Galibier. Charly Gaul won the stage by nearly fourteen minutes, and Roland Barthes wasn't alone in contrasting Gaul's apparently God-given abilities with Bobet's all-too-human suffering: 'Bobet is an entirely human hero, with no debt to the supernatural. His victories are achieved using purely earth-bound qualities, improved on through that most human of attributes: will power. Gaul incarnates the arbitrary, the fantastic, the divine. Bobet embodies the just, the human. Gaul is an archangel, Bobet is Promethean, a Sisyphus who'd tip the rock over the very gods who have condemned him to being nothing but magnificently human.'

**Jean Malléjac survived his brush with death on the Ventoux,
but the warning signs were quickly forgotten.**

When the scene changed to Mont Ventoux, however, the human prevailed over the divine. Ferdi Kübler started the Ventoux at a sprint. Raphaël Géminiani came alongside and said, 'Wait a minute, Ferdi, the Ventoux isn't like other mountains.' Kübler replied, 'Ferdi, too, not a champion like others. Ferdi great champion. Ferdi win at Avignon.' Within ten kilometres, Kübler was zigzagging: 'Ferdi taken too much dope. Ferdi going to explode.' Later, he told the press in his pidgin French: 'He is too old, Ferdi. He is sick. Ferdi killed himself on the Ventoux.' The same was nearly true of Jean Malléjac, who collapsed in the heat. After reviving him, the race doctor announced his determination to sue someone for poisoning: Malléjac, too, had been doped to the eyeballs. It emerged that other riders, including Charly Gaul, had taken the same product as Malléjac. Nicolas Frantz, the winner in 1927 and 1928, now directing Gaul's team, told *L'Équipe*:

'Gaul is the victim of attempted murder. Whoever convinced him to dope has committed a crime.' Over the coming years, we'd hear more of this sort of talk from team managers: whoever convinced him to dope indeed!

**'He is too old, Ferdi.
He is sick.
Ferdi killed himself
on the Ventoux.'**
Kübler's career Tour
ends in farce

With Gaul incapacitated, Louison Bobet was the first to the top, and the first to cross the finish line at Avignon. It had been a gruelling day, capped by victory, although, as Bobet later commented, 'A son at the summit of Mont Ventoux is not a sight to show his mother.'

The Tour organisers responded with a set of recommendations for the team managers: 'They must closely inspect the treatment given to their riders; they must monitor the activities of the soigneurs attached to their teams; they must oppose the use of certain products administered without prescription.'

Twenty-four hours later, and somewhat prematurely in view of the events of the following half-century, *L'Équipe* wrote: 'The fight against doping seems to have been won... According to our information, everyone who was in possession of "explosives" got rid of them straight away.' Still, the Tour had avoided tragedy, by the skin of its teeth. Malléjac, Kübler and Gaul had got away with their lives – and Bobet had got away with the Tour, despite his saddle sores.

1955   4,476.1 km

	Podium	Nationality	Time	Av speed (kph)
1st	Louison Bobet	France	130h 29m 26s	34.30
2nd	Jean Brankart	Belgium	+4m 53s	
3rd	Charly Gaul	Luxembourg	+11m 30s	
Mountains: Charly Gaul		Luxembourg		
Green jersey: Stan Ockers		Belgium		

1956
A Win for a Nobody

Roger Walkowiak, a Polish descendant on the North-East/Centre team, was a provincial nobody supported by a posse of even lesser bodies. Under normal conditions, these were the anonymous, undifferentiated particles in the primal sporting sludge out of which higher, more sophisticated organisms were expected to evolve as the Tour progressed. That was the theory. It all started to go wrong before the race had even begun.

Louison Bobet had two magnificent legs, but only one beleaguered crotch, and an operation for his persistent saddle sores ruled him out of the Tour. Jean Robic was convalescing from an accident, and Coppi and Kübler were getting too old for this sort of thing and stayed away as well. The favourites, then, were Charly Gaul of Luxembourg, Belgium's Jan Adriaenssens and the French co-leader Gilbert Bauvin. Co- because the other French co-, the sprinter André Darrigade, thought he could win the Tour too, or rather, instead. I should co-co. All of which boosted the chances of a provincial nobody supported – really supported – by even lesser bodies. Those chances took a skywards leap 150 kilometres into stage seven of the 1956 Tour. A huge break of thirty-one riders had formed early in the stage. After 120 kilometres, their lead had stabilised at four minutes, thanks only to a grim pursuit by the domestiques of Bauvin and Darrigade. But the French national team had been worked too hard in the opening days, and at the 150 kilometre point, it was exhausted, and gave up the chase. Over the remaining ninety-three kilometres of the stage, the gap grew and

How do you drop a nobody? If Charly Gaul can't shake off Roger Walkowiak, no one can.

grew, and, in the end, Darrigade and Bauvin crossed the finish line eighteen minutes, forty-six seconds after the stage winner Alessandro Fantini and the new yellow jersey, Roger Walkowiak.

Walkowiak, despite riding for a regional team, it quickly transpired, was more than cannon-fodder. He'd finished second to Louison Bobet in the previous year's Dauphiné Libéré, a mountainous stage race through the Alps, and at the 1955 Tour he'd been climbing with the best, before abandoning at Avignon.

Darrigade fought his way back into contention by selecting the breakaways judiciously, and by stage eleven, he was in the yellow jersey. Then, the curse of the co-leader struck. After stage thirteen, he told *L'Équipe*, 'I had a puncture ten kilometres from the finish and I found myself alone. I'm dejected. Why wasn't the car there? I had to repair it myself, and I lost more than three minutes... I'm fifth in the general classification, and I ought to have some consideration.' His *directeur sportif*, Marcel Bidot, explained that Bauvin had fallen thirty-five kilometres from the finish line, Géminiani, Malléjac and Barbotin had waited, and the car had to be with them. 'I'm sorry,' he told Darrigade, 'but I don't have the gift of ubiquity.' The row between Darrigade and Gilbert Bauvin escalated, leaving the French team deeply divided.

Stage eighteen took the Tour through the Alps from Turin to Grenoble. On the Col de la Croix de Fer, Walkowiak launched a ballsy, all-or-nothing attack, with Charly Gaul and Stan Ockers glued to his wheel. On the Col de Luitel, Gaul scampered off to win the stage, but Walkowiak finished with Nencini and Bahamontes – future Tour winners – reclaimed the yellow jersey, and kept it all the way to Paris.

Bauvin started the final stage, a 332-kilometre marathon, just one minute, twenty-five seconds behind the yellow jersey. Many hoped to see a repeat of the final stage of the 1947 Tour, when Robic attacked and won the Tour. It wasn't to be: the French favourite was exhausted, and his team was fatally divided. Walkowiak, the nobody, fully supported by his team of nobodies took the race without ever taking a stage. Critics panned his victory for its lack of panache, but for Jacques Goddet 1956 was 'one of my favourite Tours.'

1956 — 4,527 km

	Podium	Nationality	Time	Av speed (kph)
1st	Roger Walkowiak	France	124h 1m 16s	36.50
2nd	Gilbert Bauvin	France	+1m 25s	
3rd	Jan Adriaenssens	Belgium	+3m 44s	

Mountains: Charly Gaul	Luxembourg
Green jersey: Stan Ockers	Belgium

The most stylish, the most elegant
of champions: Jacques Anquetil…
and the rest.

Anquetil
and After

1957 Boy Wonder

Climber, time-triallist, climber, climber, descender.
Not the wives of Henry VIII, but the five riders
who won a Tour de France each from 1956 to 1960
– although it seriously undersells numbers two and
three in the sequence. The worldly Jacques Anquetil
was a time-trial specialist who won mountain stages.
The reclusive Charly Gaul was a climber who won
time-trials. They were succeeded by the erratic
Federico Bahamontes, a climber with a taste for ice
cream, and the fearless Gastone Nencini, a descender
and committed smoker. The Tour has always taken
all sorts.

Jean-Paul Sartre's assistant Jean Cau described Jacques Anquetil as
'Descartes on two wheels, with a heart that pumped the blood
around more slowly than a waterwheel.' A cross-country runner,
Anquetil discovered cycling late and won his first race as an
eighteen-year-old. He caught the attention of Francis Pélissier, now
directeur sportif of La Perle, who took him on a year later to ride one
race: the Grand Prix des Nations, the most prestigious time-trial
title, the last two editions of which had been won by Tour winners
Koblet and Bobet. In 1953, Anquetil, aged nineteen, won it. He
won it again the next year, and the next, and the next, and by the
time he started his first Tour de France in 1957, he was highly
fancied. Against him was not just the opposition, but the by
now customary tensions within the French team, with the brilliant
Jean Forestier riding alongside the previous year's squabblers,
Bauvin and Darrigade.

**Even in the rain, Jacques Anquetil fingers the brakes
with the touch of a concert pianist.**

But as well as a choirboy's face and that powerful heart, Anquetil
had a Machiavellian mind. He convinced his teammates – rightly, as
it turned out – that, whatever they'd achieved in the past, he'd
achieve more in the future: he was where the money was. It
worked. The incredible heat of the summer of 1957 did for the
winter-loving Gaul on stage five, but by then, Anquetil had already
taken the first Tour stage win of his career, and in his hometown,
Rouen. In Charleroi, Bauvin won the stage and Anquetil donned
the yellow jersey. Two days later, Jean Forestier took the overall lead,

wheels, with a heart
that pumped the blood
around more slowly
than a waterwheel.'
Jean-Paul Sartre's assistant Jean
Cau describes Jacques Anquetil

but through the Alps to Briançon, Anquetil made up Forestier's three-minute advantage, and added four more.

The greatest threat to his dominance came in the Pyrenees. From Ax-les-Thermes to Saint-Gaudens, on the Col de Port, the Portet d'Aspet, the Ares and the Portillon, Jan Adriaenssens, Gastone Nencini and René Dotto launched darting attacks which Anquetil could counter only with the help of his teammates Louis Bergaud, Gilbert Bauvin and André Darrigade. The following day, Anquetil launched an imprudent attack, climbing the Tourmalet at an infernal pace and dropping Nencini. Then, at the feed zone, he was handed the wrong musette; inside, instead of semolina and fruit, he found nothing but iced tea. On the Soulor, he ran out of energy. For twenty-five kilometres, he rode at a snail's pace, as Janssens sped away in his bid for the yellow jersey. Da Silva, a Portuguese rider on the Luxembourg/Mixed team, led him through his crisis; ten kilometres from Pau, Anquetil recovered, and powered towards the finish line. He had lost time, but the yellow jersey was safe. By dominating the final time-trial, Anquetil increased his winning margin to nearly fifteen minutes.

1957   4,683.8 km

	Podium	Nationality	Time	Av speed (kph)
1st	Jacques Anquetil	France	135h 44m 42s	34.50
2nd	Marcel Janssens	Belgium	+14m 56s	
3rd	Adolf Christian	Austria	+17m 20s	

Mountains: Gastone Nencini   Italy
Green jersey: Jean Forestier   France

1958 **Supernatural!**

Raphaël Géminiani was a brilliant, blustering rider with a proud, accusative nose and an even bigger personality. He was also a potential Tour winner, which meant a potentially destabilising influence in the French national team, so Jacques Anquetil told the French selecter Marcel Bidot he would accept either Bobet or Géminiani, but not both. Géminiani was left out of the team, and at the Universal Exhibition in Brussels he delighted the press by posing beside a donkey called Marcel. He started the Tour anyway, in the colours of the French regional team Centre-Midi.

Part two of his offensive was a bruising attack on stage six to Saint-Brieuc which took him into third place overall, and then a tactical ride to Pau on stage thirteen, that ended with Géminiani in the yellow jersey. 'It doesn't worry me or weigh me down,' he told *L'Équipe*. 'Far from it. The race lead will galvanise me and, even if I lose it between Pau and Gap, I'll get it back in the Alps. I'm not saying I've won: we'll see things more clearly at Luchon, but above all, I'm waiting for the Ventoux to see what Gaul can do.'

There was clairvoyance in Gém's predictions: the Italian climber Vito Favero took the yellow jersey the following day at Luchon, and kept it until the mountain time-trial up Mont Ventoux. There were two winners that day: Charly Gaul took the stage, and Raphaël Géminiani took back the race lead. Everything was going according to plan. Until...

Charly Gaul had been having a miserable time. The day after the time-trial up Mont Ventoux, he'd had a mechanical problem, then

One transitory headache for André Darrigade, one mortal blow for Constant Wouters, General Secretary of the Parc des Princes. He never regained consciousness and died eleven days later.

he'd wrongly identified Bobet as the man to watch, allowing Gastone Nencini to get away, and then he'd fallen off his bike, arriving at Gap crying like a man who'd lost the Tour de France. The following day, he limped up the Izoard with a throbbing knee. That evening, Gaul, a quiet man who detested publicity and said as little as possible, especially to journalists, made a prediction: 'Tomorrow, if it's raining, I'll attack on the Luitel.' It was. He did.

The conditions, and the five-mountain, 220-kilometre hoof across the Chartreuse massif from Briançon to Aix-Les-Bains, were all Gaul needed. Jean Bobet wrote: 'What drove him was a mystery; his performances were unfathomable. He brought with him a sort of fragility and insecurity that made us fear both for the rider and the man.' Antoine Blondin observed, 'He climbs with vacant eyes, his hat worn back to front, like a distinguished street urchin.' With a thin smile stretched across his lips, he extended his lead over Géminiani: five minutes, thirty seconds on the fog-bound Col de Port, seven minutes, fifty seconds on the Cucheron, twelve minutes, twenty seconds on the Granier, fourteen minutes, thirty-five seconds at Aix-les-Bains.

Bobet either couldn't or wouldn't relay the ailing Géminiani, who broke down in tears on the finish line, and spat at his compatriots: 'Judases...' Bobet was too amazed at Gaul's performance to take much notice of Géminiani. He marvelled, 'Charly isn't like other riders. Raphaël lost fourteen minutes. I lost nineteen and Jacques, who I escorted for a while on the Granier, lost twenty-three! You just don't have margins like these any more; they belong to the pre-war Tours, and they make me think Charly is an old-style rider lost among us. In fact, I don't think Charly's human at all: he's a supernatural being.'

The yellow jersey temporarily passed to Italy's Vito Favero, who had a thirty-nine-second advantage over Géminiani and one minute, seven seconds over Gaul – who was by far the best time-triallist of the three. Before the final time-trial began, Anquetil, coughing up blood, abandoned leaving Gaul to win the stage, a seventy-four kilometre jaunt from Besançon to Dijon, and the Tour.

1958 — 4,319 km

	Podium	Nationality	Time	Av speed (kph)
1st	Charly Gaul	Luxemb'g	116h 59m 5s	36.92
2nd	Vito Favero	Italy	+3m 10s	
3rd	Raphaël Géminiani	France	+3m 41s	

Mountains: F. Bahamontes	Spain
Green jersey: Jean Graczyck	France

1959-60 **Cat and Mouse**

Tom wants to deal with Jerry, but at the crucial moment, Spike or Butch – or whatever the bulldog's called – wades in. He gives Tom a thorough mauling and Jerry walks off with the cheese. That was the 1959 Tour, more or less, with Jacques Anquetil and Roger Rivière playing Tom and the dog, with Federico Bahamontes as Jerry and the cheese courtesy of a sniggering cow. A year later, Gastone Nencini took over from Bahamontes as the mouse, with Rivière as Tom, giving too eager a chase. Unfortunately, cartoon crashes, translated into real life, mean serious injury or death: didn't anyone say, 'Don't try this at home'?

Rivière, two years younger than Anquetil, was the new world hour record holder: he'd pulverised Anquetil's record in September 1957. Now, he wanted to win the Tour de France. It had taken an Alfredo Binda to bind Bartali and Coppi into a team. The French national selector, Marcel Bidot, did what he could to mould two champions who spent the rest of the year riding against each other, Anquetil with Helyett-Potin, Rivière for Géminiani's Saint-Raphaël team, but Anquetil was quite clear: 'I'll ride against him anyway!'

The French team imploded with meticulous abandon. Its members took turns to snatch individual moments of glory, but their disarray made Tom and Jerry look like the Trooping of the Colour. André Darrigade won stage one, and took the yellow jersey. Robert Cazala won stage three, and took it. Stages five, six and seven went to Graczyk, Rivière and Hassenforder, before Darrigade won another at Saint Gaudens.

Bahamontes can't suppress a smile as Anquetil (left) and Rivière slug each other into senselessness.

Henry Anglade, riding for the Centre-Midi regional team, had joined Roger Hassenforder's stage-winning twelve-man breakaway on stage seven, which gained five minutes on the rest. On stage thirteen, he was part of a seven-man group including Anquetil, Bahamontes and Huddersfield's own Brian Robinson. They gained four minutes on the rest, which put Anquetil ahead of Rivière, and Anglade in a potentially winning position.

Sure, Bahamontes won stage fifteen, a mountain time-trial up the Puy-de-Dôme, then finished second behind Gaul at Grenoble, which gave him the yellow jersey and a five-minute advantage over Anglade. But Bahamontes, even at his brilliant best, was hopelessly erratic. He'd even been known to top the climb, and then buy an ice cream while he waited for his colleagues. Here's *L'Équipe*'s Pierre Chany: 'Racing in the mountains, he accompanies his blows to the pedals with a pendulum movement of the head, and looks back every fifty metres to assess the damage. On his good days, he evokes the talented toreador. On his bad days, a tramp crossing the bridge at Tage after a day's labouring under the Castilian sun. This dark skinned, quick-witted man from Toledo could have gypsy blood: but he doesn't. In conversation, he speaks in the third person, in pidgin French: "As for me... he was strong today" or "As for me... he couldn't get away."'

Years later, Charly Gaul remembered, 'Bahamontes was made for the mountains. He often made me suffer and I remember a day when I had to let him go on the Tourmalet. But he lacked what made Louison Bobet a champion: brains! Federico couldn't take it easy. When he attacked, I let him go... I just kept a close eye on him. More often than not, Federico would be in trouble before the top.'

It should have been all over for him on stage eighteen, when Anquetil and Rivière joined a breakaway that had dropped Bahamontes by four minutes. If they'd forced Bahamontes to race himself out in pursuit, they could then have chased down Anglade, and one or other of them might have won the Tour. Instead, Tom and Spike refused to work together, allowing Jerry to sneak back into contention. The cheese was his!

Anglade, sacrificed to the infighting between Anquetil and Rivière, took second place, with the 1957 winner as happy to have beaten Rivière to third place as Bahamontes was surprised to have won. Roger Rivière, fourth in his first Tour, resolved to win the next one. Like most resolutions, it was never realised, but the way it was never realised is a cautionary tale to match anything Fred Quimby ever produced.

1959   4,358 km

	Podium	Nationality	Time	Av speed (kph)
1st	Federico Bahamontes	Spain	123h 46m 45s	35.21
2nd	Henry Anglade	France	+4m 1s	
3rd	Jacques Anquetil	France	+5m 5s	

Mountains: F. Bahamontes	Spain
Green jersey: A. Darrigade	France

The Tour claims another victim: Roger Rivière, like a Renaissance Christ taken down from the cross.

1960

Like Charly Gaul, Jacques Anquetil missed the 1960 Tour de France. He had just become the first Frenchman to win the Tour of Italy, leaving his great rival, Roger Rivière, with a problem: the only way left open to him to trump Anquetil's Italian success was to win the Tour. But the French team was still deeply divided, and Rivière didn't inspire everyone's confidence. Before the Tour began, Henry Anglade commented ominously, 'He'll make mistakes. He'll try to follow Nencini on the descents, and one day it'll go wrong.'

The French reporter René Mauries was following stage fourteen: 'The Col du Perjuret seemed harmless. The road wound through a chestnut wood and we reached the brow of the hill almost without realising it. The map said the village of Fraissinet-de-Fourques was nestling in the green-gold valley bellow. The cyclists plummeted down to find it, among them, the two pretenders to the crown:

France's Roger Rivière and Italy's Gastone Nencini. Nencini crouched low over his handlebars to increase the speed to a pace the French call "into the empty tomb". Rivière took up the gauntlet and passed him. We sped from one hairpin to the next, like tobogganists: right, left, right, left. Glued to their bikes, our men were intoxicated with speed. One hairpin hid them, another brought them back. Suddenly, there was a squealing of brakes and we came a brutal halt. There were choruses of swearing and a great orchestra of crumpled wings, crushed coachwork and broken glass. A big devil, tall and gnarled like a cypress, Louis Rostollan by name, called from the side of the road, his bicycle in his hand: "Roger is there, in the ravine."'

His back was broken. Palfium, a painkiller, was found in his veins and in the pocket of his jersey. He later admitted he'd used stimulants throughout his career. They'd helped him to his world hour record – but they'd deadened his reflexes on that tragic last day of his cycling career. Roger Rivière died of throat cancer aged forty in 1976.

'**Doping is now in the arsenal of the champion, and the lesser rider. They dope to finish twentieth, they dope for the time-trials, they dope to climb a mountain, they dope to overcome their nerves. Then they dope to get to sleep at night.**' *L'Équipe*

1960   4,173 km

	Podium	Nationality	Time	Av speed (kph)
1st	Gastone Nencini	Italy	112h 8m 42s	37.21
2nd	Graziano Battistini	Italy	+5m 2s	
3rd	Jan Adrainsens	Belgium	+10m 24s	

Mountains: Imerio Massignan   Italy
Green jersey: Jean Graczyck   France

1961-4 The Caravelle Prophecies

In April 1961, just before his sixth professional bout, Cassius Marcellus Clay made the first of his knock-out predictions: he'd end the fight in round two, he said – and he did. Clay wasn't Ali yet: he was only the Olympic champion, not yet 'The Greatest'. Even so, it was audacious stuff, and, soon enough, it would be the stuff of legends. Jacques Anquetil had been saying he'd win the Tour since the winter, which became, 'I want to win it with panache.' Then, two months after Clay's prophecy, on the eve of the Tour, Anquetil made a prediction of his own: he'd take the yellow jersey on day one, and keep it to the end.

1961

It didn't have Ali's surreal humour – it wasn't 'If Charly Gaul even dreams he can beat me, he better wake up and apologise' – and it wasn't delivered in rhyme, 'Luxembourg and Italy, prepare to be diminished, Anquetil is here to lead from start to finish', but it was as close as a dogged endurance sport for the sons of peasant farmers will ever get to Ali's pizzazz. And a lot can go wrong in three weeks, so in some ways Anquetil's prediction was even bolder. In any case, like Clay's predictions, Anquetil's, too, launched a sporting legend.

L'Équipe reported, 'Jacques Anquetil has made no attempt to hide his ambitions. He has an extremely simple, and quite insolent plan – the sort of plan only people who are certain of their superiority come up with…The French team intends to control the race from

'Modern riders, including the contenders for this Tour – Anquetil excepted – are dwarfs. Yes, repulsive dwarfs, either impotent, like Gaul, or submissive, satisfied with their mediocrity…'

Jacques Goddet

the first turn of the pedal to the last. If they'd only kept it to themselves, it would have been one thing. But it's quite another, now their undisputed leader has made it public. More than a warning, it's a challenge.'

The *L'Équipe* team wandered the landscape of the Tour, collecting expert punditry. Like Ali, Anquetil raised hackles: the old French champion Adolphe Deledda called Anquetil 'daring, if not downright presumptuous.' Jan Adriaenssens, third in 1960, observed, 'It's far easier to say than to do.' The Belgian's team director, Georges Ronsse, thought it would play into his hands: 'I couldn't have hoped for anything better.' And another Belgian, Émile Masson, fifth in the Tour as long ago as 1920 and now covering it as a journalist, commented: 'Jacques Anquetil has the same chances of winning the 1961 Tour as Bobet had in 1955. The difference is, Bobet had the wisdom to keep his mouth shut.'

Only the French rider Jean Dotto saw reason in Anquetil's arrogance: 'He might do it. He's strong, and, more than that, he's got by far the strongest team at the Tour.'

The time-trial on the afternoon of day one allowed him to put his plan into action. But first, in the morning's semi-stage, Anquetil joined the winning breakaway and dropped the likes of Gaul, Adriaenssens, Massignan and Planckaert by more than five minutes. Then he won a twenty-nine kilometre time-trial through Versailles by two and a half minutes. Six days later, between Belfort and Chalon-sur-Saône, a breakaway by seventeen riders gained a huge lead, but Anquetil launched a devastating counter-attack, riding on the front of the chasing group for thirty kilometres. His superiority intimidated the opposition.

Charly Gaul's bid for victory came in the Chartreuse, where he'd won despite torrential rain in 1958. But this year, the elements were against him – and Anquetil loved the heat. Gaul won the stage, but gained less than two minutes on the yellow jersey.

The last chance to attack came between Luchon and Pau, on stage seventeen. Tour director Jacques Goddet described it, and Anquetil's rivals, in full Desgrangian style: 'The second Pyrenean stage, the most majestic of stages following a legendary route, only confirmed, in the most abject fashion, what we didn't dare entirely believe: that modern riders, including the contenders for this Tour – Anquetil excepted – are dwarfs. Yes, repulsive dwarfs, either impotent, like Gaul, or submissive, satisfied with their mediocrity, happy to go through the motions.' Emerging from the Pyrenees, Anquetil rode the final time-trial like a master, distancing Gaul by three minutes and extending his winning margin over the dwarfs to more than twelve minutes.

1961 — 4,397 km

	Podium	Nationality	Time	Av speed (kph)
1st	Jacques Anquetil	France	122h 1m 33s	36.0334
2nd	Guido Carlesi	Italy	+12m 14s	
3rd	Charly Gaul	Luxembourg	+12m 16s	
Mountains: I. Massignan		Italy		
Green jersey: A. Darrigade		France		

1962

The ease of Anquetil's victory in 1961 – the impression of calculation, and suffocating control – made Anquetil an unpopular champion. In 1962, the man who would become Anquetil's greatest rival, and who would dwarf him in popularity, precisely because success would repeatedly escape him, appeared. Raymond Poulidor was Eugène Christophe's reincarnation. Born in 1936 at Léonard-de-Noblet near Limoges, he was the son of poor sharecroppers at the bottom of the rural ladder. Hardened by manual labour he rode a bike from village to village, went into the army, then took up cycling seriously and turned professional in 1960. He was leading the World Championship road race that year when he punctured. Poulidor's back luck continued when he broke his left hand in training and had to start the Tour in a plaster cast. It didn't prevent him winning the great Alpine stage from Briançon to Aix-les-Bains by two and a half minutes, and taking third place in the Tour. But Anquetil was untouchable.

Anquetil didn't attempt to repeat the previous year's dominance: he didn't seize the yellow jersey until stage twenty, of twenty-two. But when he did, it was in unprecedented style, and merited unprecedented reporting. *L'Équipe* wrote: 'You have to have seen something like it once in your life to understand what perfection means in the world of cycling. The sight of Jacques Anquetil speeding towards his conquest of the yellow jersey, pulverising the speed records for road-racing, eclipsing the best of his adversaries, this unforgettable, overwhelming sight: we saw it, between Bourgoin and Lyon. The eager witnesses of this matchless performance will one day wonder if they didn't dream it: Jacques Anquetil catching Raymond Poulidor in under forty kilometres.'

The moment Anquetil passed Poulidor, the television commentary provided France with one of those classic lines that define a historical moment: Al Michaels' 'Do you believe in miracles?', or Kenneth Wolstenholme's 'They think it's all over'. The line was '*C'est la Caravelle qui passe!*' – 'It's the Caravelle coming past!' The Caravelle was the first truly successful jet airliner, designed and built in France. It symbolised French industry, as Anquetil symbolised French sport. And it was true: Poulidor was formidable in every way – but Anquetil flew past him like a jet aircraft.

'It's the Caravelle!' Poulidor can only watch as Anquetil flies by.

The English rider Tom Simpson described what it was like to be overtaken by Anquetil in the middle of a time-trial: 'You can hear him catching you. You don't have to look round. There is the hoarse sound of breath being drawn in gulps, and then he's past you. Then, it's like being in a thunderstorm, with the sweat simply pouring off him as he goes by.'

L'Équipe continued, 'When an athlete achieves a result like this, he earns comparison with other epochs. In the closed world of time-trialling, in which he excelled as a youngster, Jacques Anquetil certainly deserves to be considered number one, the position held by Fausto Coppi for many years. He dominates his rivals with his economy, he displaces them with the unity of his action, he obliterates them with his mastery.'

The 1962 Tour was not free of scandal, though. On the morning of the stage from Luchon to Carcassonne, a dozen riders, including the 1960 winner Gastone Nencini, abandoned the race. They blamed a fish meal served the previous evening at their hotel, but the Tour doctor, Dr Dumas, discovered that the most seriously ill riders had not touched the fish – and that many of those who did were unaffected. At Montpelier, Dumas issued the following communiqué: 'The medical service of the Tour de France, concerned at the number of ill riders... can only draw their attention to the dangers of certain types of care and preparation.' A cartoon in *L'Équipe* showed the sick riders assembled around a fish skeleton with syringes for ribs.

1962   4,274 km

	Podium	Nationality	Time	Av speed (kph)
1st	Jacques Anquetil	France	114h 31m 45s	37.32
2nd	Joseph Planckaert	Belgium	+4m 59s	
3rd	Raymond Poulidor	France	+10m 24s	

Mountains: F. Bahamontes	Spain	
Green jersey: Rudi Altig	Germany	

1963

In the final time-trial of the 1963 Tour de France, the margin of Anquetil's victory – barely over a minute – raised eyebrows. The explanation was simple: as well as the best time-triallist, Anquetil was now as good as the best climbers in the sport. His victory through the Pyrenees to Bagnères-de-Bigorre (stage ten) was won, not climbing – Bahamontes had him in trouble on the Aubisque – but descending, and on the run in to the stage finish. But the win at Chamonix ten days later was tactically perfect. The stage took in the Forclaz, an unpaved goat-track with gradients that reached eighteen per cent. The regulations allowed for no changes of equipment except after mechanical failure. But at the foot of the climb, as Poulidor fought a violent headwind, Antequil called for assistance.

A rocky road over the Aubisque: Anquetil braves the dust and the camera-bikes on his way to victory at Bagnères-de-Bigorre.

'My derailleur!'

'*Merde!*' choked his director, Raphaël Géminiani. 'Antequil's in trouble!'

His mechanic leapt out of the car, adroitly severed the gear cable with wire-cutters, and passed Anquetil a lighter machine set up for climbing. Bahamontes attacked, Anquetil followed and Poulidor collapsed. By the time they reached the summit, the mechanic had restrung the gear cable, allowing Anquetil to descend on his original, robust machine. At Chamonix, he took the stage and yellow jersey, just ahead of Bahamontes.

Jacques Goddet compared him with the racing driver, Argentina's Juan Manuel Fangio: 'He conducted himself like Fangio, the greatest racing driver ever seen: he took no unnecessary risks, he avoided mechanical problems, and limited himself to answering each rival with the reply required to shut him up.'

Two days later, Anquetil scored another superb time-trial victory, and on 14 July, claimed his fourth Tour before a Parisian public that was finally warming to him. Even so, there was criticism: he was too controlling; he lacked flamboyance. Goddet defended him: 'He is calculating: he adjusts his racing to ensure victory without taking unnecessary risks.' It won him a special 'Head and Legs' Trophy, awarded in memory of Henri Desgrange to the rider who showed most courage, allied to intelligence. Desgrange would surely have approved: Anquetil's all-round skills made him just the sort of rider Desgrange was looking for – even if he did use a freewheel and a derailleur.

1963   4,140.6 km

	Podium	Nationality	Time	Av speed (kph)
1st	Jacques Anquetil	France	113h 30m 5s	36.48
2nd	Federico Bahamontes	Spain	+3m 35s	
3rd	José Perez-Frances	Spain	+10m 14s	

Mountains: F. Bahamontes	Spain	
Green jersey: Rik Van Looy	Belgium	

1964

The 1964 Tour was so stuffed with incident it might just have been the greatest Tour ever. If you're French, then no other Tour even comes close.

In June, he'd won the Tour of Italy: now, Jacques Anquetil had the opportunity to emulate his hero Coppi with the Giro-Tour double, as well as winning a record fourth consecutive Tour and a record fifth Tour in total. His stage win at Monaco, nine days in, put him in the fop five. Two days later, victory in the first long time-trial moved him up to second place. It all seemed to be going according to plan. Sunday 5 July was a rest day in the Pyrenees, and Anquetil accepted an invitation from Radio Andorra to a 'méchoui' – a traditional meal of lamb roasted whole on a spit. The solid food was accompanied by a drinking competition with his *directeur sportif*, Raphaël Geminiani. Anquetil's dietary deviations were legend: Pierre Chany once wrote of them: 'Jacques Anquetil isn't a difficult man, he just does what he pleases, or rather, what pleases him. One of his greatest successes lies in giving Louison Bobet a complex: Louison eats grilled food, Jacques prefers marinated oysters; Bobet drinks mineral water, Anquetil sends the champagne corks flying; Bobet sleeps ten hours, Anquetil spends half the night driving, then appears at the start of a criterium the following day, fresh as a cucumber.' Anquetil's own summary was more succinct: 'To prepare for a race, nothing beats a good pheasant, champagne and a woman.'

> **'To prepare for a race there is nothing better than a good pheasant, some champagne and a woman.'**
> Jacques Anquetil

But the following day, Anquetil seemed to have lost the Tour.

The stage started in thick fog, and Anquetil started nervously. On the Port d'Envalira, the first climb of the day, he recalled, 'I had to stop. I was six kilometres from the summit. I thought, I'll never make it. What was wrong? The rest day had harmed me. I never ride on a rest day. I regret it; I should have. From the bottom of the climb, I was in trouble. It was a nightmare. I'm going to confess something to you. Even if it sounds a bit ridiculous, this really affected me. An astrologer predicted I'd abandon on the fourteenth stage. It had been preying on my mind for days, and when I realised it was all going wrong, I thought: "This is it. He was right."'

His teammate Louis Rostollan – the man who'd witnessed Rivière's back-breaking fall four years before – came alongside.

'I've never seen Jacques like that,' he said, later. At one point, he

It still grips, half a century on. Anquetil and Poulidor, the greatest episode of the greatest rivalry in Tour history.

said: "I'm completely empty. I'm stopping." So I said, "*Merde*, remember your name's Anquetil.'"

It was enough to bring him round, and with Rostollan's help, he began the chase. 113 kilometres into the stage, he regained the peloton. Then, Poulidor stopped to change a wheel. As the peloton accelerated to take advantage of Poulidor's problem, the queue of race vehicles slowed as the team directors took a closer look, leaving a gaping void between Poulidor and the peloton, speeding away into the distance. By the stage finish, Poulidor had lost two and a half minutes to Anquetil.

The following day saw the Tour's third excursion into the Pyrenees. On the final climb, the narrow, severe Portillon, Poulidor launched an unanswerable attack, tearing through the remnants of an earlier breakaway with a series of sudden, impulsive accelerations. At the finish line in Luchon, his margin of victory was one minute, forty-three seconds. In *L'Équipe*'s words, 'He hasn't merely evoked the great climbers of the past in brutal, wonderful tones, and saved himself, in less than twenty kilometres, from straits we frankly considered hopeless; he's made himself Jacques Anquetil's one true successor.'

Twenty-four hours later, the curse of Eugène Christophe returned. Poulidor called his mechanic. Antonin Magne, his team director, stopped the car. The mechanic, thrown off balance by the abrupt braking, tripped, throwing the replacement bike at Poulidor's feet. Without losing a second, Poulidor picked it up and set off, only then realising the steering was out of true. He stopped again to allow the mechanic to straighten and tighten the bars, but the mechanic, in a state of shock, forgot to push him and Poulidor, off-balance, couldn't get his feet into the pedal straps, losing all impetus. At the stage finish, he complained: 'You'd think I was cursed. The smallest problem becomes a catastrophe when it happens to me. Jacques has gained thirty-seven seconds. I still think I can win the Tour, in spite of everything. There's only the Puy-de-Dôme left.'

The Puy-de-Dôme, an ancient volcano in the Auvergne, was where, in 1648, Pascal proved that atmospheric pressure varies with altitude. On Sunday, 12 July, Anquetil and Poulidor made their own contribution to France's atmospheric pressure. The first

> '**We are side by side. I slowed down, he slowed down. I accelerated, he responded. He truly amazed me.**'
> Poulidor on his duel with Anquetil on the Puy-de-Dôme.

232 kilometres of the stage are forgotten. All that remain are the final four: no – three of the final four. And the stage winner is forgotten, too: the Spanish climber Julio Jiménez, ahead of Bahamontes, still brilliant at thirty-six. Behind them, Poulidor and Anquetil rode so hard, they resembled drunks, at times leaning into each other, any pretence of composure destroyed by their exertions

'**Here are the high-wire artists of the soul, people who can do the impossible, who are on another plane. They are flawless only in the expression of their excellence.**'
Eric Cantona on Jacques Anquetil, Diego Maradona and Arthur Rimbaud.

as they compressed the entire Tour into those few kilometres. Each rode against the other, and against every instinct of self-preservation demanding that they relent from their self-mutilating efforts. Poulidor, the great ascender, needed to gain at least ninety seconds on his rival if he was to have any chance of winning the Tour. But Anquetil held on: as Poulidor later described it, 'We are side by side. I slowed down, he slowed down. I accelerated, he responded. He truly amazed me.' Only at the red kite marking the final kilometre did Poulidor begin to edge ahead. As the force field that had held them together began to ebb, Anquetil, diminished now, bored ahead on will power alone. At the finish line, he had lost forty-two seconds and Jiménez and Bahamontes had deprived Poulidor of the time bonuses. Anquetil had held his race lead: Poulidor lay fourteen seconds behind him.

Jacques Goddet wrote, coldly but perhaps rightly, that Poulidor lost the Tour because 'he showed himself incapable of doing violence to his nature.' Two days later, Anquetil, the supreme masochist, won the final time-trial, his fifth Tour, and the Giro-Tour double.

1964 4,504 km

	Podium	Nationality	Time	Av speed (kph)
1st	Jacques Anquetil	France	127h 9m 44s	35.42
2nd	Raymond Poulidor	France	+55s	
3rd	Federico Bahamontes	Spain	+4m 44s	

Mountains: F. Bahamontes	Spain	
Green jersey: Jan Janssen	Netherlands	

1965 Afterglow

In June 1965, Jacques Anquetil won the gruelling eight-day Dauphiné Libéré stage race in the Alps, and then, in the evening of the final stage, he flew across France in De Gaulle's presidential aircraft, started the 480-kilometre Bordeaux-Paris shortly after midnight, and won it the following day. It was his way of upstaging the Tour, which he had no intention of riding.

He justified his absence with a calculating rationale: 'My contracts won't increase if I win a sixth Tour. And if I fail, I've everything to lose.' The truth might be that the 1964 Tour had been won at too high a price, and that the superstitious fears that nearly cost him the race on the Port d'Envalira had come back to torment him.

With no Anquetil to smother him, all the signs were that Raymond Poulidor's time had come. The crux of the Tour was stage fourteen, from Montpellier to the top of Mont Ventoux. Poulidor's target was Felice Gimondi, a wide-eyed twenty-two-year-old from Bergamo in northern Italy, who had won the previous year's amateur Tour de France, and finished third in the 1965 Tour of Italy, a month earlier.

'I didn't even want to ride the Tour,' Gimondi said. 'I thought it would be far too hard for me. It was only when Fantinato had a knee problem and Babini was taken ill that I agreed to be part of the team. It happened the Thursday before the Tour, the evening after a time-trial at Forlí in which I finished second to Jacques Anquetil. I hurried back to the family home in Sedrina, near Bergamo, threw some things in a suitcase and it was already time to leave for Cologne', where the Tour started.

Like Anquetil in 1957, Gimondi took the yellow jersey with a

Poulidor ('Mercier-Hutchinson') and Gimondi ('Salvarani'). But can there be any doubt that Poulidor was the greater of the two?

stage win at Rouen. The abandon of his putative team leader, Vittorio Adorni, on the Aubisque, allowed the race leader to become the leader of his team. The Pyrenees took other victims, eleven riders, including the yellow jersey of Bernard Van de Kerckhove, quit the race during the same stage. Lucien Aimar collapsed, apparently suffering from sunstroke and Federico Bahamontes lost over thirty-seven minutes and abandoned the next day. Like the 'poisoned fish' incident of 1962, many suspected that doping was behind the carnage.

By the time the race reached Mont Ventoux, Gimondi was still there, with ten yellow jerseys in his luggage – one for each day he'd been leading the race.

For Poulidor, the 'Giant of Provence' was the cue for the all-out assault, which would, he hoped, win him the Tour. He had an ally in Bahamontes' mountain-climbing successor, Julio Jiménez, who wanted to shore up his leadership of the mountains competition. The two men made a molehill of the mountain: in the French poet Francis Huger's version, 'Poulidor devoured the Ventoux with the voracity of a cannibal swallowing an archbishop's calf.' He gained a minute, thirty-eight seconds on Gimondi, and moved into second place overall, thirty-four seconds behind the young Italian.

> **'Poulidor devoured the Ventoux with the voracity of a cannibal swallowing an archbishop's calf.'**
> Francis Huger conjures a poet's vision

In *L'Équipe*, Marcel Bidot, the old director of the French national team, was bullish: 'I told you yesterday that Poulidor needed, as soon as possible, to win a stage in style: he's done so, like a real patron. And I told you he needed to win by dropping the two Italians, if he was to believe in final victory: he's done that, too. He's proved that no one in the peloton can touch him in the hills. Poulidor will take the yellow jersey when he wants, but I don't think he'll be in any hurry: there are two time-trials in which no one will worry him, and one of them, on Mont Revard, is uphill. Frankly, I can tell you: Poulidor can't lose this Tour.'

Confident of victory on Mont Revard, Poulidor rode passively through the Alps. On the Col de Vars in the Alps, he led Gimondi by thirty seconds, but allowed the younger man to come back. On the next climb, the Izoard, he lacked sparkle, and allowed Gimondi to steal five seconds from him at the stage finish at Briançon. The next day, through the Chartreuse hills, Poulidor did nothing but bide his time.

'**Frankly, I can tell you: Poulidor can't lose this Tour.**'
Marcel Bidot after the Mont Ventoux stage

Bidot was right: the mountain time-trial from Aix-les-Bains to Mont Revard, twenty-seven kilometres away, decided the Tour, in about an hour – a little less for Gimondi, slightly more for Poulidor. Only twenty-three seconds separated them: thirty-three, when the bonus seconds were reckoned.

As well as losing time, Poulidor lost heart. The final stage was a flat time-trial from Versailles in Paris: Gimondi defeated him again, and this time, by nearly three minutes. Gimondi's team director, Luciano Pezzi, who rode the 1949 and 1952 Tours de France alongside the great Coppi, wiped a tear from his eye and said, 'Today, on the road from Versailles, I thought I was watching Fausto.'

Some were unforgiving with France's 'eternal second'. In 1965 alone, Poulidor had also finished second in the Vuelta a España, the Dauphiné Libéré, the Critérium International and the French Championships. It was even asked, given his lack of tactical finesse, whether, far from being subjugated by Anquetil's tyranny, he had actually benefited from it, forgetting that Gimondi had shown a remarkable ability to recuperate from gruelling stages.

1965 — 4,188 km

	Podium	Nationality	Time	Av speed (kph)
1st	Felice Gimondi	Italy	116h 42m 6s	35.89
2nd	Raymond Poulidor	France	+2m 40s	
3rd	Gianni Motta	Italy	+9m 18s	

Mountains: Julio Jiménez — Spain
Green jersey: Jan Janssen — Netherlands

1966 Big Brother

After the Paris–Nice stage race earlier in the year, won by Anquetil for the fifth time, Poulidor had accused him of unsporting conduct. The two men hadn't been on speaking terms since. At the Tour start in Nancy, the enmity was still smouldering. It didn't take long to surface: on stage two, Poulidor had a banal fall. Anquetil launched a blistering attack, stringing the peloton out in his slipstream and forcing Poulidor and his teammates into a frantic chase. The hostilities had begun.

It wasn't all business as usual. Only a handful of Italians took part; among the absent was Gimondi, who didn't attempt to defend his title. It was their way of protesting at France's new anti-doping law, published on 2 June 1966: 'During a sporting competition, whoever knowingly uses one of the substances determined by the public administration, which are intended to enhance artificially and temporarily their physical possibilities and which are predisposed to be damaging to health, will be punished by a fine of from 500 to 5,000 francs.' Anyone found to have provided the drugs or incited their use was liable to a similar fine – or imprisonment of anything from a month to a year.

Anquetil reluctantly agreed that he'd cooperate if required. Poulidor, likewise: 'It's the law. I just hope the analyses are carried out within the law, too.' Rik Van Looy, though, was defiant: 'I won't accept the procedure, even if I'm asked to.' But his team had been exempted, anyway, so he was merely posing.

The first anti-doping controls since *L'Équipe* had announced the war on doping won in 1955, took place at Bordeaux on 28 June

**The strike after the drug test before: Jacques Anquetil argues
for doping laissez-faire the day after the first controls.**

1966. The chemistry was elementary compared with today's tests,
but the procedure was far more stringent. The anti-doping doctors
chose who they'd test. As well as giving urine, riders were checked
for signs of injections and their suitcases were searched. The selected
riders were mostly youngsters, but Poulidor found himself involved
when all his teammates disappeared in the nick of time. Anquetil,
the great alpha-male of the Tour, reserved his urine for marking his
territory, and the following day, he did so by leading a riders' strike
in protest. A year later, presumably on the same grounds, Anquetil

**Anquetil bids adieu to his Tour career... but not before
he has masterminded Raymond Poulidor's umpteenth defeat.**

would refuse to give a urine sample after beating the world hour
record, which meant his time was never ratified.

But his contribution to the 1966 Tour was more than merely
upping the ante in the anti-anti-doping movement. Anquetil was
surrounded by a formidable team: his director Raphaël Géminiani
had Julio Jiménez, the best climber around, and a promising
youngster called Lucien Aimar, in reserve. Which was just as well,
because Jacques was more interested in pursuing his feud with
Poulidor than in winning the Tour – shades of 1959.

On stage ten to Pau at the foot of the Pyrenees, Aimar joined a large breakaway. Both Poulidor and Anquetil lost seven minutes. Antonin Magne, Poulidor's *directeur sportif*, criticized Anquetil for failing to lead the chase. Géminiani retorted, 'It wasn't up to Jacques to chase down his teammate. It was Poulidor's mistake, yet again.'

Poulidor bounced back to beat Anquetil – by seven scarce seconds – in the Vals-les-Bains time-trial, and the following day, in torrential rain, Anquetil, with bronchitis, conceded another minute. Recognizing that he had lost the Tour, Anquetil played big brother to Aimar, who caught Janssen and Poulidor off guard on the road to Turin, and broke away to capture the yellow jersey. Tour co-director Félix Lévitan blamed himself for handing Aimar the Tour: 'My job was to make sure I kept the journalists' cars away from the riders. Going through a small village, I hesitated before shouting "Cars move away!" A handful of riders, including Aimar, seized the opportunity to follow in our slipstream.' In Lévitan's telling words, 'That day, a rider won the Tour, which he didn't deserve.'

Between Ivrea and Chamonix, Poulidor escaped and gained time, but Aimar, with Anquetil's support, was always in control. A day later, Anquetil, weakened by a cold and weathering yet another rainstorm, took a comb from his pocket and tidied his hair before stepping off, in front of the cameras, on the Côte de Serrières, near Saint-Étienne. He'd never start another Tour.

1966 — 4,328.8 km

	Podium	Nationality	Time	Av speed (kph)
1st	Lucien Aimar	France	117h 34m 21s	36.82
2nd	Jan Janssen	Netherlands	+1m 7s	
3rd	Raymond Poulidor	France	+2m 2s	

Mountains: Julio Jiménez — Spain
Green jersey: W. Planckaert — Belgium

1967 Image and Reality

'Riding alone into the wind for twenty-nine kilometres.
That's what killed me!' was how Raymond Poulidor
described the episode that lost him the 1967 Tour, but
it could have been anyone, bandying about metaphors
of life and death without a second thought. Then Tom
Simpson collapsed on Mont Ventoux, and metaphors
– the sport itself – suddenly seemed senseless.

Jean-Marie Leblanc, the future director of the Tour de France, met
Tom Simpson early in his career. 'In 1966, I rode the Tour de
l'Hérault. The morning before one stage, I was looking for
somewhere to sit. I found the end of a bench, and sat down. Guess
who was next to me? Tom Simpson, the reigning world champion.
He looked at me and asked: "What's your name?" – "Where are you
from?" – "Ah, from the north...!" Very kind. You see? You're a little
amateur rider without a team, and the world professional champion,
with the rainbow jersey across his chest, talks to you like a friend!
Unforgettable!' Leblanc added, 'I don't want to sound as if I'm saying
this because he's dead, but, truly, I recall his extreme kindness. I
remember everyone liked him.'

Within two years, this courteous, gentle man was dead.

'We left Tom Simpson, full of joyful wisecracks, in front of the
town hall in Marseille,' wrote *L'Équipe*, the day after Simpson's death.
'We saw him again a few hours later, stiff and already cold, in case
number three of the 'Sainte-Marthe' Hospital in Avignon.' Simpson
fell two kilometres from the top of Mont Ventoux where he may or
may not have told his mechanic Harry Hall, John Wayne-style, 'Put
me back on the bloody bike.' At 5.40 p.m. that evening, mouth-to-
mouth, heart massage and a helicopter ambulance to hospital

The face of a man condemned by talent, ambition – and doping.

Tom Simpson wavers on Mont Ventoux.

notwithstanding, his death certificate was signed. There were amphetamines in his pockets and in his blood. Permission to bury his mortal remains was withheld. 'Everything that men can do to try to save another man had been done,' said *L'Équipe*. Or had it?

After Malléjac's drug-induced collapse on the Ventoux in 1955, Rivière's drug-induced fall on the Perjuret in 1960, Aimar's drug-induced crisis on the Aubisque in 1965, and who knows how many other close shaves, it was a signposted, statistical certainty that doping would cost a rider his life sooner or later. The race director, Jacques

Goddet, believed the Tour was worth defending: 'I wondered for a long time whether we should continue, and I concluded that the moral benefits of the Tour are greater than its damaging aspects.' But could the Tour's moral dimension – its great, protective, unifying metaphor – justify the health risks on which it rested?

Eddy Merckx later defended Simpson: 'In the peloton, he wasn't considered a doper. The thing was, in 1967, he was no longer a rider. He'd invested so much money in Corsica, he had so many worries, that he'd forgotten his profession. So, to compensate for his lack of training, he took something at the Tour... That doesn't mean he took something every day.' But it was too late: doping had emerged from semi-secrecy and acquired a face, a sacrificial victim and an icon.

The winner, Roger Pingeon, was an ibis of a man who soared out of a group of twelve riders on stage five, from Roubaix to the Belgian town of Jambes (French, appropriately enough, for 'legs'), gaining more than six minutes on all the favourites in sixty kilometres. Poulidor achieved his annual avoidance of victory by falling the following day and Jean Bobet summed up the rest of the Tour like this: 'Gimondi lost it, like Poulidor, on a descent in the Vosges, as Janssen did on the Galibier, and as Aimar did, losing a little at every point. Pingeon won the Tour at Jambes and then, he didn't lose it.'

But the 1967 Tour is remembered, not for Pingeon's victory, but for Simpson's loss.

1967   4,780.4 km

	Podium	Nationality	Time	Av speed (kph)
1st	Roger Pingeon	France	136h 53m 50s	34.92
2nd	Julio Jiménez	Spain	+3m 40s	
3rd	Franco Balmamión	Italy	+7m 23s	

Mountains: Julio Jiménez	Spain
Green jersey: Jan Janssen	Netherlands

1968 Fifty Ways to Lose the Tour

Flat-worlders, snake-oil salesmen and management theorists prove that some people will believe anything. Francis Pélissier's belief that the Tour would never be won by anyone who wore glasses wasn't the most outlandish theory going. A bespectacled Dutchman named Jan Janssen finally proved Pélissier wrong in 1968, but the theory would have emerged intact from the 1968 Tour if Raymond Poulidor hadn't been charting new ground in how to lose the Tour. After fifteen stages of scrupulous tactical care, Poulidor was brought down by a race motorbike. His face-first fall left his nose, and his prospects of victory, in tatters.

Fearing a repeat of the previous year's tragedy, the Tour organisers left out Mont Ventoux and nicknamed the race the 'Tour of Good Health'. It started at the mineral water town of Vittel. This may or may not have had two consequences: the first was that none of the winners of the three most recent Tours of Italy, Gianni Motta, Felice Gimondi and Eddy Merckx – the comfortable winner of that June's Giro, and the reigning world champion – started. The second was that Poulidor's calamity was the chief point of interest in a race so staggeringly dull, the journalists protested by going on strike. Their boycott of the first seventy-two kilometres of stage ten from Bordeaux to Bayonne must be unique in sporting history.

Fourteen stages in, Poulidor was in fifth place overall and the best positioned of all the contenders. At the time of the accident, he was

The latest episode in the Poulidor soap opera:
has any athlete in any sport matched his sheer bad luck?

surrounded by teammates at the front of a small group giving chase to a lone attacker, Roger Pingeon. A slight gap had opened behind them when the blackboard bike carrying race information tried to pass. At that moment, the roadside crowd edged forward, and the motorbike swerved to avoid a careless spectator, taking the Spanish climber Aurelia González side on, and just clipping Poulidor's rear wheel. He landed on his face, breaking his nose and slashing his lips, eyebrows, elbows and knees.

Then the motorbike struck his right leg.

'How can you attack a rider who's injured? How can
you take advantage when a man's down and badly
hurt, to take even more out of him?'

Raymond Poulidor

Poulidor had believed his luck had changed, and he could finally
win the Tour but the fall brought his brain into contact with reality,
in more ways than one. Hard man that he was, he picked himself up
and, despite the pain, raced away with unbelievable speed and
courage. 'I was fuelled by desperation,' Poulidor recalled, 'but it was
difficult, because I was in a lot of pain, and my right leg was stiff. I
had to hurt myself, because the knee didn't want to bend, and the
bike was damaged. And I had no help from anyone.'

However, by then the chase after Pingeon was on, and the pace
was too high to let him regain the group. 'I was panicking, I felt that
my chances of winning the Tour were disappearing, thanks to the
state I was in. Supposing I did make it to the finish, what condition
would I be in the following morning? I was despondent.

'There's one thing I can't understand: how can you attack a rider
who's injured? How can you take advantage when a man's down
and badly hurt, to take even more out of him? There are people in
the peloton who behave like…' The next word couldn't be printed
by the French press.

As well as the four minutes, three seconds of his deficit, the
favourite to win the 'Tour of Good Health' had lost blood and skin.
Incredibly, covered in bandages, Poulidor started the next morning,
but when Lucien Aimar, the rebel leader of the France B team,
attacked, dragging fifteen riders in his wake, Poulidor was not among
them. The yellow jersey went from one of the breakaway riders to
another, until it landed on the shoulders of Belgium's Herman Van
Springel. He lost his sixteen-second lead on the final stage, a time-
trial from Melun to Paris, allowing Jan Janssen to become the first
Dutchman to win the Tour de France, despite never once having

Jan Janssen time-trials into yellow, with a little encouragement.

worn the yellow jersey. A rider wearing glasses had won the Tour for the first time, and Raymond Poulidor had lost it, for the nth time.

Capable of supreme athletic displays, which were nearly always overshadowed by something else, Poulidor's entire career was shrouded by an air of farce. In these ways, and others, he was the Tour de France made flesh, and tormented for its sins.

1968 — 4,492 km

	Podium	Nationality	Time	Av speed (kph)
1st	Jan Janssen	Netherlands	133h 49m 42s	33.57
2nd	Herman Van Springel	Belgium	+38s	
3rd	Ferdinand Bracke	Belgium	+3m 3s	

Mountains: Aurelio Gonzalez Spain
Green jersey: Franco Bitossi Italy

The Cannibal

Stage 21, 1974: One against a
hundred, Cyrano de Bergerac-
style. The inimitable, the
incomparable Eddy Merckx
rides away from the peloton
to victory.

1969-74 The Greatest Belgian Ever

Sport isn't a beauty contest, granted, but we do expect some elegance from our athletes. Anquetil, for instance, was the most graceful rider who ever lived. His record suggests that style and success might be related. Then you look at Eddy Merckx. The man who would utterly dominate the sport was less Prince Charming on a bike than King Kong, threatening to tear it apart with uncontainable brute strength.

1969

During the 1968 Tour of Italy, Eddy Merckx was sharing a room with the Italian rider Vittorio Adorni. Merckx was first overall, and Adorni was second. The third-placed rider, Felice Gimondi, was more than ten minutes behind them. Merckx opened his suitcase, pulled out a map, and showed it to Adorni: 'Look! Tomorrow, we attack here!' Astonished, Adorni stammered, 'Attack? Attack who?'

In the aftermath of the 1969 Tour, Jan Janssen compared the primate with the ballerina: 'I don't think Merckx would've dropped Anquetil in the mountains, and Jacques would've ended up winning a Tour of attrition like this.' Raymond Poulidor, suffering Stockholm Syndrome for his past tormentor, agreed. It was the only comfort left to them, after Merckx's beatings. Before taking on his first Tour de France, he'd won one Tour of Italy, three Milan–San Remos, two Gent–Wevelgems, a Tour of Flanders, a Flèche Wallonne, a Paris-Roubaix, and the World Championship. On 1 June 1969, he was suspended from the Tour of Italy for doping. He flatly denied it, and took out his frustration one month later at the Tour de France.

**Merckx sets the pace, ascending the Alps the way the
mighty Kong ascended the Empire State Building.**

Victory in the team time-trial gave him the yellow jersey. Then
he sprinted up the Ballon d'Alsace like the mighty Kong ascending
the Empire State Building. After winning the Divonne time-trial,
he allowed Pingeon to win the stage at Chamonix. Two days later,
Merckx won again at Digne: 'I descended like a race car. Only
Gimondi could stay with me. With one small col to go, Gimondi
refused to take his turn riding at the front. He thought he had me,
but I sprinted from the *flamme rouge*, and he was helpless.' But he had
saved the best till last – or first, if you take his career as a whole.

On 15 July 1969, through the Pyrenees from Luchon to Mourenx-Ville Nouvelle, he took perhaps the greatest stage win in Tour history. Over the Peyresourde and the Aspin, his team, Faema, set the pace, thinning out the leading group. Then, on the Tourmalet, his Faema teammate Martin Van den Bossche accelerated. Instead of allowing him to win the King of the Mountains points, Merckx attacked. Van den Bossche had accepted an offer from a rival team, so Merckx decided to humiliate him on his favourite terrain. He won the sprint for the mountains prize, then, as Roger Pingeon later remembered, 'He shot down the descent like a stone. A small gap opened, and gradually grew: first ten metres, then twenty, then fifty. I looked at Raymond Poulidor, and he shrugged his shoulders as if to say that Merckx had no reason to continue his break. There were still another 130 kilometres to go.' Merckx agreed: 'But each time the blackboard man – the man who indicates the gaps to breakaway riders – came past, I saw my lead had grown.'

130 kilometres on, at Mourenx, there was an eight-minute wait before the group containing Pingeon and Poulidor arrived. Gimondi and Janssen trailed by a quarter of an hour. Jacques Goddet wrote: 'Is he trying to humiliate the other riders, who seem to creep along behind him, by destroying them? Is it a sort of cyclopathic vanity that drives him to conquer all he surveys? He's a champion ruled by pride, that much is certain, because without pride, there's no panache.' The Tour had been blown apart, and not just the Tour; Merckx's competitors would never quite get over it. In Paris, the last Belgian Tour winner, Sylvère Maes, recalled: 'My return to Belgium after winning the Tour was a national holiday, and the King invited me to the Universal Exhibition at Brussels. But for Eddy Merckx, I think it's going to be even bigger...!'

'I'd love to ride the 1969 Tour again. I'd ride it the same way. It's my most beautiful memory, by a long way.'
Eddy Merckx

1969				4,080.8 km
	Podium	Nationality	Time	Av speed (kph)
1st	Eddy Merckx	Belgium	116h 16m 2s	35.10
2nd	Roger Pingeon	France	+17m 54s	
3rd	Raymond Poulidor	France	+22m 13s	
Mountains: Eddy Merckx		Belgium		
Green jersey: Eddy Merckx		Belgium		

1970

There was a virtuosic self-confidence to Merckx that deflated his rivals. On the way to victory at Grenoble in stage twelve of the 1970 Tour, Dany Rebello of *France Soir* wrote, 'He performed a little mechanical adjustment on the descent from the Col de Porte. With the handlebars in one hand and an Allen key in the other, plummeting downhill at seventy kilometres an hour, he waited for a short straight section of road, and quickly lowered his saddle, which he judged a tad high.'

But he'd been suffering aches and discomfort since September 1969, when he crashed on the track at Blois. Merckx suffered a gaping head wound, but more seriously, the accident had jarred his pelvis and left him nursing back pain for the rest of his career. 'Medical treatment wasn't as effective then as now... My body became less flexible and the mountains made me suffer even more,' he said. 'Before, climbing had almost been a pleasure. Afterwards, it became a source of torment.'

Not that you'd have believed it, seeing him climb the Ventoux during the 1970 Tour. He had taken the yellow jersey on day one in Limoges, surrendered it days later to a teammate, then won it back when the Tour entered his native Belgium. Three days later, on

Jean-Marie Leblanc, the future Tour de France Director, leads Merckx during the 1970 Tour.

the road to Divonne-les-Bains, Merckx flexed his muscles. Among the few riders able to follow him was a little-known rider, the Dutchman Joop Zoetemelk, leader of the Flandria team. In Provence, the Tour returned to the ominous slopes of Mont Ventoux for the first time since Tom Simpson's death – and death, again, was in the air. Merckx's former manager, Vincenzo Giacotto, had passed away. Giacotto had taken Merckx to the Italian team Faema, where he had learnt discipline and polished his skills. Wearing a black armband in Giacotto's memory, Merckx dropped Poulidor, France's Bernard Thévenet and the Belgian Lucien Van Impe as he approached the Chalet Reynard, then his former teammate, Martin Van den Bossche, and finally Portugal's Joaquim Agostinho. With no competition left, he removed his cap as he passed the Tom Simpson memorial, then his pedalling became increasingly irregular.

The French war reporter Lucien Bodard saw it first hand: 'In the middle of the hysterical crowd that swelled on the platform built

On his way to the stage win, Eddy Merckx crosses himself at the very moment Jacques Goddet lays a wreath in Tom Simpson's memory.

around the summit, the triumphant Merckx suddenly stumbled, and revealed that he was only a man, that he had limits.' He was escorted to an ambulance and given oxygen – but was the crisis real, or was it part of the mind games Merckx played with his rivals? Merckx later revealed, 'I only spoke to Belgian television, then I climbed into the ambulance, which allowed me to reach the hotel early!'

1970   3,877.6 km

	Podium	Nationality	Time	Av speed (kph)
1st	Eddy Merckx	Belgium	119h 31m 49s	32.44
2nd	Joop Zoetemelk	Netherlands	+12m 41s	
3rd	Gösta Petterson	Sweden	+15m 54s	

Mountains: Eddy Merckx	Belgium
Green jersey: W. Godefroot	Belgium

The glorious injured: Luis Ocaña had Merckx on the ropes until the foul conditions delivered the knockout blow.

1971

The 1971 Tour started with more displays of crazed despotism from Eddy Merckx. He won the Prologue, then decided that stage two, finishing on a cinder track in Strasbourg – madness on the part of the organisers – had to be his. Merckx remembered, 'Roger [De Vlaeminck] loved grass tracks, and I could see he wanted to win. I couldn't take any risks: it was before the Alps, and it would have been stupid to fall there. I should have stayed with the peloton. But I was motivated, and I wanted to annoy De Vlaeminck. I'm not ashamed of saying it: I took great risks that day. I went into a corner at top speed, in an insane duel. I shouldn't have, but I won and I took great pleasure in it. My great rival had it coming to him!'

Everything went according to Merckx's totalitarian designs until stage eleven, from Grenoble to Orcières-Merlette in the Alps. That day, for the first time of his career, Merckx took a beating from a Spanish flyweight named Luis Ocaña. In 1969, team disunity had cost Ocaña the Tour of Spain. He had won the pre-Tour Midi Libre, but a heavy fall on the Ballon d'Alsace had prevented him from challenging Merckx. In 1970, Ocaña had won in Spain, but sickness had again prevented him from challenging for the Tour. In 1971, weeks before the Tour, Ocaña had had Merckx on the ropes in the mountains of the pre-Tour Dauphiné Libéré. 'I shook him off climbing the Granier, but I couldn't finish off the job on the next climb, because it started to rain.' At the Tour de France, there was, for once, an aura of uncertainty around Eddy Merckx. Not: 'Could he win the Tour?' But: 'Could he lose?' Ocaña thought so. He won stage eight on the Puy-de-Dôme, then seized the moment on the stage from Grenoble to Orcières-Merlette. Ascending with remarkable agility, Ocaña, the leader of the Bic team, gained nearly nine minutes on Merckx and took the yellow jersey.

In the *Journal du Dimanche*, René Barjavel wrote, 'After their exertions, the two men look alike. Their faces are marked with the same creases, the same fevered look in the vanquisher and the vanquished. The Spanish long occupied Flanders: could it be that the Belgian and the Spaniard issue from a common ancestor, a contemporary of Philip II? On the now famous road of the Merlettes, they demonstrated their qualities as men as well as athletes. Ahead, Ocaña, relaxed, comfortable, faced the solitary conquest of those terrible

> '**Whatever happens, I have lost the Tour. There will always be doubt.**'
> Merckx on Ocaña's exit

summits with tranquil resolution. Behind, Merckx, isolated, choked, dehydrated and surrounded by enemies, dragged them like a ball and chain to his calvary, jeered by the mediocre who reproached him not for losing, but for winning too often. On the finish line, each paid homage to the other.'

On the next stage, Merckx responded by attacking at the stage start immediately, accompanied by a dozen riders. Two hundred and

'**Guimard attacked me in the mountains when I wasn't
well. I decided he could forget the green jersey.**'
Merckx wins stage seventeen at Bordeaux

fifty kilometres later, Merckx entered the old port of Marseille. The
mistral blew them into town so fast, no one was there to greet
them. Yet he had regained just two minutes.

Three days later, on the Pyrenean stage from Revel to Luchon,
Ocaña was expected to attack again. But it was Merckx who went
on the offensive. Each time he accelerated, however, Ocaña matched
him. As they battled, a storm gathered. Soon streams of mud flooded
the road; hailstones pounded the riders' backs. Their brakes became
useless, and they had to use their feet. Merckx was the first to fall, but
he was quickly back in the saddle. Then Ocaña went down. As he
picked himself up, Zoetemelk glissaded into him at high speed. The
collision was sickening; Ocaña bent double and collapsed into the
dirt, muttering unintelligibly. Perhaps remembering Roger Rivière's
accident in 1960, Maurice De Muer, Ocaña's *directeur sportif*, later
commented: 'I feared the worst: a spinal damage, paralysis...' Merckx
learned of Ocaña's plight at the foot of Le Portillon, under a hail of
spittle and stones; Ocaña's fans held him responsible for their idol's
downfall. At Luchon he refused to don the yellow jersey, out of
sympathy for Ocaña. Merckx considered abandoning, and in an
evocative interview after the stage, expressed his bitterness.
'Whatever happens, I have lost the Tour. There will always be doubt.'
Ocaña's misfortune had put him in the lead but deprived him of the
opportunity of winning the Tour in honest, man-to-man combat.

Merckx finished the Tour as he'd started it: with two stunning
victories. He held off the entire peloton to win the millpond-flat
stage into Bordeaux: 'Guimard attacked me in the mountains when
I wasn't well. I decided he could forget the green jersey. I attacked
fourteen kilometres from the finish-line and I won – and took the
green jersey.' Then he won the final time-trial, from Versailles to Paris.

1971			3,584.7 km
Podium	Nationality	Time	Av speed (kph)
1st Eddy Merckx	Belgium	96h 45m 14s	37.05
2nd Joop Zoetemelk	Netherlands	+9m 51s	
3rd Lucien Van Impe	Belgium	+11m 6s	

Mountains: Lucien Van Impe Belgium
Green jersey: Eddy Merckx Belgium

1972

At the end of stage fifteen, on the finish line of Mont Revard, Merckx made a beginner's mistake: as he celebrated the stage win, the Frenchman Cyrille Guimard threw himself past and four-inched it. Guimard was known as a sprinter, but this was his second consecutive win in the Alps, and his fourth of the Tour, and it put him into second place. The galling thing was, Merckx was so dominant, a little complacency made no difference. Guimard was still six minutes behind, and the stage had also seen Luis Ocaña quit.

Ocaña had picked up painful injuries and a lung infection on the road to Pau. Swinging out of a bend to find a line of cars blocking the way, he threw himself at the road to avoid the collision. Injured, but intact, he got up and sped towards the finish. 'I only lost a minute,' he recalled, 'but I couldn't find a *soigneur* in the hotel, and went to look for one, sweating and exhausted. That was probably how I picked up the infection, which ruined any chance I had.'

Nonetheless, the luckless Spaniard soldiered on, and lay second overall, three minutes behind Merckx, at the start of stage thirteen, through the Alps from Orcières-Merlette to Briançon. Attacking the descent from the Vars, Merckx dropped Ocaña, who then punctured. But Merckx was already far away and Guimard was with him, making sure he'd inherit second place when Ocaña abandoned.

Strength, determination and, for once, some good luck:
Ocaña leads José Manuel Fuente up the Télégraphe.

But Guimard's knees were going the way of Ocaña's lungs: daily injections of novocaine – which would get him banned these days – took him to the Alps, but he had to be carried to the stage starts in a sedan chair. It couldn't last, and on stage eighteen, he was forced to abandon. That left Merckx in a metaphorical sedan chair, no serious challengers left, cruising to his fourth Tour victory, with the points and the combined classifications into the bargain. In Paris, he offered the green points jersey to Guimard, who burst into tears on behalf of everyone whose career coincided with the mighty Kong.

1972			3,846 km
Podium	Nationality	Time	Av speed (kph)
1st Eddy Merckx	Belgium	108h 17m 18s	35.52
2nd Felice Gimondi	Italy	+10m 41s	
3rd Raymond Poulidor	France	+11m 34s	

Mountains: Lucien Van Impe   Belgium
Green jersey: Eddy Merckx   Belgium

1973

In 1973, King Kong varied his diet. In the spring he completed a historic double by devouring the Tours of Spain and Italy. Sated, he decided not to defend his title at the Tour. For Luis Ocaña, the stage was set for what Pierre Chany would describe in *L'Équipe* as 'a massacre, a sort of collective annihilation.'

Ocaña could have been forgiven for thinking he was cursed by the gods. A fall on the Ballon d'Alsace had ruined his 1969 Tour; the storm on the Col de Mente had cost him victory in 1971; the downpour on the Soulor had forced him out in 1972. On stage two of the 1973 Tour, even man's best friend was against him: a dog brought him down, but he escaped with a few bruises.

Stage three was one for burly classics specialists, over the cobbles from Roubaix to Reims. But Ocaña hadn't read the script, and joined Cyrille Guimard and four of Guimard's Bic teammates on the attack over the unfamiliar cobblestones of Querenaing, near the Belgian border. Guimard won the stage, his teammate José Catieau took over the yellow jersey, but the real victor was Ocaña. He had gained two minutes on Thévenet, Zoetemelk, Van Impe and the evergreen Poulidor, and seven on the fine Spanish stage racer José Manuel Fuente.

After his coup over the northern cobbles, Ocaña entered the Alps with an appetite for victory. He won the short stage from Divonne to Gaillard, then took up José-Manuel Fuente's challenge on the road to the ski station at Les Orres. It was an epic duel. At the top of the climb to Les Orres, Ocaña emerged the victor, but was so exhausted that he went straight to his room, too tired to eat or change his clothes. Thévenet and his compatriot Mariano Martinez had managed to limit their losses, but among the rest of the peloton, the race schedule of three severe mountain stages in two days had wrought havoc. The Tour had been decimated, and the peloton was bristling with defiance. Ocaña was among them. 'If you take the coach and train transfers into account, we get less than six hours' sleep a night. And after that, they ask us to climb mountains!' The Spaniard consolidated his lead over the Pyrenees to Luchon, on a stage that almost proved fatal to Poulidor. On the descent from the Portet d'Aspet, the thirty-seven-year-old Frenchman plunged into a ravine, crawling out with a helping hand from the race director Jacques Goddet.

By the time the Tour arrived in Paris, Ocaña had taken six stage victories. There can be little doubt that he, like everyone else, rode in the massive shadow cast by Eddy Merckx; but, proud and persistent, Ocaña lived less in his shadow than most.

1973 — 4047.8 km

	Podium	Nationality	Time	Av speed (kph)
1st	Luis Ocaña	Spain	122h 25m 34s	33.06
2nd	Bernard Thévenet	France	+15m 51s	
3rd	José-Manuel Fuente	Spain	+17m 15s	

Mountains: Pedro Torres — Spain
Green jersey: H.Van Springel — Belgium

1974

'Can 40 million Frenchmen be wrong?' asked the *Daily Mirror* in July 1974, when the Tour de France made a rather lacklustre visit to Britain. In cycling terms, the English Channel was more of an ocean separating France, where the Tour ruled the streets, from Plymouth where it was restricted to an unopened bypass. The long, unpleasant

> **'I won at Aix-les-Bains because I didn't want to miss the World Cup final that evening.'**
> Eddy Merckx, in a hurry

ferry trip there was followed, the same evening, by the long, unpleasant ferry trip back. The Tour waited until the Channel tunnel was built before it came back.

The stage result – the only victory of Dutchman Henk Poppe's professional career – had less influence on the Tour de France than the soccer World Cup, held in Germany, for which England hadn't even qualified. Eddy Merckx stretched his race lead to two minutes on the stage to Aix-les-Bains because, he said, 'I didn't want to miss the World Cup final that evening.'

Neither Luis Ocaña, nor Joop Zoetemelk started the 1974 Tour. The Spaniard was in dispute with his sponsor, the Dutchman was recovering from serious injuries after crashing, in an all-out sprint, into a badly parked car during the Valras–Plage stage of the Midi Libre. The man who moved into second place that day was none other than the irrepressible and apparently immortal Raymond Poulidor. Poulidor dropped Merckx on the ascent of the Mont du Chat, only to falter on the Galibier, but he spared the Tour from monotony by winning at Saint-Lary-Soulan in the Pyrenees. Still, even he could offer no sustained challenge to Merckx.

The day after winning the Tour of Switzerland, Merckx had undergone a delicate operation on his perineum. At Brest for the Grand Départ of the 1974 Tour de France, the wound had still not healed. 'After the Prologue, the lining of my racing shorts was soaked in blood. It was to stay that way for the duration of the Tour,' he recalled. That didn't stop him winning the Prologue, stage seven at Chalons-sur-Marne, stages nine and ten in the Alps, stage fifteen through the Pyrenees, and stage twenty-one, from Vouvray to Orléans. Merckx's victory at Orléans was an extraordinary *coup de théâtre*: with fourteen kilometres to go, he simply rode away from the rest of the peloton. Jacques Anquetil, providing colour commentary for French radio, expressed his amazement. 'I have known a few champions in my time – Coppi, Van Looy and Altig – but none of them could have dropped the entire peloton like Merckx today. On the other hand, it is not good enough for the peloton to wave the white flag. There must be riders out there lacking in self-esteem!' It was hardly surprising. Merckx paid for his efforts later that afternoon, when an ungainly young Belgian named Michel Pollentier defeated him in the Orléans time-trial. The next day, on the final run into Paris, it was business as usual: Merckx took the stage, won the Tour and set a new record of thirty-two stage wins, passing André Leducq's previous record of twenty-five. Poulidor's late flowering gave neither victory nor a taste of the yellow jersey, but he did finish the Tour second overall. He snatched the runner-up's spot from the veteran Spaniard Vicente Lopez-Carril by five seconds.

1974 — 4,098 km

Podium		Nationality	Time	Av speed (kph)
1st	Eddy Merckx	Belgium	116h 16m 58s	35.24
2nd	Raymond Poulidor	France	+8m 4s	
3rd	Vicente López-Carril	Spain	+8m 9s	

Mountains: D. Perurena	Spain
Green jersey: Patrick Sercu	France

1975-7 Eddy's Final Act

Eddy Merckx started the '75 Tour imperiously, tearing the peloton to shreds on the Côte d'Alsemberg, one of the feared, cobbled climbs from the Paris–Brussels classic, and on the cobblestones of Roubaix. Victory in the first time-trial won him the yellow jersey, and a narrow, nine-second win over Thévenet in the second, at Auch, seemed to confirm his dominance. Then, suddenly, it started to go wrong.

1975

Merckx was thirty, now, and came to the Tour with a new record of six Tour wins in his sights. But the years had weakened his body and death had dealt his morale a serious blow: his long-standing manager, Jean Van Buggenhout, a lightning conductor who had attracted many of the pressures of success away from the champion, died shortly before the Tour. The burden would begin to tell.

He started and finished stage eleven in the yellow jersey, but the stage winner, Joop Zoetemelk, observed, 'Merckx didn't seem to be himself, nor Ocaña, who'd been excellent on the Tourmalet. Thévenet was the best.'

Like Merckx, Bernard Thévenet was riding his sixth Tour de France. He started stage eleven two minutes, twenty behind Merckx. He ended it one minute, thirty-one behind him. That's the way it stayed until stage fourteen, finishing on the Puy-de-Dôme. Dropped by Van Impe and Thévenet, and with Zoetemelk hot on his heels, Merckx was attempting to close the gap when, 150 metres from the finish line, a spectator leapt from the crowd and threw a punch into his kidneys. Doubled up by the violence of the blow,

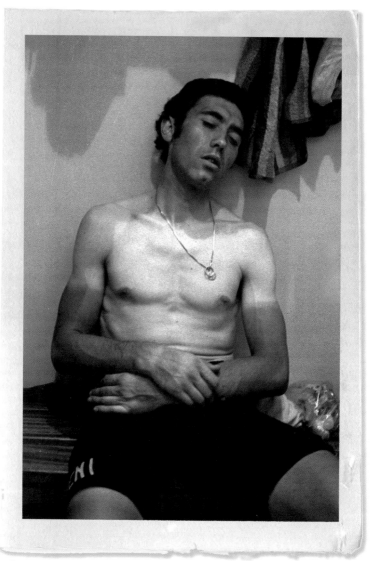

At the Tour, success is no guarantee of popularity: Merckx saw his slim chance of victory in 1975 dissolve after taking a punch from a roadside spectator.

Merckx finished the stage barely able to breathe. His assailant made the mistake of walking up to the finish line area. There, Merckx recognised him, and had him arrested. Thévenet moved to within a minute of the yellow jersey – and so it stayed until the Alps.

Stage fifteen took the Tour from Nice to ski resort of Pra-Loup. Thévenet described the stage: 'I tried to drop Merckx on the Col de Champs. He took everything I could throw at him. Then, on the Allos, he counter-attacked. The final 700 metres of the col were terrifying. Merckx gave it everything he had, I tried to ride in his slipstream, but I literally blew up! When I started the descent, I was on the edge, as they say – in a black hole. I don't think I've ever descended that badly.'

At the foot of the climb, Thévenet had lost one minute, thirteen seconds to Merckx. 'I thought it was important to limit my losses. It was obvious they would have doubled, at the very least... My initial deficit would have had catastrophic consequences.'

'I glimpsed Merckx around a corner. I sat in his slipstream for a moment, then [my director] shouted: "Go, Bernard! He's burnt out." I didn't hesitate. And it was true: Eddy was rooted to the spot.'
Bernard Thévenet profits from Merckx's first great collapse

It was a performance from the Eddy Merckx of legend, and the Tour seemed to have been decided when the unthinkable happened; on the final climb of the day, Merckx simply ran out of energy. An incredulous Felice Gimondi was the first to catch him up, soon followed by Thévenet, who then set off to win the yellow jersey.

'Suddenly, after I'd passed Van Impe, then Zoetemelk, I glimpsed Merckx around a corner. I sat in his slipstream for a moment to recover, then [my director] Maurice De Muer shouted: "Go, Bernard! He's burnt out." I didn't hesitate. And it was true: Eddy was rooted to the spot.

'When I reached Gimondi, I did the same thing. The moment I dropped him, I thought about winning the stage, nothing more.'

With the stage, Thévenet took the yellow jersey: 'It's the first time I've worn it, in my sixth Tour de France. And to think that Poulidor has never put it on! But the hardest part is still to come.'

The following day, Thévenet won the second big Alpine stage: 'In the last five kilometres of the Izoard, I said to myself "I could be winning the Tour de France," and I gave it everything.' Merckx was beaten. Later it became apparent that he was suffering from the blood-thinning effect of medication prescribed after the punch on the Puy-de-Dôme. Then, at the start of stage seventeen, Merckx collided with Denmark's Ole Ritter and fractured his jaw. He refused to abandon; to do so would have devalued Thévenet's victory. Thévenet was greeted as a hero by the French crowds when the race reached its first ever conclusion on the Champs-Elysées.

1975 — 4,000 km

	Podium	Nationality	Time	Av speed (kph)
1st	Bernard Thévenet	France	114h 35m 31s	34.91
2nd	Eddy Merckx	Belgium	+2m 47s	
3rd	Lucien Van Impe	Belgium	+5m 1s	

Mountains: Lucien Van Impe Belgium
Green jersey: Rik Van Linden Belgium

1976

Lucien Van Impe had won the mountains competition three times, and had finished on the final podium twice. But it was only when he won the time-trial from Morzine to Chatel at the 1975 Tour, beating Merckx and Thévenet on the way, that he convinced himself he could one day win the Tour de France. But he nearly didn't start the 1975 race. During the Midi Libre, a pre-Tour stage race, he rode so disinterestedly that his team director, Merckx's old rival Cyrille Guimard, threatened to leave him at home during the Tour. Guimard was a wise old bird, and Van Impe's 1976 performance was to a very great extent due to Guimard's prompting.

With Merckx absent through injury, on paper, the way was open for Thévenet, who had just won the pre-Tour Dauphiné Libéré, and Ocaña, who had lost the Tour of Spain by barely a minute in May. But the Tour isn't won on paper.

Before the favourites slugged it out for victory, another Belgian with Eddy in his name – Freddy Maertens – won four stages.

Then came the punishing, 258-kilometre marathon that finished on the slopes of Alpe d'Huez. Zoetemelk and Van Impe attacked and counter-attacked in a fascinating piece of choreography that allowed Zoetemelk to gain just three seconds on his rival. Van Impe took the yellow jersey for the first time in eight Tours.

Twenty-four hours later, Zoetemelk won again at Montgenèvre ahead of Thévenet, Van Impe, and five more riders including Thévenet's thirty-three-year-old teammate Raymond Delisle. When the 1975 Tour winner fell ill, Delisle attacked on the ascent to the ski station at Pyrenees 2000, won the stage by seven minutes and borrowed the race lead. Then, it was stage fourteen, from Saint-Gaudens to Saint-Lary-Soulan, over the Col de Mente, the Portillon and the Peyresourde. Guimard decided to send Van Impe on a long-range attack, to impose himself on his rivals.

A stinging attack by Luis Ocaña shattered the peloton. Ocaña launched himself on the Col du Portillon in pursuit of the leading group; behind him, Guimard sent Raymond Martin to give his leader the order to attack. Van Impe ignored him. Then he sent Alain Meslet to give the order: again, Van Impe did nothing. Finally, Guimard himself drove past the peloton and told him himself: this time, Van Impe obeyed. He hated long efforts, and, from the foot of the Col du Portillon, there were eighty kilometres to cover.

**An Old Pro Remembers: Jean-Marie Leblanc, future director of the Tour,
asks the forty-year-old Poulidor what he makes of the modern world.**

On the other side of the mountain, Guimard came alongside and
said: 'You're one minute, fifty seconds ahead of Delisle and
Zoetemelk. Do you want to win the Tour de France or not?'

Van Impe flew over the Peyresourde, passing the remnants of the
early breakaway until he reached Luis Ocaña. The two men rode
together before Van Impe attacked for victory and the yellow jersey.
Zoetemelk finished in second place, but over three minutes down.

Before the riders reached Paris, Freddy Maertens won four more
stages, equalling the record held for stage wins in a single Tour by
Gino Bartali and Eddy Merckx, and taking the green points jersey.

On the final stage, Raymond Poulidor inched ahead of Delisle in
the general classification, and finished the Tour in third place.
Fourteen years had elapsed between the first and the last time he
finished third in the Tour. If misfortune is the precondition of all
humour, Poulidor had been France's greatest comic for a decade.
Now, he bowed out, never having worn the yellow jersey.

1976			3,930.6 km
Podium	Nationality	Time	Av speed (kph)
1st Lucien Van Impe	Belgium	116h 22m 23s	33.78
2nd Joop Zoetemelk	Netherlands	+4m 14s	
3rd Raymond Poulidor	France	+12m 8s	

Mountains: Giancarlo Bellini Italy
Green jersey: F. Maertens Belgium

1977

The '77 Tour took the riders over the Pyrenees on only the second day of racing. With the favourites Zoetemelk, Van Impe and Thévenet in check, the young German Dietrich Thurau was the principal beneficiary. Victory in the Prologue and stage two secured him the yellow jersey for seventeen days, until the mountain time-trial on the slopes of the Avoriaz revealed his limitations and the race began in earnest. Van Impe won the stage, but Thévenet took the race lead.

Van Impe, his confidence bolstered by victory the previous year, was more audacious than ever, and chose stage seventeen, across the northern Alps from Chamonix to Alpe d'Huez to try to reverse the situation. He attacked sixty-five kilometres from the stage finish, six kilometres from the Col du Glandon. He led by over a minute at the summit, and after a virtuoso descent, by two minutes, and by nearly three minutes at the foot of the Alpe – despite a fierce headwind. His three main adversaries, Thévenet, Zoetemelk and Kuiper, should have pulled him back on the twenty kilometre descent from the Glandon and the fifteen kilometers of valley roads before the final climb. But Zoetemelk and Kuiper refused to work. At the stage finish, Thévenet denigrated them as 'little men'.

But Van Impe's swashbuckling escapade was to come to a premature end. On the final ascent of the Alpe, he lost a large part

The seconds pass like years, and Eddy Merckx struggles to hold them back.
Ahead, Bernard Thévenet is climbing to Tour victory.

of his hard-earned lead when a television reporter's car struck him from behind and threw him into the ditch. He rose immediately and set off without hesitation, only to have his rear wheel collapse. As his mechanic changed it, Van Impe could only watch in distress as Hennie Kuiper passed, pursued by Thévenet.

Thévenet lost forty-one seconds to Kuiper's attack six kilometres from the finish, keeping the yellow jersey on his shoulders by just eight seconds. For Van Impe, third across the line two minutes, twenty-five seconds behind the yellow jersey, the Tour was lost. Still further back, Eddy Merckx accumulated nearly a quarter of an hour's deficit and thirty-one riders finished outside the time limit and were eliminated.

Merckx wasn't his normal self. At Fribourg four days earlier, he had been diagnosed with dysentery and had steadily been losing time on the leaders. He was philosophical in defeat: 'It had to happen one day. You'd have to be foolish to think otherwise. Between now and the end of the Tour, I'll have better days than this. I'll try to profit from them – not to win the Tour, obviously, but for my honour. We're not at Paris yet.' Merckx knew how to lose as well as how to win; he knew that to abandon would detract from the winner's achievement, and he insisted on finishing. Sixth place overall in the Tour de France, beyond the aspirations of most professional cyclists, represented the end of Merckx's Tour de France career. At Saint-Étienne, Merckx was even awarded the stage win after Joaquim Agostinho and Antonio Menéndez, the first and second placed riders on the stage, were disqualified after failing anti-doping tests. Indeed, the Tour ended, not for the first – and not for the last time – in an atmosphere of suspicion. A list of riders suspected of doping circulated clandestinely. The organisers responded to rumours by publishing a statement making it clear that Bernard Thévenet, who had tested positive in March during the Paris–Nice, was 'above suspicion'. However, some months later, while being treated in a Paris hospital, Thévenet admitted to one of his journalist friends that he had taken cortisone, a substance as yet undetectable by tests. In 1979, he expanded on his confession: he'd used the drug for three years, with the result that he was no longer even physically capable of riding a bike. Criticised by his employer and his peers, Thévenet never again played a major role in the Tour de France.

1977 — 4,096 km

	Podium	Nationality	Time	Av speed (kph)
1st	Bernard Thévenet	France	115h 38m 30s	35.42
2nd	Hennie Kuiper	Netherlands	+48s	
3rd	Lucien Van Impe	Belgium	+3m 32s	

Mountains: Lucien Van Impe Belgium
Green jersey: Jean Esclassan France

The Years of the Badger

Bernard Hinault wears the
look of a man obsessed as he
leads the pack in the Alps.

1978-9
The Tetch Offensive

Some tetchiness is to be expected in a champion, but Bernard Hinault had tetch by the ton. Once, thumping the door of the anti-doping caravan, he threatened to piss on the steps if they didn't open up. He hated being slapped on the back so much he talked about making a prickly vest using drawing pins and slipping his shirt over the top. Nor did he have any patience with mythmakers. At a press conference in the Alps during the 1982 Tour, he was asked about the legend he was creating. 'What use is a legend?' was his response. 'What good does winning the Tour by ten or twenty minutes instead of six, do?'

But Bernard had his soft side: before stage eleven of the 1981 Tour, a mother with a sick son gave a note to one of his team staff. Her sick son was in hospital; would Hinault be able to visit him. Jean-Marie Leblanc, still editing *L'Équipe*'s cycling pages, not yet directing the Tour, was asked his opinion. 'Merckx would have gone,' he said. Without a word to anyone save the chief cycling correspondent of France's biggest selling newspaper, Hinault paid his visit.

In 1975, at the end of his first year as a professional, during which he'd finished seventh in Paris-Nice and first in the Circuit de la Sarthe, Hinault commented, 'One day, I'll be the champion of France, the winner of the Tour and the world champion.' After stage eight of the 1978 Tour – his first – *L'Équipe*'s headline read, 'He's the champion we've been waiting for.' He rode that day's time-trial to perfection, with a negative split – the second half faster than the first

**A man apart: highly strung, totally committed – Bernard Hinault
leads the strike against late nights and early mornings.**

– to beat Freddy Maertens, who started too fast and led for the first
three-quarters of the route. By stage eleven, the headline writers
made the ultimate comparison: 'Hinault: cold-blooded like Anquetil.'

Hinault's honeymoon with the press finished five days later. The
Tour had been planned with repeated transfers between stages
which left the riders hurrying their meals and travelling instead of
sleeping. At the town of Valence d'Agen, they staged a strike. Their
spokesman was André Chalmel, who told the press, 'We're not
circus animals on display from town to town.' But everyone was
looking at Hinault. The town magistrate, not an avid reader of
Socialist Worker, told him: 'You're unworthy of the jersey of the
French champion.' Hinault took it to heart. 'I couldn't get over it.
All the accounts singled me out for criticism. I became hyper-
nervous and I slept badly for several nights. That's the state I was in
when I started the time-trial at Puy-de-Dôme. I suffered a blow

there' – he lost one minute, forty seconds to Joop Zoetemelk, but added – 'It helped me for the rest of the Tour.'

The following day, Hinault, who had ridden the Pyrenees with the best of the climbers, won the bunch sprint into Saint-Étienne, ahead of the great specialists Sean Kelly and Freddy Maertens.

Stage sixteen, from Saint-Étienne to Alpe d'Huez, saw the drama of the climb descend into farce. Belgium's lanky Michel Pollentier won the stage to Alpe d'Huez and declared, 'The Tour is now between Zoetemelk, Hinault and me.' Then he went for the anti-doping test, and was caught twitching like an apprentice bagpiper as he attempted to squeeze urine from a balloon secreted in his armpit down a pipe and into the sample bottle. His exclusion left Zoetemelk in the yellow jersey, fourteen seconds ahead of Hinault. The Dutchman commented: 'If I don't leave the Alps with a two-minute advantage over Hinault, I won't win the Tour.' He didn't.

Hinault rode stage twenty, the time-trial from Metz to Nancy, four full minutes faster than Zoetemelk, and finished so fresh he said, 'I could ride another three months like this, I feel so good – better and better each day.'

He had started the Tour with a plan. 'Take advantage in the time trials and eliminate my rivals one by one.' It had worked to a tee. Yet, no sooner had he won his first Tour, than Hinault was talking of retirement: 'I give myself eight or nine years more to compete at the top level. But I won't try to do what Merckx did, and win everything. Each year, I'll set myself a few goals, and I'll stick to them, without being excessive. I love nature, I can't live without space, trees and wind. When it's time to retire – because I already think about it – I'll choose something that will keep me rooted to the land I love. I'm a happy man.'

> **'I could ride another three months like this, I feel so good – better and better each day.'**
> By stage twenty of his first Tour, Bernard Hinault was just warming up.

1978			3,920 km
Podium	Nationality	Time	Av speed (kph)
1st Bernard Hinault	France	108h 18m 0s	36.20
2nd Joop Zoetmelk	Netherlands	+3m 56s	
3rd Joaquim Agostinho	Portugal	+6m 54s	
Mountains: Mariano Martinez	France		
Green jersey: Freddy Maertens	Belgium		

1979

The 1979 Tour started deep in south-west France. The World Champion, Holland's Gerrie Knetemann, won the Prologue, and the following day, Hinault's teammate Jean-René Bernaudeau took over the race lead. Then Hinault sprang into action: victory over the thirty-seven-year-old Portuguese rider Joaquim Agostinho in the Superbagnères time-trial gave him the yellow jersey.

When Pau saw his second stage win the following day, his second Tour de France success seemed certain. The excellent performance of his team, Renault-Gitane, in the two team time-trials – the speciality of the powerful Dutchmen of TI-Raleigh – reinforced the conviction.

Then, on stage nine, over 100 kilometres from Roubaix, Hinault suffered a puncture. As his main rival, Joop Zoetemelk, sped towards the stage finish in a small group of powerful riders, Hinault pursued them alone, losing nearly three and a half minutes. Two weeks later, on the Champs-Élysées, Jacques Anquetil observed, cryptically, 'Hinault won the Tour that day. Or rather, he didn't lose it. Which he might have, without that extraordinary resilience in adversity.'

However, even before the Alps, Hinault had whittled Zoetemelk's lead down to forty-nine seconds. There, a mammoth mountain time-trial from Evian to the purpose-built ski centre at

**The perfect finale: numbers one and two in the general classification,
Bernard Hinault and Joop Zoetemelk, slug it out on the Champs-Élysées.**

Avoriaz awaited. It saw one of the most remarkable exploits of
Hinault's career. Far longer than a conventional mountain time-trial,
the 54.2-kilometre stage had been designed to deliver huge
differences between the protagonists. During the time-trial through
the northern Alps from Évian to Morzine-Avoriaz, Zoetemelk had
to change bikes twice. Hinault, in a one-piece, yellow-topped
bodysuit, left Zoetemelk nearly two minutes behind in the general
classification. Still, he was one of only seven riders who finished

within five minutes of Hinault. Alpe d'Huez welcomed two stage finishes on consecutive days. The stage winners, Agostinho on stage seventeen and Zoetemelk the following day, ensured that the podium roster would repeat the previous year's result: Hinault,

> **'He seems improved in the mountains, he's stronger on the flat than anyone, and he's among the best sprinters. If he carries on like this, he could match Merckx.'**
>
> Zoetemelk on Hinault

Zoetemelk, Agostinho. Hinault used the final time-trial around Dijon to extend his lead. That evening, Zoetemelk reflected, 'No regrets. Hinault is stronger than me... He seems improved in the mountains, where he's developed a climber's pedal action. He's stronger on the flat than anyone, and he's among the best sprinters. If he carries on improving like this, he could match Merckx.'

Then, on the final day, the Tour reached the perfect conclusion, as Hinault and Zoetemelk, first and second in the general classification, found themselves in a two-man breakaway on the Champs-Élysées, slugging it out for the final stage win. Zoetemelk had made a gallant final attack as the riders closed in on Paris. Hinault had reacted strongly, and crossed single-handed to the Dutchman. In the sprint, Hinault took his seventh stage of the Tour. Classic stuff!

1979   3,719.4 km

	Podium	Nationality	Time	Av speed (kph)
1st	Bernard Hinault	France	103h 6m 50s	36.07
2nd	Joop Zoetemelk	Netherlands	+3m 7s	
3rd	Joaquim Agostinho	Portugal	+26m 53s	

Mountains: Giovanni Battaglin — Italy
Green jersey: Bernard Hinault — France

1980
In Through the Out Door

The underdogs live in the shadow of the superstars: sad, ragged figures, serious about everything they attempt, no matter how futile or foolish they may appear. Poulidor was one, pummelled by Anquetil, and then by Merckx. Joop Zoetemelk was another. He inherited Merckx, then faced Hinault. But neither man ever submitted. They clung to the tiny, forlorn spark of hope still glimmering in their soul, which made them keep trying. In 1980, Zoetemelk struck a victory for the Christophes, the Viettos, and the Poulidors of this world.

For the French writer Lucien Bodard, Joop Zoetemelk had 'a griffin's head and a smile that had to be wide to contain his enormous teeth. His was the philosophy of small steps – they had to be small to allow Merckx to ripen, age, and retire before he had a chance at glory.' Caricatures aside, Zoetemelk had a remarkable Tour de France record. In his first Tour in 1970, he'd finished second behind Merckx. The following year, he did the same. Second again in '76, '78 and '79, fourth in '73 and '75 and fifth in '72, his record was testimony to remarkable athletic gifts, and to the unfortunate timing of his career. In 1979, he had won the Tour of Spain; now, aged thirty-three and on his tenth Tour, Zoetemelk had his last chance.

Yet Bernard Hinault's first Prologue win of his career brought a sense of inevitability down on the race. Merckx's years of domination had followed close on those of Anquetil. Now a new era of dominance had begun to suffocate the spirit of sporting tension. In

The race leader, minus yellow jersey. Joop Zoetemelk refused to wear it the day after Hinault's abandon.

the first individual time-trial, he sped to victory, his Renault colours suddenly at home on the smooth asphalt of the Spa-Francorchamps racing circuit. The next day, the longest stage of the race took in the jarring cobblestones of north-east France between Liège and Lille. Hinault hated cobblestones, and at the stage start, rumours abounded that he was organising some sort of protest. He took exception: 'It's got nothing to do with me. I've been saddled with enough criticism to get involved in anything like that. I'll ride, even if I think there are too many miles of cobbles.' To hammer home his protest, he won the stage – then complained: 'It's close to inhuman, what they've made us do today. The cobblestones, when it's dry, are OK, but when it rains continuously like this, it isn't racing.' He continued, 'I suffered at the front. What must it have been like for those at the back?'

Zoetemelk's TI-Raleigh team won the team time-trial and temporarily deprived Hinault of the yellow jersey, which passed to Belgium's Rudy Pevenage after a swashbuckling breakaway through driving rain on the stage from Frankfurt to Metz. Appalling conditions characterised the entire first half of the Tour, and tendinitis soon reached epidemic proportions. Bernard Hinault felt the first twinges during the stage from Lille to Compiègne.

Two days later, during the second team time-trial, the normally flamboyant Hinault hid behind his teammates, to the disappointment of his fans. TI-Raleigh took the semi-stage and gained a minute and a half on Renault-Gitane. That afternoon, Hinault somehow found the strength to react to a darting acceleration from Zoetemelk in the closing stages of the semi-stage from Beauvais to Rouen, and in the long time-trial between the Gascon villages of Damazan and Laplume, he finally retrieved the yellow jersey, despite riding far below his usual level and managing only fifth place behind the winner, Zoetemelk.

On 9 July, as the Tour reached the Pyrenees, Hinault was wearing the yellow jersey. At 5 p.m., in Place de Verdun in the middle of Pau, Hinault had said he'd carry on. He was lying: 'Fifty kilometres into the stage from Agen to Pau, I'd made up my mind. I understood, at

'a griffin's head and a smile that had to be wide to contain his enormous teeth. His was the philosophy of small steps – they had to be small to allow Merckx to ripen, age, and retire before he had a chance at glory.'

Zoetemelk, by French writer Lucien Bodard

that moment, I'd never get through the Pyrenees.' So at 10.30 that night, he loaded his suitcases into a car and disappeared without a word. 'I didn't have the heart to face a

> **'One false question, and I'd have been capable of violence.'**
> Hinault avoids a press conference

press conference. I was in such a state of tension, I wasn't sure I could control myself. One false question, and I'd have been capable of violence. In the face of pain, I'm just a man like any other, with the same limits. I could have started at Pau, but I'd only have stopped on the first climb and watched the peloton pass.' Hinault took refuge at the home of his teammate, Hubert Arbes, in the outskirts of Lourdes. That night, it snowed in the Pyrenees.

The man who inherited the race lead, Joop Zoetemelk, refused to wear the yellow jersey for the stage from Pau to Luchon out of respect for the champion. But he still complained, 'If he really had a bad knee, he obviously had to abandon. But, in my opinion, he didn't choose the right way to do it. I don't think my victory was cheap because of it.'

With the strongest team in the race to protect his lead, Zoetemelk added authority to his win by taking the final time-trial around Saint-Étienne. He was the first Dutchman to win the trophy since Jan Janssen in 1968; their compatriot, Hennie Kuiper, came second.

1980 — 3,945.8 km

	Podium	Nationality	Time	Av speed (kph)
1st	Joop Zoetemelk	Netherlands	109h 19m 14s	36.09
2nd	Hennie Kuiper	Netherlands	+6m 55s	
3rd	Raymond Martin	France	+7m 56s	

Mountains: Raymond Martin France
Green jersey: Rudy Pevenage Belgium

1981-2
The Killer Glance

Hinault had recovered from the Tour to win the World Championship. History had proved him right – and made him more unbeatable, and unbearable, than ever. The slightest criticism, he answered with words to the effect of, 'I race to win, not to please people. If someone thinks he can do better, put him on a bike.'

He arrived at the Grand Départ at Nice as the outstanding favourite. His rivals were all older than him: Zoetemelk, as ever; Agostinho, and the 1976 champion Van Impe. Hinault's former teammate Jean-René Bernaudeau, two years his junior, had moved to Peugeot, and led the new generation.

Hinault took the yellow jersey on day one, winning the Prologue by seven seconds, a wide margin given the length of the stage. In stage 1b, TI-Raleigh won its sixth consecutive Tour de France team time trial, winning the yellow jersey for Gerrie Knetemann. Three days later TI-Raleigh made it seven consecutive team time-trial wins.

Hinault's rivalry with Bernaudeau didn't quite materialise, but an unexpected adversary emerged in Phil Anderson, an aggressive, twenty-three-year-old Australian riding his first Tour. By matching Hinault in the Pyrenean stage to Saint-Lary Soulan, Anderson became the first Australian to wear the yellow jersey. By distancing Anderson by just thirty seconds in the Pau time-trial the following day, Hinault won it back. It was sweet revenge for having had to abandon there the previous year, and it was the first of three time trial victories for Hinault at the 1981 Tour. The second, at Mulhouse, nine days later, gave him a decisive lead before the Tour

Freddy Maertens shows the aggression that made him the most feared sprinter in the sport.

even reached the Alps. There, Hinault contented himself with a steady, controlling ride since his margin was so great. On Alpe d'Huez, where the semi-professional Dutchman Peter Winnen gained eight seconds on Hinault, Lucien van Impe, second overall, was already more than nine minutes down; Robert Alban, the winner at Morzine and third overall, more than ten.

Then came stage twenty, from Alpe d'Huez to Le Pleynet. Hinault had already won three time-trials – including the Prologue at Nice – and his adoring fans were demanding a fourth win, this time in the high mountains, in the style of Coppi, Bobet or Anquetil. He'd been looking at the Alpe d'Huez stage, but the race had gone otherwise. In any case, he achieved his main goals: Phil Anderson and Joop Zoetemelk had lost time, and Bernaudeau had lost more. The following day, the question was, how much he had left in the tank? And what would be the best tactic to shake off the riders intent on hanging on his wheel?

With master tactician Cyrille Guimard's guidance, Hinault decided to ride gently for the first hour of the stage, over the Col de Luitel, where Charly Gaul had destroyed Raphaël Géminiani in 1958. He wanted them to believe his appetite for victory was sated. Then, on the first slopes of the Col des Moulins, he surged out of the pack. Only Fons De Wolf could go with him. The two men devoured the Col des Mouilles at top speed, in pursuit of the leading, two-man breakaway of Juán Fernández and René Bernardeau. The catch took place at the foot of the climb to the ski station at Le Pleynet. The catch was part one. Part two was the stage win. With fifteen kilometres to go, Fernández cracked. Hinault led for the next ten kilometres, then, on a left-hand hairpin, he flashed the other riders a murderous look, and accelerated. De Wolf reacted, but a second quickening saw him fall away, defeated. Hinault won the stage, and extended his overall lead to twelve minutes on Lucien Van Impe.

The time-trial at Saint-Priest allowed Hinault to seal his third Tour de France victory. The formidable Belgian sprinter Freddy

Maertens won his third green jersey with five stage victories, including the final stage on the Champs-Élysées, but Hinault's Prologue and four stage wins had earned him victory over Lucien Van Impe by fourteen minutes, thirty-four seconds, the greatest margin of victory recorded between 1973 and 2003.

1981   3,365.8 km

	Podium	Nationality	Time	Av speed (kph)
1st	Bernard Hinault	France	96h 19m 38s	34.94
2nd	Lucien Van Impe	Belgium	+14m 34s	
3rd	Robert Alban	France	+17m 4s	

Mountains: Lucien Van Impe   Belgium
Green jersey: Freddy Maertens   Belgium

1982

Hinault had won his second Tour of Italy in June; tendinitis had robbed him of the Italian-French double at the 1980 Tour, and now he intended to rectify the matter; victory would also take him past Louison Bobet's milestone of three Tour wins. He pursued his goals with such singularity of purpose that the opposition barely made any impact. After Hinault won the Prologue, Australia's Phil Anderson took the stage from Basel to Nancy and wore the yellow jersey for ten days. But Anderson's leadership merely played into Hinault's hands: he allowed Anderson's Peugeot team to dictate the pace, knowing he was vastly superior against the clock. Hinault won two more time-trials at Martigues and Saint-Priest, where he covered the last kilometre in precisely one minute: sixty kilometres

'What use is a legend? What good does winning the Tour by ten or twenty minutes instead of six, do?'
Bernard Hinault

Sweatbands and bulging muscles are in: the unstoppable Bernard Hinault.

an hour! Even more memorably, he triumphed on the Champs-Élysées again, three years after his memorable breakaway with Zoetemelk. This time he beat the whole peloton in a bunch sprint, proving his unquestionable superiority. As the victor of the Tour of Italy, Hinault also emulated Coppi, Anquetil and Merckx by completing the double after winning his fourth and easiest Tour.

1982   3,501 km

	Podium	Nationality	Time	Av speed (kph)
1st	Bernard Hinault	France	92h 8m 46s	37.99
2nd	Joop Zoetemelk	Netherlands	+6m 21s	
3rd	Johan Van Der Velde	Netherlands	+8m 59s	
Mountains: Bernard Vallet		France		
Green jersey: Sean Kelly		Ireland		

1983-4 Mister Merckx? Who he?

Just when Hinault seemed to have no natural enemies, two turned up at once. The first was tendinitis, which kept him out of the 1983 Tour. The second was a Parisian student with glasses, an angel face and a headband: Laurent Fignon. Merckx, watching from the sidelines took an instant dislike. Fignon shot back, deadpan: 'Merckx, you say? Don't know him.'

Fignon had been the revelation of the 1982 season, when he celebrated his professional debut by winning the Critérium International. But he had to wait for his moment of glory. First, he helped Hinault win the Tour of Spain in May. Then, he started his first Tour de France – the first 'open' Tour (open, that is, to amateur teams), which allowed a Colombian national team to take part. Their best rider was Edgar Corredor, fifth at Luchon, sixth in the Puy-de-Dôme mountain time-trial, third to Alpe d'Huez, third to Morzine, ninth to Morzine-Avoriaz, and sixteenth overall.

So much for the amateurs. The semi-professionals yielded the Prologue winner, Belgium's Éric Vanderaerden. Then came the overseas visitors: Kim Andersen became the first Dane in Tour history to wear the yellow jersey, before Scotland's Robert Millar emerged as a feisty climber who could rival Hinault for tetchiness. This is his take on journalists: 'Those guys see the race on TV, then ask you what's happened. You see them sleeping during the day because they've been drunk the night before. If I think they're useless, I tell them so.' Yet it was Millar's Peugeot teammate Pascal Simon who assumed the race lead after finishing third at Pau. The

'Those guys see the race on TV, then ask you what's happened. You see them sleeping during the day because they've been drunk the night before. If I think they're useless, I tell them so.' Robert Millar on his friends, the journalists

next day, the complexion of the race changed to wrinkled and grimacing when Simon fell and broke his shoulder blade.

The yellow jersey plays games with your mind. This is Jacques Anquetil, in 1957: 'Intense joy, a feeling of power. That evening, in my room, I looked at myself in the mirror with the jersey on my shoulders. I'd grown bigger, but at the same time, I was full of doubt. To keep the jersey, I'd have to suffer.' Simon suffered more than most: he soldiered on for six days, as the Tour crossed the Massif Central; his pains were heroic but in vain. The mountain time-trial on the Puy-de-Dôme sealed his fate. With the real race being decided behind them, the Spanish and Colombian climbers dominated the stage. Pascal Simon, meanwhile, struggled pitifully up the steepest sections. 'All I cared about was one thing: my time loss to Fignon. One minute lost after eight kilometres. I knew it was in my pocket: he couldn't regain more than two minutes in the rest of the stage. But my day was horrendous.' He lost three minutes, ten seconds of his four-minute, fourteen-second lead over Laurent Fignon, keeping first place overall. But it was only a matter of time before he was overhauled; unable to put on the yellow jersey without intense pain, he was permitted to dispense with post-stage jersey presentation.

The following day, between Issoire and Saint-Étienne, the peloton accelerated on the Côte de Lavet. Simon didn't have the strength to follow, yet, surrounded by teammates, he gave chase, and after nineteen kilometres, regained the group. But it was his last reprieve.

Simon's ordeal ended on stage seventeen, on the slopes of La Table, shortly after leaving La Tour-du-Pin for Alpe d'Huez, Simon finally abandoned. Four hours later, Fignon approached the finish line two minutes, seven seconds behind Peter Winnen, who had won on the Alpe in 1981. Fifth in the stage, Fignon was first on GC, six days from the Champs-Élysées.

He was going to win his first Tour, like Coppi in 1949, Koblet in 1951, Anquetil in 1957, Merckx in 1969, Hinault in 1978. But less glorious names were those who had won the Tour without winning a stage. Fignon took his in the final individual time-trial.

1983			3,860 km
Podium	Nationality	Time	Av speed (kph)
1st Laurent Fignon	France	105h 7m 52s	36.72
2nd Angel Arroyo	Spain	+4m 4s	
3rd Peter Winnen	Netherlands	+4m 9s	
Mountains: Lucien Van Impe	Belgium		
Green jersey: Sean Kelly	Ireland		

1984

At Alençon, before the first long time-trial of the 1984 Tour, Laurent Fignon appeared wearing a helmet out of a TV science-fiction comedy. The aerodynamic advantage, with a little help from his thighs, brought him victory over Sean Kelly by sixteen seconds, and Hinault by forty-nine. The news wasn't all good: victory foreshadowed eventual defeat by an analogous hi-tech ruse some years later, although we'll get to that in good time.

The 1984 Tour de France was presented as a generation gap allegory, with Old Man Hinault, twenty-nine, fighting from the grey corner, and Laurent Fignon, twenty-three, with a light blue bodysuit and a rattle, and playing peekaboo with Cyrille Guimard, the surrogate father he'd stolen from Hinault. Actually, Hinault was the one who'd walked, joining a new team, La Vie Claire, owned by a flamboyant and controversial businessman named Bernard Tapie,

Smiles all around, but the body language tells a tale: Hinault's arm around Fignon's neck, Fignon's right arm in a defensive gesture.

who brought in the values of big business, and wages in line with other global sports. Guimard, meanwhile, had nurtured little Laurent to second place in the Tour of Italy. It should have been first – he lost the lead on the final stage – but he made up for it by starting the Tour in the jersey of the champion of France.

First blood went to the oldies, when Hinault won the Prologue, three seconds ahead of Fignon. Guimard's riders won stage two (through Marc Madiot), the team time-trial the following day, and then took over the yellow jersey when Vincent Barteau finished second on stage four, seventeen minutes ahead of the peloton. His advantage raised the possibility of a Walkowiak-style Tour.

Guimard exploited the situation, keeping Fignon in the wings and dispatching Pascal Jules, Pascal Poisson and Pierre-Henri Menthéour for stage wins. Barteau showed strength and stamina in the Pyrenees and held on to the yellow jersey until the Alps.

The contest for overall victory, meanwhile, had began in earnest with the long individual time-trial on stage six. The route should have favoured Hinault, but it was Fignon, the behelmeted boychild, who won it. Then, in the Alps, Fignon won three stages out of five: the mountain time-trial at La Ruchère, twenty-five seconds ahead of Lucho Herrera, the brilliant Colombian apparently made of extruded glass; at La Plagne, convincingly and alone; and Crans-Montana.

Then came the stage to Alpe d'Huez. Hinault attacked immediately – much to Fignon's amusement: 'When I saw him attack I laughed to myself.' Over the next few switchbacks, Fignon reeled Hinault in with injurious ease. Hinault had attacked too early on the Alpe, but he didn't need telling: 'We both took risks. I lost, but that's the game. As long as I have breath left in me, I'll attack.' Hinault was talking a good race because he could no longer ride one: Fignon confidently bided his time and overwhelmed his rival, despite an irresistible ascent by Lucho Herrera, who, on the Tour's most mythical climb, achieved the first stage win by an amateur and the first for a rider from a developing nation in Tour de France history.

The transfer of power felt definitive; Fignon, seven years Hinault's junior, took his second Tour win in Paris. Hinault finally won favour with the French public, not, as he saw it, by losing the Tour, but by showing such bravery and panache in defeat. In third place, Greg LeMond became the first American to climb the podium in Paris.

1984 — 4,021 km

	Podium	Nationality	Time	Av speed (kph)
1st	Laurent Fignon	France	112h 3m 40s	35.88
2nd	Bernard Hinault	France	+10m 32s	
3rd	Greg LeMond	USA	+11m 46s	
Mountains: Robert Millar		Great Britain		
Green jersey: Frank Hoste		Belgium		

1985-6 Not Dead Yet

As Hinault missed the 1983 Tour, Fignon did in 1985: an operation on an inflamed Achilles tendon deprived him of his title defence. That left the man who'd been a geriatric a year before as the outstanding favourite. What the years hadn't withered, the Saint-Étienne road surface assaulted on stage fourteen.

Hinault was the worst hurt of a group which went down in a pointless sprint behind stage winner Lucho Herrera. He sat on the road, his eyes unfocussed, his face covered in blood, rising only minutes later to cross the finish line at last.

Two hours later, he walked into the foyer of his hotel, swaggering like a prize fighter. 'You see? Nothing! They just put two stitches in it. Don't I look a bit like a boxer?' It was Hinault's first ever fall during a three-week Tour. 'Its also the first time I've broken anything. But don't let's make a meal of it. I could have got up quicker if I hadn't known I'd be classified in the same time as my rivals... It could have been worse. I came out of it pretty well. I've still got two arms and two legs. I'm not dead yet.' Not dead, but in difficulty breathing – and he still had to get over the Pyrenees.

In the Pyrenees, as Hinault struggled up the Aubisque, La Vie Claire's *directeur sportif*, Paul Koechli, had to forbid Hinault's American teammate Greg LeMond from co-operating with the stage leader Stephen Roche. The atmosphere was tense and LeMond declared on American radio: 'Koechli made me lose the Tour on the day I could have won it!'

Hinault emerged from the Pyrenean mountains with his race lead intact, and although Greg LeMond won the time-trial around the lake of Vassivière-en-Limousin, the first American stage win in

**Hinault carries the injuries incurred in his fall at Saint-Étienne.
They wouldn't stop him winning the Tour.**

the Tour, he gained only five seconds on Hinault, who played down the drama, and blamed it on American TV reporters who didn't understand cycling: 'There was no clash. Greg reacted like any young, ambitious rider. The CBS reporters egged him on, and made him believe he'd been deprived of the yellow jersey, when the gaps simply weren't there. But I'm telling you outright, there's not so much as a shadow between us.'

The 1985 Tour had been designed with Hinault in mind. It started in his region, Brittany, at the tiny village of Plumelec in the cycling-mad Morbihan, where Hinault won his fifth Tour Prologue before his home crowds. Three days later his team, La Vie Claire, took the team time-trial at Fougères.

'**Koechli made me lose the Tour on the day I could have won it!**'
Greg LeMond criticises his team director

Hinault took the race lead after taking his rivals to the cleaners in the time-trial between Sarrebourg and Strasbourg: his winning margin over Ireland's Stephen Roche was two minutes, twenty seconds. On the first alpine stage, Hinault kicked so strongly only Herrera could go with him. The two men shared the lead for most of the day, and when the Colombian darted away in the final stages, Hinault didn't fight him. The following day, Herrera spent eight more hours at the front with his countryman Fabio Parra, who took another Colombian stage win.

> '**Without my fall at Saint-Étienne, it would have been easy.**'
> Hinault on 1985's Tour

Then, the fall – and the Pyrenean stages, where Hinault was proved right: it was nothing, and he did look like a prize fighter. On the Aubisque, Stephen Roche subtracted a minute and a half from his five-minute deficit. And that was it. LeMond won the final time trial (Hinault was five seconds behind, or 'a broken nose' as it might be known, but isn't) and Hinault's fifth Tour win (and second Giro-Tour double) was in the bag.

Jean-Marie Leblanc pointed out that the black eyes and scars only added to his charisma. Hinault responded with his usual venom. 'Maybe. But that's hogwash. I don't need it. Without my fall at Saint-Étienne, it would have been easy,' he added. 'Nuff said.

1985 — 4107.3 km

	Podium	Nationality	Time	Av speed (kph)
1st	Bernard Hinault	France	113h 24m 23s	36.22
2nd	Greg LeMond	USA	+1m 42s	
3rd	Stephen Roche	Ireland	+4m 29s	
Mountains: Luis Herrera		Colombia		
Green jersey: Sean Kelly		Ireland		

1986

Some say they got it the wrong way round. In 1985, LeMond was the stronger man, but Hinault had been promised the Tour, and in 1986, vice versa. That may be. But Hinault had made a promise: 'In eighty-six, the Tour will be for you. I'll be there to help you.' And the Frenchman was so iconoclastic, gifting the Tour to his teammate was as good a means as any to underline the scale of his superiority. He seized the opportunity with both hands.

The moment the race reached the Pyrenees, Hinault powered out of the peloton. The Spanish climber Pedro Delgado, not yet a contender for the overall classification, took the stage win. Hinault ended the day with a four-and-a-half-minute advantage over his teammate LeMond, and more over the other pretenders to his throne. It's worth quoting the exact advantage – four minutes, thirty-six seconds – because, uncannily, LeMond made up that time to the second the following day. Hinault attacked on the descent from the Tourmalet, and had a further couple of minutes on LeMond

> **'There was no clash. Greg reacted like any young, ambitious rider. The CBS reporters egged him on, and made him believe he'd been deprived of the yellow jersey, when the gaps simply weren't there.'**
> Hinault's damage limitation exercise

at the top of the Aspin, but he was caught and dropped before the final climb to Superbagnères, where LeMond won the stage. Hinault emerged from the Pyrenees in yellow, but the atmosphere in La Vie Claire was tense, despite the efforts of the media-conscious Bernard Tapie to play down the discord.

LeMond took the yellow jersey from his teammate on stage seventeen over the Col du Granon, but these were uneasy times for the American. The second Alpine stage took in three great mountains: the Galibier, the Croix de Fer and Alpe d'Huez. If

'This one's for you' – but behind the smiles, teammates
LeMond and Hinault were bitter rivals.

LeMond feared Hinault's opportunism, his fears were confirmed on the descent from the Galibier. On the Télégraphe, that steep ramp that leads down from the Galibier, Hinault attacked. LeMond allowed the Swiss rider Urs Zimmermann – his closest rival, Hinault apart – to burn energy, leading him back to his teammate. Then, Hinault attacked again, gaining a hundred metres or so, and taking three riders with him. Zimmermann lost LeMond on the descent, where the American started a swashbuckling, 100-kilometre pursuit of Hinault. By St Michel de Maurienne, at the foot of the descent, LeMond had gained a minute on his rival, and joined his teammate. By the start of the Croix de Fer, Zimmermann was two and a half minutes down.

For the next eighty kilometres, Hinault rode with LeMond in his slipstream. Behind them, Zimmermann rode in solitary pursuit. Hinault led his protégé up to Alpe d'Huez, where LeMond gestured him ahead to become the first Frenchman to win on the Alpe.

And that was how America won its first Tour. Bernard Hinault took the credit, with all the tetchiness we'd come to expect of him: 'Thanks to me, Greg has become a very good rider. In future, he'll benefit greatly from the psychological war I've waged against him. From now on he'll be capable of winning the toughest races. I've taught him a lot. He'll be able to defend himself on every terrain, and that, too, he owes to me. I don't regret what I've done. It was all for his own good.' Hinault, with a little Desgrange!

1986   4,093.4 km

	Podium	Nationality	Time	Av speed (kph)
1st	Greg LeMond	USA	110h 35m 19s	37.02
2nd	Bernard Hinault	France	+3m 10s	
3rd	Urs Zimmermann	Switzerland	+10m 54s	
Mountains: Bernard Hinault		France		
Green jersey: E. Vanderaerden		Belgium		

1987-8 In Absentia

Greg LeMond ensured the staggered, and staggering,
run of defaulted title defences continued by standing in
front of his brother-in-law's hunting rifle in April 1987,
and taking a back-full of grapeshot that lodged in his
back, legs, intestine, liver, diaphragm, and heart lining.
His right lung collapsed and he lost three quarters
of his blood supply before a helicopter evacuation to
a hospital specializing in gun shot wounds saved his
life. By the start of the 1987 Tour, in still-divided
Berlin, LeMond was on the road to recovery, but not
yet on the road; Hinault had retired from the road
– he was farming in Brittany – and Laurent Fignon
had forgotten what to do on the road, especially in
the time-trials. The Tour was more open than ever.

Gorby, the Pope, Ronald Reagan, Mrs Thatcher... There are stronger
claimants to responsibility for the fall of the Berlin Wall than the Tour
de France, but the fact remains: there was prescience in the decision
to start the 1987 Tour in West Berlin. For some reason, Colombia's
Lucho Herrera was the most popular rider to photograph against the
backdrop of the wall – leaning, as it happens, by a piece of graffiti
reading 'Fuck the USSR', the Tour's first salvo in the Cold War, in at
the death. Not its last, though, because Lech Piasecki, the Pole who
finished second in the Prologue, took the yellow jersey the following
day, no doubt sending shock waves through the Kremlin.

   The yellow jersey has never graced so many backs in a single
Tour: the 1987 Tour went down in the annals as the one about the
Dutchman, the Pole, three Frenchmen, a Swiss, a Spaniard and an

A globalised, but divided world: Lucho Herrera, a rare representative of the poor world at the Tour, beside the wall that separated Eastern and Western Europe

Irishman. More specifically, it's the one in which the Irishman comes off best, right at the very end.

It was also the last Tour directed by Jacques Goddet. Goddet had first directed the Tour in 1936, more than half a century earlier. He'd taken over permanently after Desgrange's death, from the 1947 Tour onwards – but he was never a conformist. He had a lunatic edge, and dozens of wild ideas about how to develop the Tour. He didn't like Tours crammed full of meaningless sprint stages; 'But they tell me the first ten days are necessary to wear down Lucho Herrera.' But he didn't think the Tour should be a climbing championship either. His ideal was Sean Kelly, the tough Irish buccaneer who could win anywhere but in the high mountains. He favoured stages through the Ardennes, Beaujolais and the Swiss borders, 'landscapes for all-rounders – and why not also a marathon stage?'

Kelly's best effort was fourth in 1985, although a likelier Irish Tour prospect finished one place above Kelly that year: Stephen Roche. The real race hierarchy was established during the incredibly long Saumur-Futuroscope time-trial (eighty-seven kilometres). Ireland's Stephen Roche won it, but France's Charly Mottet took the yellow jersey, and wore it through the Pyrenees. Roche laid the foundations for victory in the 1987 Tour on Mont Ventoux. Herrera was the favourite for the time-trial up its slopes, but he never found his rhythm, and the Frenchman Jean-François Bernard won the stage. Roche lost over two minutes, but finished among the climbers – Delgado, Parra – men he could crucify in the final, flat time-trial. Even so, Bernard took the yellow jersey, and looked likely to wear it all the way to Paris until he punctured the next day, and was dropped by the leading group. Delgado won at Villard-de-Lans the following day, but it was Roche who took the yellow jersey.

> '**All of a sudden, I wanted to actually look at the mountains.**'
>
> Fignon needs a holiday

The duel continued on Alpe d'Huez, where Delgado wrestled back the race lead, and on the next day's epic stage to La Plagne, where Roche attacked into a headwind, far too early in the stage. On the Col de la Madeleine, he was caught, and on the final climb, Delgado launched his counter-attack. Half way up to La Plagne, Delgado's lead had reached a minute and a half. Yet, just four seconds after he crossed the finish line, Channel Four's commentator, Phil Liggett, gasped in surprise: 'And who is that in the background. It looks like Stephen Roche! IT LOOKS LIKE STEPHEN ROCHE!' Roche had to be given oxygen, but he'd saved the Tour, and on stage twenty-four, a twenty-four-mile time-trial around Dijon, Roche sealed victory by forty meagre seconds. 'Before the time-trial, I only knew that is would be the turning point of my career – that I could do something few can achieve.' He didn't win the stage – Jean-François Bernard did that – but Ireland took the Tour home.

1987			4,231.6 km
Podium	**Nationality**	**Time**	**Av speed (kph)**
1st **Stephen Roche**	Ireland	115h 27m 42s	36.65
2nd **Pedro Delgado**	Spain	+40s	
3rd **Jean-François Bernard**	France	+2m 13s	
Mountains: Luis Herrera	**Colombia**		
Green jersey: J.-P. Van Poppel	**Netherlands**		

1988

After the 1987 Tour, Stephen Roche commented: 'It won't change my life. To stay at the top for four or five more years, which is what I want, I'll have to ride, eat and sleep.' But rather than prolonging his reign, Roche missed the 1988 Tour (another title defence forfeited) and Pedro Delgado slipped into the breach. The unassuming Spaniard took the yellow jersey on Alpe d'Huez, and kept it to Paris. But at Bordeaux, with five days to go, rumours started flying.

Jacques Chancel, a French TV journalist, had spoken to Pedro Delgado shortly after the stage:

'Pedro, are you certain you'll get to Paris in yellow? Are you afraid of anything? An accident?'

'No, I'll be in yellow at Paris.'

No joy there. So Chancel closed his transmission with these words: 'Tomorrow, despite the short stage that will take us to Limoges, there will be a storm at the Tour. I have the impression' – he said, looking at the sky – 'something is going to happen.'

An hour later, 'Journal du Tour', the post-stage TV analysis

> **'You know, we all take bottles from the public at the roadside. Why not a "sinister hand"? It's the only explanation.'**
>
> Pedro Delgado's reaction to his positive anti-doping result

Which one's the doper? Gert-Jan Theunisse (left) would be penalised, but not Pedro Delgado.

on Antenne 2, broke the news: 'We have a major story that was only a rumour this morning, and is developing. We have learnt that, in the coming hours and days, there will be a statement making public a positive control against Pedro Delgado, the yellow jersey.'

Jean-Marie Leblanc, in his last year before taking over as its director, rehearsed his future role by pronouncing, very correctly, 'It was a television scoop, although we know that to preserve the dignity of the athlete, the anti-doping rules say that the rider must be informed first, and that he has the right to a second test before the matter can be made public.' But Tour coverage was reaching saturation point, and news like this – the Tour winner, positive! – could hardly be kept under wraps for long.

Delgado, meanwhile, knew nothing: he heard the news from the television, in his hotel room, and by the time he went down for dinner, the hotel was full of journalists. 'You know,' he told them, 'we all take bottles from the public at the roadside. Why not a "sinister hand"? It's the only explanation.'

The official communiqué, when it came, cut both ways. 'Regarding the medical control of Pedro Delgado, the counter-analysis... confirms the result of the first test, i.e., the presence of probenicid. However, this product does not figure on the list of substances prohibited by the UCI [cycling's world governing body]. As a result ... there is no question of sanctioning Pedro Delgado.'

Probenicid, a diuretic, could be used as a masking substance to prevent the detection of anabolic steroids in anti-doping exams. It was on the IOC's (International Olympic Committee's) banned list, but the UCI list hadn't been updated (it would be a month later). Leblanc's boss, Jean-Pierre Courçol, railed, 'I now know that the letter can replace the spirit of the law, and that the regulations can be played with in order to give the appearance of utter innocence. Today, I'm ashamed; tomorrow, perhaps I'll have to tell my children not to go too far in competitive sport.'

Leblanc himself complained: 'The decision that has been taken will please the world of cycling, which has such sensitive skin, and perhaps the wider public, whose memory is short. But look deeper, and it's a dismal verdict. It rewards transgression, it encourages fraud, it lowers sport.'

1988 — 3,288.8 km

	Podium	Nationality	Time	Av speed (kph)
1st	Pedro Delgado	Spain	84h 27m 53s	38.94
2nd	Steven Rooks	Netherlands	+7m 13s	
3rd	Fabio Parra	Colombia	+9m 58s	
Mountains: Steven Rooks		Netherlands		
Green jersey: Eddy Planckaert		Belgium		

1989-90
Against the Odds

In 1989 and again the following year, four former winners started the Tour: Roche, Delgado, Fignon and LeMond. LeMond started a long US tradition by having more to overcome than his immediate rivals: he still had more than thirty shotgun pellets imbedded in his body. Not to be upstaged, Delgado started his title defence by missing his start time for the Prologue and started his title defence with a self-imposed handicap of two minutes, forty seconds – and adding to it the following day, when a catastrophic loss of form left him nearly ten minutes behind the race leader. Meanwhile, Laurent Fignon, the winner of the Giro in June, and second in the prologue, was looking invincible.

LeMond had set himself the challenge of winning back the Tour de France, despite his injuries. The odds were stacked against him. At the 1988 Tour of Italy, his comeback stalled when he was near-paralysed by leg pain. To overcome his physical impairments, he used science. With LeMond, wind tunnel testing, heart rate and power output monitors, protective eye wear and aerodynamic helmets changed the look, and the ethos, of professional cycling for ever. At 8 a.m. on the morning of stage five, the seventy-two kilometre time-trial from Dinard to Rennes, the commissaires ruled to allow LeMond's time trial bike, equipped with triathlon handlebars. Despite the advantage the bars gave him, he beat Delgado by just twenty-four seconds, and Fignon by less than a minute. Still, it gave Greg the yellow jersey.

Cyrille Guimard, working with Fignon, recognised that LeMond was back: 'I saw him finish the Giro.' – second in the final time-trial to Poland's Piasecki – 'I didn't realise he was our main rival only today; I said so before the Tour. I saw how he rode into form during the Giro, and I know Greg by heart.'

Delgado, meanwhile, staged a gutsy fightback, especially in his beloved Pyrenees. On stage nine, between Pau and Cauterets, as his teammate Miguel Induráin won the stage alone, Delgado clawed back twenty-seven seconds on LeMond and Fignon. On stage ten, to Superbagnères, he gained three and a half minutes on the new race leader, Laurent Fignon. On stage fifteen, a time-trial to Orcières, he gained another eight seconds on LeMond and nearly a minute on Fignon. But by then, the yellow jersey was pinging back and forth between the two protagonists, who were pouring their strength into numbing ground strokes from the back of the court.

Fignon held serve by finishing ahead of LeMond, but with the same time, in the Prologue, and forced the American out of position in the team time-trial, which gave him a fifty-one second lead. LeMond made an audacious return by winning back that time, and five seconds more, in the first individual time-trial. Fignon moved to the net after gaining seven seconds and the yellow jersey at Superbagnères, only for LeMond to deliver a strategic lob on stage fifteen – that Orcières time-trial – in which he gained forty seconds on his rival, and gained another thirteen seconds time the following day at Briançon. But Fignon stayed in the game with two flamboyant cross-court forehands: on Alpe d'Huez, he regained the yellow jersey by twenty-six seconds; and at Villard-de-Lans, he moved in for the kill with an unforgettable solo attack.

A kilometre or so from the top of the climb at Saint-Nizier-du-Moucherotte – twenty or so kilometres from the stage finish – Fignon sensed weakness in the group around him. He seized the moment, and rocketed away. Quickly, he led by a hundred metres, as Delgado and LeMond looked at each other. One of them had to

Greg LeMond: the face of a man who's just won the Tour – by eight seconds!

respond: the Spaniard was unwilling; the American unable. Fignon's audacious move gained him just twenty-four seconds on LeMond (a little more on Delgado), but stretched his overall lead to fifty seconds. And so it stayed, for three more stages, until the final day of the Tour, a 24.5 kilometre time-trial from Versailles to the Champs-Élysées.

LeMond talked himself up: 'Fifty seconds to make up in fifteen miles isn't *a priori* an insurmountable handicap. Remember, I left him one minute fifty behind in fifty-five kilometres during the Giro, and I gained fifty-six seconds on him between Dinard and Rennes.' But LeMond recognised his rival's class: 'It would be wrong not to recognise that Fignon was better than me in the mountains. Everyone saw it the afternoon he dropped us all on the Côte de St Nizier; Laurent is so strong, he's capable of anything – including beating me on Sunday in Paris! I saw it right when I told you last Sunday that he wanted this Tour de France more than anyone else... But where there's life, there's hope, isn't there?'

The two men raced towards the Place de la Concorde in breathless heat and dazzling sunlight, LeMond aerodynamically tucked over his tri-bars, Fignon suffering from problems with his undercarriage: 'For two days, I haven't been able to sit down. I have an

> **'Laurent is so strong, he's capable of anything – including beating me on Sunday in Paris!... But where there's life, there's hope, isn't there?'**
> Greg LeMond, before the final time-trial

inflammation of I don't know what.' After ten kilometres, LeMond had made up nineteen seconds of his fifty-second deficit. After thirteen, he'd made up twenty-two. After fourteen kilometres, twenty-four. After 18.5 kilometres, he'd made up thirty-five seconds. Three kilometres from the finish line, Fignon retained five seconds left of his lead. At 4.38.57, LeMond crossed the line. Not wanting to smile, he watched anxiously as the seconds passed. Fignon appeared in the Place de la Concorde – but eight seconds before he crossed the line, LeMond had exploded into joyous laughter.

LeMond had set a new speed record for a Tour de France time trial. But, as he said, 'I didn't give a damn about the split times. I gave it everything I had. That's it.' Fignon was more laconic: 'I should have gained ten more seconds somewhere else. There are a thousand places where I lost this Tour, and a thousand places where Greg won it.'

1989   3,285.3km

	Podium	Nationality	Time	Av speed (kph)
1st	Greg LeMond	USA	87h 38m 35s	37.49
2nd	Laurent Fignon	France	+8s	
3rd	Pedro Delgado	Spain	+3m 34s	

Mountains: Gert-Jan Theunisse Netherlands
Green jersey: Sean Kelly   Ireland

Present and future: Greg LeMond (right) leads Miguel Induráin up to Luz-Ardiden.

1990

On stage one of the 1990 Tour, the entire peloton followed Delgado's 1989 example by turning the race into an almost hopeless handicap. Olaf Ludwig, a twenty-nine-year-old East German who'd never competed against professionals, won the bunch sprint that day, but ten minutes, thirty-five seconds after four riders, three of them potential Walkowiaks, had crossed the line. The only one of the four who would not get to wear the yellow jersey was the stage winner, Holland's Frans Maassen. Steve Bauer, with the best Prologue time of the four, took the overall race lead, and wore the yellow jersey all the way to the Alps. He'd finished fourth in the 1988 Tour, but his bid to better that ended at Saint Gervais on the slopes of Mont Blanc, when Ronan Pensec, seventh in the 1988 Tour, celebrated his twenty-seventh birthday by stripping Bauer of the race lead.

When Pensec finished tenth on Alpe d'Huez the following day, forty-eight seconds behind the stage winner Gianni Bugno, many began to believe he could win the Tour de France, despite the ambitions of his teammate and leader, Greg LeMond. The mountain time-trial at Villard-de-Lans dispersed those illusions: Pensec lost his race lead to the fourth member of the stage one breakaway, Claudio Chiappucci, who'd won the climbers' category in the recent Tour of Italy. He duly showed some panache on the major Pyrenean stage, attacking on the Col d'Aspin, retaining a slight lead at the Tourmalet, but slipping back at Luz-Ardiden, allowing Greg LeMond to creep to within five seconds of the yellow jersey. LeMond could do no better than fifth in the final time-trial, but he was still a couple of minutes faster than Chiappucci, and took his third Tour de France title, without winning a stage.

Going back to the stage between Le Puy-en-Velay and Millau, in the Massif Central, Pedro Delgado paid tribute to his young teammate, Miguel Induráin, who finished second that day. 'Because he stayed with me in the main bunch, I think I deprived Miguel of the stage win. I salute him. He's my right arm, my left arm, and my legs as well. I owe him so much, and he provides me with all the protection I need.' Very soon, their roles would be reversed: Induráin's time was nigh.

1990				3,403.8 km
	Podium	Nationality	Time	Av speed (kph)
1st	Greg LeMond	USA	90h 43m 20s	37.52
2nd	Claudio Chiappucci	Italy	+2m 16s	
3rd	Erik Breukink	Netherlands	+2m 29s	
Mountains: Thierry Claveyrolat		France		
Green jersey: Olaf Ludwig		Germany		

Richard Virenque, thrown off the
1998 Tour. It would take him two
years to confess to EPO doping.

The Modern EPOch

1991-5
Chance the Gardener

The eccentric French playwright Alfred Jarry once wrote: 'The bicycle is a new body part, like a mineral or metal extension of our bone structure.' He could have been talking about Miguel Induráin, bolted onto his futuristic time-trial machine, the 'Spada'. Where mechanism became man was hard to tell. Induráin's great heart, reputed to pulse just twenty-eight times a minute at rest, seemed more like an early industrial miracle than a human organ. Yet Miguelón – Big Mig – was a gentle man whose face, when relaxed, loosened into a mild, herbivorous smile. Surprisingly for a man who annihilated the opposition with predictable élan, he had few enemies. If there were other secrets behind his success, no one's telling.

Miguel Induráin first rose out of the lumpen peloton by winning two Tour de France mountain stages, at Cauterets in 1989 (he finished seventeenth overall) and on Luz Ardiden in 1990, when he made the top ten in GC. He quickly became the principal exponent of the new cycling era ushered in by Greg LeMond, with wind-tunnel testing, aerodynamic time-trial bikes, teardrop helmets, low-friction bodysuits, Uncle Tom Cobley and all, which suddenly gave larger, more powerful physiques the decisive edge. On long, flat time-trial stages, they could gain five minutes or more on any diminutive climber – yet, in the mountains, they could keep the climbers in sight and their losses to a minimum.

On the Tourmalet, LeMond sees the Tour escape him as
Induráin accelerates.

That, in any case, was Induráin's formula – and his first victim was LeMond himself, five hundred metres from the top of the Tourmalet, in stage twelve of the 1991 Tour. Induráin's team car, blazoned with Banesto logos, came alongside, and the Spaniard asked, 'Who's looking bad?' His team director, José Miguel Echávarri, gave him the names of the last two race leaders: '[Luc] Leblanc. LeMond, too, I think...' And Induráin lifted the pace.

LeMond had come to the 1991 race determined to win his fourth Tour. Third in the Prologue, and third in stage one, he wore the yellow jersey on day two, for one night only, but won it back a week later when he finished eight seconds behind Induráin in the first long time-trial. For four days, the American held the race lead. On the fifth – stage eleven, through the Pyrenees to Jaca in Spain – he slipped into second place behind Luc Leblanc, still the best placed of the contenders.

Then came his crisis on the Tourmalet. The leading group crossed seventeen seconds ahead of him; he made up the tiny gap on the descent. But by then, Induráin had slipped away with Claudio Chiappucci, and was blowing the race apart, on the descent. Then, up the climb to Val Louron, the Italian headed for a mountain-top stage win; as so often during the next five years, the Spaniard didn't dispute the sprint. His was the greater prize: the yellow jersey, and pole position overall. LeMond eventually finished ninth in the stage, over seven minutes behind. It was the end of his reign – the next American to wear the yellow jersey would be Lance Armstrong.

'With his body and weight, it's just awesome. I'm not talking just about steep little hills or winding drags, I'm talking about Tour mountains, the Dolomites, the Pyrenees, the toughest paved summits in the world. I had to see it to believe it.'

Eddy Merckx on Induráin

The acceleration on the Tourmalet was pure Induráin. According to his biographer, Javier García Sánchez, 'Miguel not only knew the Tour; he was the Tour. Each heartbeat of the Tour was his, and every startled jump was controlled by him. He was its family doctor, its orthopaedic surgeon and even its neurosurgeon. When an executioner was required (according to the law of competitive sport) he acted quickly and it was soon done.'

It wasn't just LeMond who suffered: Lucho Herrera lost nearly thirteen minutes that day, and Pedro Delgado waved goodbye to his hopes of a repeat win. Five or six switchbacks up the Tourmalet, Delgado recalled, 'I understood that the Tour was over for me. Miguel felt very good, and he said so. So I decided to ride for him.'

Between Alès and Gap, Chiappucci, Bugno and Fignon escaped, and gained a minute. Induráin told Pedro Delgado he was in trouble: the 1988 Tour winner paid back past favours by bridging the gap, with Induráin in tow. A day later, Miguel had recovered, and sealed his first Tour win on Alpe d'Huez. Every time the Italian Gianni Bugno twitched, Induráin moved alongside and looked down at Bugno's front wheel, as if to say: 'There's nothing you can do.' Even so, at the top, he allowed Bugno the stage win.

Predictably, Induráin won the final time-trial. His brilliance against the clock made his name. But to Eddy Merckx, what made him remarkable was his climbing: 'With his body and weight, it's just awesome. I'm not talking just about steep little hills or winding drags, I'm talking about the Tour mountains, the Dolomites, the Pyrenees, the toughest paved summits in the world. I had to see it to believe it.'

1991				3,914 km
	Podium	Nationality	Time	Av speed (kph)
1st	Miguel Induráin	Spain	101h 1m 20s	38.74
2nd	Gianni Bugno	Italy	+3m 36s	
3rd	Claudio Chiappucci	Italy	+5m 56s	
Mountains: Claudio Chiappucci	Italy			
Green jersey: D. Abduzhaparov	Uzbekistan			

1992

Miguel was the master of a mystical form of tedium. With flotation-tank lungs and the sleepy manner of the plankton-feeder, his essential talent was not the jolting acceleration, the sudden, perceptible transition from one state to another, but something altogether harder to discern: sustained, unchanging speed. He defied the invisible resistance of the air, and the pleasure in observing Induráin at work was the blissful contemplation of changelessness. Never was this ability more clearly displayed than during the time-trial. After following stage nine of the 1992 Tour de France in an official car, race director Jean-Marie Leblanc described Induráin as 'Powerful, supple,

**Man and machine in perfect harmony: Miguel Induráin
at the peak of his time-trialling powers.**

magnificent to behold: the aesthetic perfection of the cycling
machine.' Laurent Fignon 'saw a missile fly past'; Charly Gaul thought
it was an angel; he professed to having been pierced by some sort of
light which penetrated his longstanding state of depression and
allowed him step out into the world after years of self-imposed
withdrawal. Miguel won that day by three clear minutes: remarkable!

Five days later, the riders faced a taxing, five-mountain marathon
from Saint-Gervais, looking up at Mont Blanc, across the Italian
border to Sestriere. Claudio Chiappucci unleashed a bizarre attack
on the first climb of the day, and built up a formidable lead. Induráin
waited and waited, panicking Bugno into leading the chase and
burning himself out. Induráin closed to within half a minute of
Chiappucci, who somehow got away again, and finished the stage
one and three-quarter minutes ahead of the Spaniard. Bugno was
another minute back.

On Alpe d'Huez, Induráin's fans' hearts skipped a beat: on the first section of the climb, before the first switchback, Chiappucci opened a twenty-metre gap. It was hard to believe, and probably hardest of all for Chiappucci himself: instead of powering off into the distance, he stared uncomprehendingly over his shoulder. But it was no physical crisis: Induráin's chain had come off. He slipped it back on himself, and sped back up to the Italian. The Tour was his.

As the years have passed, a fog of suspicion has enveloped Chiappucci's attack on the way to Sestriere. Between 1992 and 1995 his name, and that of Gianni Bugno, appears in the computer files of a rogue Italian doctor named Conconi; their blood test results show marked, inexplicable surges in red cells, timed perfectly to coincide with the most important dates in the cycling year. For many, Chiappucci's tireless sprint over the Alps, single-handedly holding off the entire peloton, heralded the advent of a new form of corruption in world sport: EPO abuse. EPO was a copy of a natural hormone which multiplied the red blood cells that carry energy-giving oxygen to the muscles. Coupled with blood transfusions, also illegal, also undetectable, it became synonymous with cycling – although, in all probability, it transformed every other elite professional sport. Cycling seemed to believe, like Nietzsche, that whatever doesn't kill you makes you stronger. And that was even after Dutch riders had started dropping dead, apparently due to the strain of pumping blood thick as toothpaste through their veins. Indeed, during the 1991 Tour, the Dutch team PDM abandoned the Tour en masse. They blamed food poisoning. But their team doctor, Erik Rijckaert, who later moved to Festina, confided to the Festina *soigneur* Willy Voet that PDM was already using EPO. Voet was one of many who believed that their abandon was due to illness caused by EPO treatment.

A year earlier, *L'Équipe*, without the benefit of hindsight, reported that 'Professor Conconi, who treated Moser in the past, has tested Miguel [Induráin] and concluded that 'The physical limits of this rider are unimaginable.' And so they were.

1992				3,983 km
Podium	**Nationality**	**Time**		**Av speed (kph)**
1st Miguel Induráin	Spain	100h 49m 30s		39.50
2nd Claudio Chiappucci	Italy	+4m 35s		
3rd Gianni Bugno	Italy	+10m 49s		
Mountains: Claudio Chiappucci	Italy			
Green jersey: Laurent Jalabert	France			

1993

The 1993 Tour saw the best of time-trials and the worst of time-trials from Big Mig. He'd won the Prologue in 1992; he won it again in 1993, at Le Puy du Fou in France, by eight full seconds from his Swiss rival Alex Zülle. Nine days later – twenty-four hours after Lance Armstrong became the youngest post-war stage winner at Verdun – Induráin pulverised Gianni Bugno in a fifty-eight-mile time-trial around Lake Madine. But Bugno's problem wasn't the two minutes he lost that day, but the eight he lost the next on the first Alpine stage, up the Télégraphe and over the Galibier. Overnight, Induráin's rivals were no longer Italian like Bugno and Chiappucci, but Swiss: Tony Rominger and the improving Alex Zülle.

Rominger won that first stage through the Alps, and won the second one, too, with Miguel in close attendance, third and second respectively, in the same time. But in the Pyrenees, Rominger had Induráin close to submission. The French novelist Christian Laborde wrote that there were just eight bears left in the Vallée d'Aspe. Their grandfathers had seen Octave Lapize and Gustave Garrigou. Perhaps the survivors were hanging on to see Miguel Induráin before they faced extinction. But by the time the Spaniard sped past, Rominger was threatening his natural habitat at the top of cycling's tree. On the final climb of stage sixteen, up to the ski resort of Saint-Lary, Miguel came close to asphyxiation following his Swiss rival, conceding just three seconds at the stage finish. But on the Tourmalet the following day, Rominger darted away, and this time, Induráin couldn't follow. By the brow, Rominger had a minute's advantage. In 1991, Induráin had torn the race apart on the descent of the other side of the mountain. Now, he dropped like a meteorite going to earth, and miraculously appeared on Rominger's wheel.

In his haste, Induráin had forgotten to cover up, and the wind chill factor of a 100 kph descent brought on a fever that he kept very quiet about. He rode the final time-trial with a temperature of 40 °C, losing a second per degree to Rominger that day. In terms of time lost, it was the worst of time-trials; given his illness, it was one of the best, and guaranteed him Tour number three.

We now know that EPO abuse was rife at the 1993 Tour. Richard Virenque won his first King of the Mountains title. Years later, the Festina trial would establish that he and his teammates took up to 2,000 units of EPO per day for the first two weeks of the Tour.

1993 — 3,714 km

	Podium	Nationality	Time	Av speed (kph)
1st	Miguel Induráin	Spain	95h 57m 9s	38.71
2nd	Tony Rominger	Switzerland	+4m 59s	
3rd	Zenon Jaskula	Poland	5m 48s	

Mountains: Tony Rominger — Switzerland
Green jersey: D. Abduzhaparov — Uzbekistan

1994

On stage nine, an individual time-trial from Périgueux to Bergerac, Induráin was breathtaking. His closest rival, the Swiss rider Tony Rominger, conceded two minutes. Two days later, in freezing fog, the young Italian climber Marco Pantani attacked eleven kilometres

Flash, bang, wallop – what a picture! Laurent Jalabert (left) and Fabiano Fontanelli after their collision with a gendarme armed with a camera.

from the stage finish at the ski resort of Hautacam, above Lourdes. Unfortunately for Marco, Rominger was suffering lower down on the climb, so Induráin seized the moment to attack with such impetus that two and a half kilometres from the finish line he rode straight past, taking the Frenchman Luc Leblanc with him. Induráin allowed Leblanc to win the stage; Pantani finished third, sixteen seconds behind Induráin.

Racing resumed after the rest day, when France's Richard Virenque joined a breakaway at the foot of the Tourmalet, fifty kilometres from the finish line at Luz Ardiden. When Virenque's lead reached eight minutes, Pantani drifted out of the yellow-jersey group in pursuit. Three kilometres from the brow of the Tourmalet, he had pulled back two and a half minutes, but Virenque defended his lead on the descent of the Tourmalet and paced himself on the final climb to Luz Ardiden. Four minutes, thirty-four seconds after

Virenque had won the stage, Marco crossed the line in second place. He was now eighth overall.

Three days later, on 18 July, Eros Poli, a giant of a man built for anything except climbing, attacked early and gained an almost absurd lead of twenty-four and a half minutes by the foot of the imposing Mont Ventoux. It was enough to allow him to win the stage by nearly four minutes. On the mountain's lower slopes Pantani developed a gear problem. He stopped to change machines, then collided with a teammate who had waited for him, and fell, taking a blow to his right thigh. Back in the saddle, with eleven kilometres of the climb remaining, he attacked, 'to find out if the fall was serious', as he said after the stage. He quickly gained ninety seconds on the yellow-jersey group, only to be chased down by an alliance of Virenque, Leblanc, Pascal Lino and Induráin. After the stage Pantani complained: 'Induráin is still riding after me, even though I'm twelve minutes down, and he's doing it to give his Festina friends Virenque and Leblanc a hand. They're always talking among themselves and their tactics are the same. Leblanc and Virenque have already won a stage each, with Induráin's blessing, and now they're protecting their places. So it's looking increasingly unlikely that I'll win a stage or get on the podium. But Induráin's making a mistake, because he's made room for everyone except me. Now I'm going to do everything I can to blow his plans out of the water.'

> '**The '94 Tour came down to experience. I arrived there, knowing it like the back of my hand – the rhythm of the event, the Press conferences, the race organisation, the other riders, everything. It was like being in the garden at home.**'
> Miguel Induráin

On Hautacam and on Mont Ventoux he had accelerated eleven kilometres from the apex of the climb. He did so again on stage sixteen from Valréas to Alpe d'Huez. His fellow Romagnolo Roberto Conti had joined a large breakaway, attacked with sixteen hairpins to go, and crossed the finish line nearly six minutes before Marco. But Marco, who reached the foot of the climb with the yellow-jersey group, attacked with such venom that he set a record time of thirty-seven minutes, fifteen seconds for the ascent, two minutes, seventeen seconds quicker than the stage winner.

The stage of the 1994 Tour that lingers in the memory is stage seventeen, from Bourg-d'Oisans to Val Thorens. On the Col du Glandon, the first climb of the stage, as the TV cameras watched the leading group, Pantani was involved in another fall. Twenty-two kilometres into the stage, riding at high speed, he touched the rear wheel of Alberto Elli. Both men fell, hitting a wall at the roadside. Elli abandoned immediately; Marco stayed down, losing two minutes as the race doctor, Dr Gérard Porte, examined the wound and ruled out a fracture. The television footage shows Marco wiping his face, looking at his elbow. He had agreed with Roberto Conti to attack on the Col de la Madeleine, but the fall had destroyed their plan. Frustrated, angry, perhaps ready to walk away, Marco watched his knee swell, even as, with three teammates at hand, he began the chase. It lasted twenty-three kilometres. At the forty-five kilometre mark, Marco and his helpers finally re-joined the main peloton on the descent from the Col de Glandon.

Weeping with pain, Pantani dropped back to his team car three times for permission to abandon. It didn't come, so on the Col de la Madeleine he attacked, partly, as on Mont Ventoux, to test the wounded knee. The move thinned out the group. Far ahead, Ugrumov and the Colombian Cacaíto Rodríguez were already on the thirty-nine-kilometre Val Thorens climb. The pace of the yellow-jersey group was so high, no attack seemed possible. Yet five and a half kilometres from the finish line Pantani, still in pain, attacked, sprinting from the back of the group. For thirteen seconds, Luc Leblanc gave chase, before Marco's speed made him think again. At the finish line,

Cacaíto dropped Ugrumov to win the stage. Marco finished sixty-eight seconds later, third in the stage but one and a half minutes ahead of Induráin, Virenque and Leblanc. He had leapfrogged into third place overall. But he spent the night in pain and the following day, from Moutiers to Cluses, he couldn't push a big gear. Piotr Ugrumov won the stage, with Induráin and Virenque second and third. Marco was fifth, three and a half minutes down. In the general classification he dropped into fourth place, two seconds behind Ugrumov.

The penultimate stage was a mountain time-trial from Cluses to Morzine-Avoriaz. Ugrumov led at every split. Marco lost a minute and thirty-eight seconds to Ugrumov, but gained the same on Induráin. Virenque performed dreadfully and slipped from second place overall to fourth. Pantani, in his first Tour, had finished third. He stood on the podium in Paris, perched precariously with Induráin and Ugrumov, his sponsor's cap too big for him.

EPO-fuelled Richard Virenque (left) and Luc Leblanc (centre) bite Induráin's ankles on the climb up to Lourdes-Hautacam.

However, all this drama had taken place in Induráin's wake. It had been his easiest Tour, as he later said, 'The '94 Tour came down to experience. I arrived there, knowing it like the back of my hand – the rhythm of the event, the Press conferences, the organisation, the other riders, everything. It was like being in the garden at home.'

Marco Pantani's swashbuckling performance at the 1994 Tour can today be explained by blood values discovered by Italian police investigators who raided Professor Conconi's laboratory in late 1999. On 27 June 1994, just before the Tour, Pantani's red blood-cell count (6,140,000), haemoglobin (18.2 g/dl) and haematocrit (57.2 per cent) were fantastically high. Just after the Tour, another blood test showed almost unchanged values. His Tour de France performance had been EPO assisted in its entirety. In addition, the 25 July data for Marco include, for the only time in the period documented in 'dblab.wdb', a value for testosterone: 8.5, raising the suspicion of hormonal manipulation in addition to EPO therapy.

Big Mig's surprise attack on the way to Liège.

1994				3,978 km
	Podium	Nationality	Time	Av speed (kph)
1st	Miguel Induráin	Spain	103h 38m 38s	38.38
2nd	Piotr Ugrumov	Latvia	+5m 39s	
3rd	Marco Pantani	Italy	+7m 19s	
Mountains Richard Virenque		France		
Green jersey: D. Abduzhaparov		Uzbekistan		

1995

The afternoon before the first long time-trial, when Induráin was expected to wipe the floor with his rivals, the unthinkable happened. On the Côte du Rosier in the Ardennes, he sprung a trap: after a coded signal, his teammates raised the pace. As the gradient steepened, he shifted into a bigger gear, and exploded out of the group. Further on, he caught the Belgian rider Johan Bruyneel, who was sucked into the great man's slipstream as he powered past. Afterwards, Bruyneel raved, 'I felt like I was riding behind a motorbike for twenty-four kilometres, at over fifty kph.' Induráin dealt his rivals a stunning blow: Even before the time-trial had began, he led them by fifty seconds – and then won the time-trial, to boot.

Denmark's Bjarne Riis led at every split, but Miguel accelerated in the final section and had taken a dozen seconds off Riis by the finish line. Two weeks later, in the time-trial

'In the countryside there is a philosophy, a whole way of thinking. You sow and you harvest, and you're always dependent on whatever good or bad weather might come. This is the kind of philosophy I also find useful in cycling.'

Miguel Induráin as
Chance the Gardener

'I felt like I was riding behind a motorbike for twenty-four kilometres, at over fifty kph.'
Johan Bruyneel tucks in beind Big Mig

around Lac de Vassivière on stage nineteen, Induráin gained another forty-eight seconds on the Dane, making a total of a minute in the time-trials. The other six minutes he made on Riis came in just six kilometres of hard climbing at La Plagne on stage nine. Marco Pantani won the following day on Alpe d'Huez, setting a new record for the climb of thirty-six minutes, fifty seconds – a record that still stands – but Induráin was second, with only Riis and Zülle able to follow him.

Miguel's biggest panic came on Bastille Day. Three riders from the team sponsored by Spain's national institution for the blind – ONCE – had the foresight to slip into a breakaway. Australia's Neil Stephens, and Induráin's ex-teammate Melchor Mauri gave their leader Laurent Jalabert a free ride for much of the afternoon. Then, at the foot of the steep final climb into the town of Mendes, Jalabert darted away. The French crowd was shouting 'Nouveau leader, nouveau leader!' as he accelerated towards the finish. Behind him, everyone seemed to be going to pieces: everyone, but Miguel Induráin. At the foot of the climb, Riis started the action, Pantani pressed the detonator, and Miguel pushed past both of them. Jalabert needed to gain over nine minutes: only five and a half had passed when Riis, Pantani and Miguel reached the line. The crisis was over.

Two days later, Pantani celebrated Induráin's birthday by tearing into the cloud forty-two kilometres from the finish line at Guzet Neige. When asked for the secret of his climbing speed, Pantani said he was simply trying 'to shorten the suffering'. But Marco's insane inspiration still belonged to the future. For the time being, Miguel made the Tour a province of his rural idyll. After his fifth Tour de France win, Miguel reflected: 'In the countryside there is a philosophy, a whole way of thinking. You sow and you harvest, and you're always dependent on whatever good or bad weather might come. This is the kind of philosophy I also find useful in cycling.' It could have been Chance the Gardener speaking, the Peter Sellers character in the film 'Being There' who is mistaken for someone with deep knowledge of the world, and stumbles into a world of political intrigue. Miguel continued: 'You've given people and the fans a great spectacle, you've ridden a good stage, you've performed brilliantly, but in the evening when you're on your own, or in the morning, when you get up and think about it and say to yourself: What have you really achieved? You've climbed a mountain and then you've descended. First you climbed, and then you descended. That's all.... You've got a bouquet of flowers, but you haven't actually achieved anything concrete. You haven't, for instance, made anything with your own hands, like a piece of furniture.'

Five years later, the Festina trial considered an intriguing statement made by Induráin's domestique, Thomas Davy. During his years riding for Banesto, he said, 'I took EPO – I think. The doctor, Sabino Padilla, came into the riders' rooms after the stage. The syringes were prepared in advance... We asked what was in the syringes, but he never replied... No one ever found out. These injections were systematic during major races, especially the Tour de France. We imagined it must have been something stronger than recovery products... We generally rode better after those injections.' Davy was convinced EPO had been taken by all the team's riders.

1995				3,398.3 km
	Podium	Nationality	Time	Av speed (kph)
1st	Miguel Induráin	Spain	92h 44m 59s	36.64
2nd	Alex Zülle	Switzerland	+4m 35s	
3rd	Bjarne Riis	Denmark	+6m 47s	
Mountains: Richard Virenque	France			
Green jersey: Laurent Jalabert	France			

1996 Mr Sixty Per Cent

When, in 1993, Bjarne Riis won an Alpine stage in the Tour de France, a Danish newspaper dubbed him 'the Eagle of Herning'. It was a deliberately naff nickname, emphasising limitations, not prowess, in the mountains: Herning, Riis's hometown, stands on the flattest part of a flat country. But Riis, who was a thick-skinned sod, adopted the insult as a nickname. Effortlessness wasn't an illusion he perpetrated: after time-trials, he would cling to the railings, eyes bulging, gasping for breath. The day before the 1996 Tour, he told teammates he believed he could win it. His conviction was met by smirks.

Induráin's team, Banesto, had lost its doctor, Sabino Padilla, before the 1996 Tour. During his preparation, Miguel paid Padilla from his own pocket, and took him on training recces into France. Whether that was the decisive factor, we can't say: according to Induráin's team director José Miguel Echávarri, Induráin came into the 1996 Tour de France facing an enemy made more dangerous because, as it didn't have a number on its back: rain. Induráin's biographer, Javier García Sánchez, saw a lack of desire in a photo of the favourites in the pouring rain, early in the 1996 Tour. Miguel's rivals had a driven, hungry look betraying total focus on their exertions. 'Induráin's face, on the other hand, was contracted into a grin which could well have meant: "What the hell am I doing here?" [It] seemed to belong to someone who had been forced, against his will, to go on one of those pointless, stomach-wrenching fairground roundabouts.'

His bid to win six Tours came undone in the last four kilometres of the climb up to Les Arcs, one Miguel could normally have devoured with ease. Instead, something was wrong. Rominger saw it, and asked his teammate Olano to accelerate. For Riis, Jan Ullrich did the same. With that, Induráin dropped silently away from the leading group. Alex Zülle, led by Aitro Garmendia, another of Induráin's ex-teammates, came past, and Miguel tried to get on his wheel. After a few metres, he surrendered. The following day, *L'Équipe*'s headline recalled the words spoken to Louis XVI when the uprisings began: '*Sire, c'est une Révolution.*'

García Sánchez believed Miguel never really sought a sixth victory. No one – neither Anquetil, nor Merckx, nor Hinault – had won more than five, and to do so required a sort of iconoclasm, or sacrilege against cycling history. Neither was part of Induráin's temperament. When Induráin finally cracked, Riis claimed victory with a series of performances that riders with superior physical gifts couldn't match: a short sprint to Sestriere on a stage curtailed by snow; to Hautacam, after Induráin's fight-back had been sabotaged by a puncture; and the following day into Pamplona, on a stage designed to celebrate Induráin, but which became his wake.

> '**Induráin's face, on the other hand, was contracted into a grin which could well have meant: "What the hell am I doing here?" [It] seemed to belong to someone who had been forced, against his will, to go on one of those pointless, stomach-wrenching fairground roundabouts.**'
>
> Javier García Sánchez, Induráin's biographer

Riis's weren't the finest cycling genes around. Fignon, his leader for three years at the team sponsored by Super U, later Castorama, had those. In 1989, when the bespectacled Parisian lost to LeMond

The emaciated Bjarne Riis (in yellow) ends the Induráin era.

by just eight seconds, Riis was riding his first Tour; he finished ninety-fifth and he could have regarded Fignon's and LeMond's gifts only with envy. But his years as Fignon's domestique made him one of the most knowledgeable tacticians in cycling. Riis had transformed himself into a Tour winner by dint of near-pathological dedication, and a great deal of medical help.

Elite cyclists shouldn't be eating biscuits and drinking sweet tea, but that didn't stop many of them becoming blood donors. Years later, police officers in Italy seized files containing Riis's blood test results for 1994 and 1995. His red blood cell count leapt from a base level of 41.0 per cent to a staggering 56.3 per cent. Debilitating illness could have explained the increase, but Riis was one of the fittest men alive. The alternative explanations were blood transfusions, and/or treatment with the blood booster EPO. And we know from Festina *soigneur* Willy Voet that insanely irresponsible blood doping had unpleasant side effects. Voet tells a story of a Festina rider who collapsed during the night in 1996, with a red blood cell count of 66.0 per cent. Blood, in other words, as thick as strawberry jam!

If this was the state of cycling, no wonder Riis was tight-lipped. Gary Imlach, who covered the race for Channel Four, recalls: 'During that race I must have interviewed Riis after a dozen stages and got only a marginally greater number of words out of him. It became a cross between a game and a punishment – if I'd had a row with the producer he'd get even by sending me down to the finish line to interview Bjarne. He'd be taking bets on whether I'd manage to get beyond "Yes" or "No". Coming back with a full sentence on tape was a victory for me.'

The Danish prime minister described the feat as the greatest in Denmark's sporting history – perhaps not realising the practices rife in professional cycling. But it could have been worse: Riis could have taken the train.

1996 — 3764.9 km

	Podium	Nationality	Time	Av speed (kph)
1st	Bjarne Riis	Denmark	95h 57m 16s	39.24
2nd	Jan Ullrich	Germany	+1m 41s	
3rd	Richard Virenque	France	+4m 37s	
Mountains: Richard Virenque		France		
Green jersey: Erik Zabel		Germany		

1997 Wunderkind

Jan Ullrich, Riis's runner-up in 1996, aged just twenty-two, was a second Induráin: extraordinarily powerful in the time-trials, and lightning fast, even without a decisive change of pace, in the mountains. However, Induráin had been a gentle man whose face, when relaxed, loosened into a mild, herbivorous smile. He had matured slowly and, even at his greatest, it was clear that the years would erode him. Ullrich was a product of the East German sports system; he was steely, muscular, and had ten, perhaps fifteen years ahead of him.

Riis suffered a bacterial infection and, in the privacy of a tunnel on the way up to Arcalis (Andorra), he gave his German teammate Jan Ullrich permission to attack. As Ullrich tells it in his autobiography, he asked Riis, at the foot of the climb: 'What do we do now?'

'If we want to win, we have to attack now.'

'OK. How? Shall I set the pace, and then you attack?'

'No. When you can, go.'

Ullrich made a dramatic exit from the darkness, alone now, and rode away. 'The Pyrenean roads are surfaced with large-grained, rough tar. Your wheels don't go round like they should, and the going is very tough. It felt like one of those nightmares we all know: you're trying to escape from something, but you can't get away.' Warming to his theme, he added, 'My legs were as soft as a pudding.' Still, Pantani could only finish second, one minute eight seconds behind his unstoppable rival. On one climb, the succession to Induráin seemed to have been decided.

Pumped up on Arcalis: Jan Ullrich displays the musculature of the 1990s.

Then, on 18 July Ullrich won again, a fifty-five-kilometre individual time-trial starting and ending at Saint-Étienne. His margin of victory was remarkable: three minutes, five seconds. Not even Induráin himself had achieved such crushing superiority in a Tour de France time-trial.

The following day, the riders faced a 203-kilometre stage from Saint-Étienne to Alpe d'Huez. As Pantani's domestiques dropped away, Ullrich took over in person, forcing the pace on the first hairpins of the climb. Pantani followed for five kilometres, then attacked. Ullrich, Virenque and Riis gave chase. With sixteen of the twenty-one hairpins still to ride, Riis surrendered. With twelve to go, Virenque dropped back. Soon afterwards Ullrich too dropped away from Marco's wheel. Seven kilometres from the summit Pantani led Ullrich by twenty-two seconds. On the finish line, he clenched his fists and shouted in joy. Marco's time for the climb, thirty-six minutes fifty-five seconds, was only five seconds off his 1995 record – little short of astonishing at the end of such a long stage. Ullrich crossed the line second, forty-seven seconds later.

The following day, from Le Bourg d'Oisans at the foot of Alpe d'Huez to the Courchevel ski station, Ullrich took his revenge. Richard Virenque, second overall but facing a deficit of more than six minutes, attacked early on the stage. Ullrich, relayed by Riis, closed in on him, and the two men rode together to Courchevel. To Virenque, the stage; to Ullrich, even greater security for his overall lead.

But the next day Pantani attacked on the Col de Joux Plane, dived into the abyss on the other side and finished alone at Morzine after a daring descent. Ullrich and Virenque finished together, one minute, seventeen seconds later. But there was no changing the general classification now, and on 27 July Ullrich rode into Paris, the winner of the Tour, aged twenty-three.

Years later, Ullrich's name came up when an ex-rider named Erwann Mentheour was interviewed by French police. During the

Reach out and touch faith: Pantani nails Alpe d'Huez again

amateur Tour de France in 1997, Mentheour's *soigneur*, Jeff D'Hont, gave him a product, which 'brought a marked improvement in his performances' (the quotation is from the judgment of the Festina trial). D'Hont worked with Deutsche Telekom during the 1996 Tour, so Mentheour asked him 'if he'd given this product to Jan Ullrich of the team Telekom in 1996?' D'Hont's reply was affirmative.

1997			3,943.8 km
Podium	**Nationality**	**Time**	**Av speed (kph)**
1st **Jan Ullrich**	Germany	100h 30m 35s	39.24
2nd **Richard Virenque**	France	+9m 9s	
3rd **Marco Pantani**	Italy	+14m 3s	
Mountains: Richard Virenque	France		
Green jersey: Erik Zabel	Germany		

1998 Piracy

After his 1997 victory, many Germans believed he would develop into the greatest athlete of all time in any sport, according to a survey by *Der Spiegel*. However, when Ullrich wasn't pounding on the pedals, he was piling on the pounds, and his attempts to reach race fitness in the spring had descended into a vicious circle of self-starvation, illness and more weight gain.

In November and December 1997 he had suffered a heavy cold, followed by a painful inflammation of the auditory canal. In January, a high temperature had interrupted his Tour of Mallorca. He had abandoned the Tirreno-Adriatico in March after stage one due to an allergy, and the Tour of the Basque Country after three stages with bronchitis. By any standards, here was a man in need of medication. As luck would have it, medication was on its way to the Tour start in Dublin in massive supplies – until, at 6 a.m. on Wednesday 8 July 1998, three days before the start of the 1998 Tour, French customs officers stopped a Fiat Marea emblazoned with the logos of Festina, the world number one team with three Tour contenders in Richard Virenque (second in 1997), Alex Zülle and Laurent Dufaux.

As well as a driver without a driving licence – Festina *soigneur* Willy Voet had been without one since a speeding offence in January 1998 – the car was stuffed with doping products. Now, when Fausto Coppi was asked if he had taken drugs, he replied, 'Only when necessary.' When asked how often that was, he said, 'Nearly always.' According to Jacques Anquetil, 'Only an imbecile would imagine that a professional cyclist who rides 235 days a year can hold himself together without stimulants.' But even they might have been shocked by what cycling had become.

Marco Pantani was prepared to sacrifice possible Tour victory to protest against the anti-doping raids

Eighty-two vials of Saizen (somatropin, or human growth hormone), sixty capsules of Pantestone (epitestosterone), 248 vials of physiological serum, eight pre-filled syringes containing hepatitis-A vaccine, two boxes of thirty Hyperlipen tablets (to lower the amount of fat in the blood), four further doses of somatropin, four ampoules of Synacthene (to increase the rate at which corticoid hormones are secreted by the adrenal gland) and two vials of amphetamine. There were also 234 doses of recombinant human erythropoietin, made up of ten pre-filled syringes of Eprex 4000, 139 vials of NeoRecormon powder and eighty-five vials of Erantin 2000 powder. In short, potions and pills to strengthen the body and anaesthetise the conscience.

Willy Voet's mobile pharmacy had been due at Calais to sail for Dublin on the 11.45 a.m. ferry. Instead, Voet spent the day at Neuville with specialist interrogators and the night in a police cell in Lille.

At 8.30 p.m. on 17 July, a statement issued by the lawyer of Festina team director Bruno Roussel changed cycling for ever: 'Bruno Roussel has explained to investigators, who were in possession of the facts, the conditions under which the supply of doping products to the riders was managed collectively between the Festina team directors, doctors, *soigneurs* and riders. The purpose was to optimise performance under strict medical control, in order to avoid the individual and untrained provision of the riders in conditions likely to endanger their health, as might have been the case in the past.'

The lawyer then telephoned the team, to inform them of Roussel's confession and allow them to avoid the shame of disqualification by withdrawing voluntarily. Richard Virenque, the team leader and one of France's most cherished sportsmen, refused point-blank. Jean-Marie Leblanc, the Tour de France race director, issued a statement announcing the race organisers' decision to exclude Festina from the race. The following morning Virenque telephoned Leblanc to inform him that the riders didn't accept their exclusion and would start the individual time-trial. Leblanc arranged to meet them in the Chez Gillou café at Corrèze railway station. The meeting lasted an hour. Richard Virenque brazenly denied any involvement, making a mantra of George Burns' old joke: 'Sincerity is everything. If you can fake that, you've got it made.' But he emerged from the meeting in tears, and left the Tour there and then.

> **'They dope to ride 3,500km in 20 days, just as they do to run 100m in nine seconds.'**
> Jacques Goddet, *L'Équipe*

It was a turning point. When news of Voet's arrest first reached the Tour de France, the riders were generally unconcerned. As a rule, they thought of anti-doping investigations the way General Sedgwick thought of the Confederates in the American Civil War: 'They couldn't hit an elephant from that dist—.' Finally, as Philippe Gaumont recalled, 'We realised it was serious.'

That day, Ullrich rode the first long time-trial of the Tour, fifty-eight kilometres from Meyrignac to Corrèze in a bodysuit with pink arms and shoulders, white back, with the three branded stripes across the shoulders like an enormous beetle. He scuttled voraciously into the race lead.

After the time-trial, Marco Pantani appealed: 'The police and the judges will deal with the Festina affair. I hope the journalists will talk about the race.' He wasn't to know a second scandal had broken. On 4 March customs officers near Reims searching a TVM team vehicle driven by two mechanics had stumbled on a cache similar to that found in Voet's car. The products, including 104 pre-filled syringes of EPO, had been seized, the mechanics released and no further action taken. The revelations of the Festina affair had led magistrates to reopen the TVM file, eroding the reputation of the Tour – and cycling – still further.

'Everyone longs for freedom. I'm a non-conformist, and some are inspired by the way I express my freedom. I've never been meticulous or calculating, either on or off the bike. There's chaos in everyday life, and my riding is instinctive. I respond to the moment. But not everyone sees things that way.'
Marco Pantani

As the Tour approached the Pyrenees, Pantani announced: 'Everyone is asking me to save the Tour, to do something. They've finally realised that without Festina the race risks becoming less spectacular. A race with Ullrich in the yellow jersey all the way to Paris would be boring, but try telling the organisers, who repeatedly favour the rouleurs and forget the mountains. I don't ask much – just more balance.' But is was hard to keep attention on the racing, with Jacques Goddet telling his readers from the pages of *L'Équipe*, 'They dope to ride 3,500 kilometres in twenty days, just as they do to run 100 metres in nine seconds.'

The first Pyrenean stage went to Rodolfo Massi – a man later found in possession of huge quantities of doping products in a travelling salesman-style suitcase. Pantani later commented, 'If I'd won it, I'd have gone home. I'd have won my stage and I'd have returned home.' The following day, he took his stage win on Plateau de Beille: but now, one wasn't enough. He told the press, 'My main goal in entering the Tour was to win this stage because it was the most beautiful climb in the race. Now I hope to win the other stage finishing at altitude, next week in Les Deux Alpes. As for overall victory, I think I lost too much energy in winning the Giro.'

Fausto Coppi, asked if he had taken drugs:

'Only when necessary.'

When asked how often that was:

'Nearly always.'

The Pyrenees had restored part, at least, of Marco's lost time. Even so, on the morning of stage fifteen – the final uphill finish of the Tour, from the town of Grenoble to the ski station of Les Deux Alpes – Marco needed three more minutes on Ullrich just to draw level. And there was still the second long time-trial to come. He'd conceded four minutes twenty-one seconds to Ullrich in the first; he could expect to do the same again. In short, to have any chance of overall victory, Marco had one stage on which to gain seven and a half minutes on the reigning Tour de France champion. Seven and a half minutes! An insane margin: unthinkable in modern cycling. Pantani naturally accepted the challenge.

The stage to Les Deux Alpes was ridden at breakneck speed. five kilometres from the brow of the Galibier, with thirty kilometres left to ride, Pantani grimaced and flashed away from the group of contenders. Ullrich made no attempt to respond.

In the finishing straight, Pantani clenched his eyes in pain, grimaced – and spread his arms into a crucifix. Five kilometres down the mountainside, Ullrich was climbing listlessly, disconnected from the commotion of riders swarming upwards.

Over the following eight minutes, fifty-seven seconds, twenty-two filthy, sodden riders crossed the line. Ullrich was not among them. Then he appeared, shepherded home by his teammates Bölts and Riis. In his autobiography, *Ganz oder Gar Nichts – All or Nothing –* Ullrich admitted that only the extra week before the Tour had allowed him to get his weight down to seventy-one kilos – less, in fact, than in 1997, but still not the sixty-seven or sixty-eight he was aiming for. Ullrich had started the Tour starving himself in order to lose those extra three or four kilos. His collapse on the Galibier was due to the pressure of Marco's attack, but it was also the logical outcome of too-rapid weight loss.

On the morning of the final time-trial, Pantani led Ullrich by six minutes: he surrendered two and a half of them to the German, but his margin of victory was still substantial. In Paris, Jean-Marie Leblanc, the Tour director, formally thanked the man they called the Pirate for saving the Tour. Within a year and a half, Italian police had proof of EPO abuse and probable blood transfusions during much of Pantani's career. Oh, and as for Virenque, he maintained his laughable denial of doping charges, in the face of overwhelming evidence, until October 2000, when the judge in the Festina trial at last forced him into a corner. By then, his confession had a Groucho Marx quality: 'These are my principles. If you don't like them, I have others.'

1998 — 3,711.6 km

	Podium	Nationality	Time	Av speed (kph)
1st	Marco Pantani	Italy	92h 49m 46s	39.98
2nd	Jan Ullrich	Germany	+3m 21s	
3rd	Bobby Julich	USA	+4m 8s	
Mountains: Christophe Rinero		France		
Green jersey: Erik Zabel		Germany		

The Winning Habit

Total commitment from
Lance Armstrong (right), as
he drops Virenque, Jiménez
and Escartín on the way
to Hautacam in 2000.

1999
Anything's Possible

'Nothing goes to waste,' said Lance Armstrong. 'You put it all to use, the old wounds and long-ago slights become the stuff of competitive energy.' Maybe that was why he seemed to regard a day without an argument, a day wasted. But the uncompromising brashness was part of the winning package: Armstrong exploded into cycling history in 1993. In July of that year, he became the youngest Tour de France stage winner since the war. In August the same year, he was crowned the youngest ever world champion. Not yet twenty-two, his ability was clear. He lived life in such a hurry, they used to call him 'FedEx': 'When you just gotta have it overnight.'

But Armstrong seemed to enjoy making enemies. He hinted as much in an interview that winter, at his Texas home. 'I wanna say what's on my mind and people may not like it. Some people may really like it, but I think it's gonna be fifty-fifty. People are gonna love it or they're gonna hate it. The bottom line is, I'm a competitor and I like training hard and going out and kicking ass. I like it, and I got a lot more ass to kick. I'm looking forward to going back to Europe and doing the big races and winning.'

Pretty soon, the irresistible force of Armstrong's kick-ass mentality met the immovable object of life-threatening illness. In 1996, physically drained, he abandoned the Tour. In October that year, the problem was explained when he was diagnosed with a rare,

Armstrong attends the 1997 Tour, still convalescing after chemotherapy. Little do they know what he's got in store for them!

aggressive form of testicular cancer. It had already spread to his brain and lungs. Armstrong dubbed the disease 'the Bastard,' and approached it as one more challenge. But he had the help of Dr Craig Nichols, an oncologist and researcher who was part of the team that treated Armstrong, who recalled: 'We had just done the clinical trial on the drug that would fight the cancer, but spare him permanent lung damage.' Armstrong was in the right place at the right time to get treatment that would save his life and his career.

It was Armstrong's second brush with death. After a fall killed his teammate Fabio Casartelli during the 1995 Tour, Armstrong took an emotional stage win. He crossed the finish line with his eyes, and his fingers, raised to the sky. Afterwards, he admitted a little supernatural performance enhancement: 'There was no doubt in my mind that there were two riders on that bike. Fabio was with me.'

After his teammate's death, it was Armstrong's turn to stare

'There was a second supremely sweet moment of victory. As I made my way through the finish area, I passed the Cofidis team. Assorted members of the organization stood around, the men who I felt had left me for dead in a hospital room. "That was for you," I said as I moved past them.'

Lance Armstrong after winning the opening time-trial
and becoming the leader of the 1999 Tour de France

mortality in the eye. 'I didn't think too much about cycling in 1996,' he said. 'If you told me I was gonna come back I'd have said you were crazy. If you said I was gonna come back and ride the Tour I'd have said you were really crazy, and if you said I would wear the *Maillot Jaune* into Paris I'd have said you were absolutely crazy... so it's... heh, anything's possible... anything is possible.'

In 1997 he launched his cancer charity and the fund-raising Ride for the Roses – and visited the Tour as a civilian. Then, he relaunched his career with one thing in mind: victory in the Tour de France. He more or less ignored the rest of the cycling calendar, or treated it as so many training rides in the build up to the Tour. The French press excoriated him, although all he was doing was following the recipe laid down by Henri Desgrange in 1928: 'I hope I have demonstrated that the only formula that can ever ensure victory in the Tour de France consists of presenting men who are admirably prepared, who adore their work... and teams... not worn down by earlier struggles. I repeat: the Tour de France demands riders to dedicate themselves to it alone.'

Turning illness into inspiration, he won the Prologue, over the course used in 1993. Then, Induráin had taken eight minutes twelve seconds to ride to the win; now, Armstrong won in eight minutes two seconds. A week later, Armstrong won the second time-trial of the Tour, starting and finishing in Metz. The question was, what could the man who was unbeatable against the clock do in the mountains? A day later, he gave his answer, knocking them dead on the first mountain stage. Second on both days was the bespectacled Swiss, Alex Zülle. The Mr Magoo of the peloton, Zülle never knowingly passed up an opportunity to fall off his bicycle... true to form, he'd taken a tumble on stage two while crossing the Passage du Gois, a causeway that disappears into the Atlantic at high tide, and was still treacherously slimy when the riders negotiated it. Zülle lost over six minutes that day.

Having demoralised the opposition, Armstrong sat on his lead until the final time-trial, when he allowed Zülle to come within ten seconds of his winning time. After the upsets of the year before, the Comeback Kid added a fairytale touch to his recovery. It made him one of the most bankable stars in global sport, and he spoke of his achievement in the language of an advertising executive: 'It was major for cycling, but also for cancer, the combination of the two made a story. If I'd just won the Tour de France and didn't have cancer, the story wouldn't have been told as much.'

There was a whiff of scandal when corticoids – a banned steroid – were found in minute quantities in Armstrong's urine. A medical prescription was produced for a corticoid cream to treat a saddle sore, and the case was shelved. But for those whom the Armstrong story was an impossible fairytale took careful note: the test would come back to haunt him.

1999   3,882.3 km

	Podium	Nationality	Time	Av speed (kph)
1st	Lance Armstrong	USA	91h 32m 16s	42.41
2nd	Alex Zulle	Switzerland	+7m 37s	
3rd	Fernando Escartin	Spain	+10m 26s	
Mountains: Richard Virenque		France		
Green jersey: Erik Zabel		Germany		

2000
'I Don't Speak French'

In 2000, the Armstrong legend was on everyone's lips.
A best-selling, award-winning, if ghost-written, book
had brought him the veneration of millions. But he had
his critics. Some believed you couldn't win the Tour
and not be on something illegal. Others rubbished his
1999 Tour win because the two previous Tour winners,
Jan Ullrich and Marco Pantani, had both been absent.
And the French protested that a Tour de France winner
should speak more French. Armstrong was angrier than
ever – and an angry Armstrong was a dangerous one.

Ullrich had damaged a knee in the months before the 1999 Tour,
and stayed away. Pantani had imploded after a test during the Tour
of Italy raised suspicions of blood doping. Armstrong had never
ridden a Tour time-trial against Ullrich, or climbed against Pantani.
Few believed he had much chance against them.

The Prologue wasn't a prologue, but a proper, sixteen-kilometre
time-trial. Armstrong gained twelve seconds on Ullrich, and added
another forty seconds in the team time trial a few days later, but
there was still room for doubt. Then, they reached the mountains.

On Hautacam, in the rain, Armstrong bided his time, allowing
the likes of Zülle, Virenque, and José María Jiménez to build up a
small lead, behind a Basque rider, Javier Otxoa, who'd started the
climb ten minutes before them. Then, Pantani made his move.
Armstrong followed – dropping Ullrich like a stone – then made a
jolting acceleration, which Pantani couldn't match. The Texan rode

past the cream of world climbing, and gained nine and a half minutes on Otxoa, who deservedly won the stage. The big loser was Pantani: on the first climb of the Tour, the man who used to be the best climber lost nearly six minutes.

Hostilities resumed on Mont Ventoux, two days later. Not on the climb: Armstrong bridged the gap to Pantani, who'd attacked earlier on, and then, on the way past, turned to Pantani and spoke. They reach the summit together. Both men had pushed themselves to the very limit. Armstrong pulled ahead and looked over his shoulder at Marco. At tremendous cost Marco crossed the line first, taking his first win for thirteen months and eight days.

After the stage Pantani told Italian TV: 'I didn't like Armstrong's company. Armstrong's a great champion, but I'd have liked to have arrived alone.' Armstrong replied: 'I don't know what Pantani's thinking but ... he's just a little shit starter.' A feud began between the

Armstrong and Pantani at the limit on Mont Ventoux.
Marco said he won fair and square; Lance said it was a gift.

two men. Later, Pantani's team director Giuseppe Martinelli would say: 'Marco always respected Armstrong. The only thing he couldn't get over was Armstrong's speed. He said, "It isn't possible that, on all these climbs, he riders that much faster, given the effort I make."'

Pantani took the Alpine stage finishing at Courchevel, and leap-frogged into six place overall. Suddenly, anything seemed possible, and the following day, 130 kilometres from the finish line at Morzine, Marco launched an impossible attack. The move put Armstrong in crisis; bewildered by the madness of Marco's attack, he too suffered a physical breakdown, one of only two in his seven-year domination of the Tour de France. He even called his adviser Michele Ferrari, Conconi's old associate, for tactical advice. This time, though, Pantani's madness ended in failure. Never more than two minutes ahead of the main group, he began to suffer stomach cramps, which ended his attack. But Pantani's unpredictability had lost Armstrong one minute thirty-seven seconds to Ullrich, one minute thirty-four to Roberto Heras, and fifty seconds to Joseba Beloki. That evening Armstrong described the stage as 'the most difficult day of my life.'

The final leg of Armstrong's challenge was the time-trial from Freiburg to Mulhouse, passing through Merdingen, Ullrich's hometown. Along roads lined with Ullrich supporters, in an hour-long race, Armstrong vanquished his rival by twenty-five seconds.

2000			**3,866.5 km**
Podium	Nationality	Time	Av speed (kph)
1st Lance Armstrong	USA	92h 33m 8s	41.78
2nd Jan Ullrich	Germany	+6m 2s	
3rd Joseba Beloki	Spain	+10m 4s	
Mountains: Santiago Botero	Colombia		
Green jersey: Erik Zabel	Germany		

2001 **The Look**

Sport's proximity to insanity is little trumpeted. As well as organs of exceptional strength and efficiency, champions need an ice-cold ruthlessness bordering on the psychopathic – not to mention the sheer lunatic recklessness required to ride down mountains at 100 kilometres an hour. In 2001, more than any other year, Armstrong proved he had them all.

The defining moment of the 2001 Tour took place, as it so often did, on the stage of the first mountain finish. For a few, fleeting minutes, and the only time in their respective careers, Armstrong and Ullrich were riding together, but the Texan had nearly run out of teammates, and Ullrich was surrounded by them. They had to contend, not just with each other, but with thirteen lesser riders who had ridden away to a thirty-five-minute advantage two days before. One of them, a Kazakh named Kivilev, was an excellent climber, potentially capable of surpassing Claudio Chiappucci's 1990 performance and matching Walkowiak's achievement in 1956. On the morning of stage ten, Armstrong commented: 'We might have made a very big mistake the other day.'

Miserable weather during week one had left Armstrong's team in trouble. Two riders had fallen during the team time-trial, and several were suffering cuts, bruises, and tendinitis. With the race entering its first major day in the Alps, Armstrong, with his team director Johan Bruyneel, plotted to feign illness until the final climb, hoping to wear Ullrich's team out by bluffing them into setting the tempo.

Sure enough, on the Col du Madeleine, Kevin Livingston and Andreas Klöden upped the pace on Ullrich's command. On the Col du Glandon, Livingston, Klöden and Vinokourov paced Ullrich,

Stage 14, Luz-Ardiden: Jan Ullrich can't shake Lance Armstrong off.

while only Chechu Rubiera was on hand to help Armstrong. In Armstrong's account: 'Ullrich and his teammates took the bait – they surged to the front and started riding at a hot tempo, excited. Clearly, they had gotten the message that I was hurting. They responded exactly as Johan had predicted they would.'

But Jan Ullrich gives a different version of events: 'Armstrong told the story as if we'd fallen for his brilliant bluff... But when Rudy Pevenage switched the radio on that morning, he stumbled across the frequency of the US Postal team...We learned that US Postal, for their part, had secretly listened in to our radio communications. So we always knew what Armstrong's real intentions were.'

On the final climb up to Alpe d'Huez, as the grade steepened, Armstrong's teammate Rubiera accelerated. After a kilometre, Rubiera pulled off, leaving Armstrong in the lead. At that moment, he looked over his shoulder. 'I stared into Ullrich's sunglasses for a long moment. What I saw convinced me to make my move.'

Armstrong reached the top two minutes before Ullrich, with a brilliant Basque climber named Joseba Beloki in third place. The following day, a mountain time-trial, finished Armstrong, Ullrich, Beloki too, and so did stage thirteen, up to the ski station at Saint-Lary Soulan. It was sport as a repeatable scientific experiment, producing the same result each time.

At Saint-Lary Soulan Armstrong finally pulled the yellow jersey on, rectifying stage eight's thirty-five-minute mistake. In admiration of the American, a French writer, Gérard Rondeau, commented: 'Where others ride with nothing but their legs, Armstrong, taciturn, sure of himself, rides with doctors, dieticians, IT experts, masseurs, chiropractors, strategists, specialists, statisticians, tacticians, psychologists. He is inventing a new era: he has added Clausewitz (poor Ullrich!) to the reading matter of people more used to comic books.'

It was true: Armstrong was changing the sport. But, as well as riding a good race, he could also talk one.

2001 — 3,660.2 km

	Podium	Nationality	Time	Av speed (kph)
1st	Lance Armstrong	USA	86h 17m 28s	42.42
2nd	Jan Ullrich	Germany	+6m 44s	
3rd	Joseba Beloki	Spain	+9m 5s	
Mountains: Laurent Jalabert		France		
Green jersey: Erik Zabel		Germany		

2002 Take the 'A' Train

The days when Tour riders took the train came back in 2002. Lance Armstrong's US Postal Service team mimicked the tactics of sprinters like Rik Van Looy and Mario Cipollini. Armstrong's men were paid to transfer energy from their muscles into the surrounding atmosphere, tunnelling into the still air and creating a moving stream in their wake. In the last carriage but one of this speeding express train, Armstrong sat, watching, biding his time, deciding when to attack.

The last but one, because in 2001 Armstrong had snapped up Roberto Heras, the second-best climber in the sport, and his job was to ride behind the Texan and make sure no one rode into him. Days before the Tour, another teammate, an ex-mountain biker named Floyd Landis, had finished second in the week-long Dauphiné Libéré. Armstrong had won it. No one really believed they stood a chance against Armstrong anyway – and that was before he assembled the strongest possible team around him.

His number one rival responded with his customary single-mindedness. In the winter, the injury that had kept Jan Ullrich out of the 1999 Tour flared up. After treatment, he sabotaged his recovery by overtraining. Then, on 1 May, he had a few glasses too many, went for a night on the town, and drink-drove his Porsche into a bicycle rank outside Freiburg station. By then, it was clear his knee would not be ready, and he announced he'd miss the Tour.

Second in the Prologue behind Armstrong was Laurent Jalabert. It wasn't quite the highpoint of his Tour: unable to compete with Armstrong, Jalabert targeted the mountains competition, and exposed it for what it was: no longer the red polka dot endorsement of the world's best climber, but the red-nosed, bald-pated, baggy-trousered clown's costume of the most comic breakaway act.

As Armstrong went about his task with ruthless professionalism, the clowning carried on around him. Colombia's Santiago Botero beat him by eleven seconds in the first long time-trial. The yellow jersey at the time, Beloki's Basque teammate Igor González de Galdeano, whispered to the press that Armstrong was looking vulnerable. 'The Tour has changed,' he said. Then the anti-dopers found 1,346 nanograms of salbutamol in Igor's urine. The limit was 1,000, but Igor had a medical certificate. A row began over whether he should be allowed to continue in the race, but since the row outlasted the race, he did anyway.

Armstrong's only vulnerability was to his teammate Heras. On the way to the first uphill finish of the Tour, at La Mongie, halfway up

**The Blue Train sweeps through Europe with Captain America
biding his time in the penultimate carriage...**

the Tourmalet, first Hincapie, then Rubiera, and finally Heras led Armstrong up the climb at ever-increasing speeds, until Armstrong got into a slanging match with Bruyneel: Lance was telling Heras to take it easy, Bruyneel was telling him to get a move on. 'Goddammit, Johan, tell him to slow down!' Only Beloki could stay with Armstrong and his teammate, and even he could do nothing when Armstrong powered past, fifty yards from the line, to win the stage and take over the yellow jersey. The next day, another stage with an uphill finish, this time at Plateau de Beille, the blue train made a repeat performance. This time, Armstrong's domestique Roberto Heras beat his greatest rival, Beloki, into third place: not content with winning, Armstrong's dominance was becoming despotic.

Beloki was not good enough to worry Armstrong, but untouchable by anyone else. The battle for third place, however, was lively. Botero had slipped out of contention on Mont Ventoux, where he lost a quarter of an hour, then slipped back in again at Les Deux Alpes, where he won the stage in spectacular style. But his main rival was a Lithuanian, Raimundas Rumsas, more consistent in the mountains, and, in the final time trial, nearly a minute and a half faster than the Colombian.

Alas, Rumsas' fate proves doping ruins your sense of taste. On Sunday 29 July, as he prepared to celebrate finishing on the podium of the Tour de France, French customs officers arrested his wife near Chamonix in the French Alps. Her car was crammed with

---

Armstrong to Heras:
'Take it easy, take it easy.'
Bruyneel to Heras:
'Faster, faster.'
Armstrong to Heras:
'Take it easy, take it easy.'
Bruyneel to Heras:
'Faster, faster.'
Armstrong to Bruyneel:
'Goddammit, Johan, tell him to slow down!'
Who says radio communication makes life easier?

Armstrong leads Beloki, with Raimundas Rumsas just behind – and that's the way it would finish.

'medications that could be considered as doping products'. According to customs – and according to custom – Raimundas Rumsas blamed the doping products in his wife's car to his ill mother-in-law. How tasteless is that? Oh yes, a year later, during the 2003 Tour of Italy, Rumsas tested positive for EPO.

2002				3,483 km
	Podium	Nationality	Time	Av speed (kph)
1st	Lance Armstrong	USA	82h 5m 12s	42.43
2nd	Joseba Beloki	Spain	+7m 17s	
3rd	Raimundas Rumsas	Lithuania	+8m 17s	
Mountains: Laurent Jalabert		France		
Green jersey: Robbie McEwen		Australia		

2003 Pride after a Fall

In 2003, Ullrich was back – although, with Ullrich, it was never quite that simple. He'd turned his back on Deutsche Telekom's lavish sponsorship, and managed to find himself a team that went bankrupt before the Tour had even begun. Luckily, his bike supplier, Bianchi, stepped in, convinced that this could be Ullrich's year. It so nearly was.

The 2003 Tour was the Centenary edition. It was also Armstrong's chance to join an elite club, with Anquetil, Merckx, Hinault and Induráin: the five-timers. In the spring, Armstrong was voted World Sportsman of the Year. In his pre-race press conference, he eulogised the Tour: 'I think the race has everything. I think it has difficulty. It has joy. It has excitement. It even has death.' Not this year, although Armstrong's former domestique Tyler Hamilton, now leading the team founded by 1996 winner Bjarne Riis, contrived to break his collarbone in a mass fall on stage one. Amazingly, he rode on, attacked, won a mountain stage and finished fourth. Deutsche Telekom was led by a Kazakh, Alexander Vinokourov, who outrode Armstrong and Ullrich on stage eight to Alpe d'Huez, the following day to Gap, and again on stage fourteen through the Pyrenees to Loudenvielle. By then, Joseba Beloki had fallen and fractured his femur. Armstrong narrowly avoided him, swerved off the road, ploughed across a field, dropped back into the leading group one hairpin down the mountain and didn't even puncture. Someone up there was smiling on him.

The fire inside Armstrong continued to burn: perhaps even to the point of dehydration during the first long time-trial. Armstrong's face was covered with salt as he finished the stage; he'd been unable

The face of a man who has given everything: Lance saves Tour number five.

to drink, and came close to cracking. He still finished second, but Ullrich beat him by a minute and thirty-six seconds. If the feat could be repeated, the German might just have won his second Tour.

Two days later – sixteen days, sixty-one hours of racing, into the Tour – just eighteen seconds separated Armstrong, Ullrich and Vinokourov. It had never been this close!

Stage fifteen took them over the Col d'Aspin and the towering Tourmalet, down to the village of Luz-Saint-Sauveur, then up fifteen writhing kilometres to the finish line at the ski resort of Luz-Ardiden. It was one of most unforgettable stages in Tour history.

On the Tourmalet, Ullrich, like a power-lifter tensed for the weight, accelerated with incredible power. Armstrong elected to follow him at a distance. When the German began to run out of clout, Armstrong reeled him in. Afterwards, he ridiculed his rival: 'Tactically, it was not the time to go.' But Ullrich defended his tactics: 'On the Tourmalet, I felt very good. I launched a surprise

'No one trains like me. No one rides like me.
This jersey's mine. I live for this jersey. It's my life.
No one's taking it away from me while I'm around.
This fucking jersey's mine.'

Lance Armstrong, after his victory at Luz-Ardiden

attack, exactly in Armstrong's style. Unfortunately it wasn't one of Armstrong's bad days. If he'd collapsed, probably everyone would have talked about Jan Ullrich's fantastic attack.'

Vinokourov had been dropped on the climb, but re-joined Armstrong and Ullrich on the descent. As soon as the final climb began, Iban Mayo jumped out of the group. Reacting immediately, Armstrong flashed past him into a three-length lead, still bobbing over the saddle. Mayo somehow wrung more speed from his slight physique, piloting Ullrich into Armstrong's slipstream. The trio was fifty seconds clear of the chasing group.

A yellow blur appeared beside Armstrong's right hand: a replica feedbag, attached to a little boy in a green T-shirt and blue-peaked baseball hat. If the boy had only opened his hand and surrendered his souvenir, the moment would have passed. But the kid, like everyone else, had been standing there for hours in the hope of a glimpse of the riders as they sped past. Losing his memento would mean losing any certainty that he'd witnessed the Tour de France at all. He held tight. The strap tightened over Armstrong's brake lever, and he was suddenly in free fall. Before he hit the ground, Mayo ran into his rear wheel, and came to a halt sitting upright, beside Armstrong. Ullrich swerved around them, and continued climbing.

Armstrong's chain was jammed. It took him nearly half a minute to pull it free. The riders ahead of him were stretched out along seventy metres of the climb. Ullrich's version of waiting was so fast Vinokourov had to stand on the pedals to keep up.

That was fall number one. Fall number two came seconds later: Armstrong's right foot slipped out of the pedal, and his sternum struck the handlebars. He recovered, clicked into the pedals again, and began to pedal, staring down at his feet in disbelief. Then Mayo attacked again, and Armstrong responded in an exact repetition of what had taken place four minutes before. Armstrong rode straight past Mayo and was on his own, heading for the summit.

On the finish line at Luz-Ardiden, he threw his bike forward like a sprinter desperate to gain a few extra centimetres. His eyes, sunken into the skull, were small and crossed; deep furrows scarred his cheek bones. Armstrong had gained fifty-two seconds on Ullrich – less than 300 metres. Vinokourov came in two minutes, seven seconds behind.

After the stage, Lance stormed up and down the aisle of the team bus, punching the seats and shouting, 'No one trains like me. No one rides like me. This jersey's mine. I live for this jersey. It's my life. No one's taking it away from me... This fucking jersey's mine.'

The fall led to a difference of opinion between Armstrong and Ullrich. The German claimed he had slowed to allow the American time to recover: 'I had seconds to decide what to do. It was instinct: I had no choice. I waited.' Lance initially accepted Jan's story, and thanked him for his good manners. Later, he wasn't so sure: 'I'm not so sure he did wait. In replays, he seems to me to be riding race tempo.' Whatever the truth, the Centenary Tour had been a truly Desgrangian affair: hard-fought, and replete with terrible collapses, bitter argument and boys' own heroics.

2003   3664 km

	Podium	Nationality	Time	Av speed (kph)
1st	Lance Armstrong	USA	83h 41m 12s	43.78
2nd	Jan Ullrich	Germany	+1m 1s	
3rd	Alexander Vinokourov	Khazakstan	+4m 14s	
Mountains: Richard Virenque		France		
Green jersey: Baden Cooke		Australia		

2004 'I Can Destroy You'

By 2004, Lance Armstrong's second book was on the shelves. 'When your life is constantly measured, and you're compensated for it, as an athlete is,' he wrote, 'you can get confused and start equating winning with a good and happy life.' Was it the preamble to some sort of confession? Well, yes, actually – his relentless dedication had taken its toll on his marriage. But, as the Tour came round, cycling was reeling from other sorts of suspicion.

Lance Armstrong had raised millions of dollars for cancer research and helped thousands of cancer patients, often quietly, out of the public eye. He was an inspiration to people all over the world. He'd been invited to downtown Manhattan in the days after 9/11 to gee up the firemen. He was instantly recognisable, and fantastically rich (he was said to be due a bonus of $10 million from his team alone if he won the 2004 Tour, more from the likes of Nike, Trek and Oakley). He was also the best cyclist on earth. But he received no gifts from two respected sports journalists who, on 15 June 2004, published *LA Confidentiel*, a book that promised, but didn't quite deliver, revelations about Lance Armstrong and doping. Available only in French, the book provided hundreds of pages of inconclusive, circumstantial evidence, but absolutely nothing of any substance. On the cover was a quote from Greg LeMond: 'If Lance is clean, it's the greatest comeback in the history of sport. If he isn't, it would be the greatest fraud.'

> 'If Lance is clean, it's the greatest comeback in the history of sport. If he isn't, it would be the greatest fraud.'
>
> Greg LeMond

Seven days later, the Scottish rider David Millar was taken in for questioning by French police. Like a gentleman-spy, he'd cut a cavity out of a book, hidden two empty EPO syringes inside, and kept the book on his shelves at home in Biarritz. A squad of forensic speed-readers bent on identifying the literary influences of the modern stage racer had burst into his flat, raided the bookshelves and unearthed the incriminating tome. Millar admitted to taking three one-week courses of the drug, a semi-confession for which he eventually took a two-year rap. Meanwhile, the scandal rumbled on, and the serpent of doping twisted itself inextricably into the DNA of professional cycling.

Whatever else was on the market, doping accusations seemed to have a wonderful performance enhancing effect on Lance Armstrong. The harder things got, the more he enjoyed himself – and that included rain and cold. His rivals just fell away. The first victim was Iban Mayo, the Basque mountain specialist. He fell and lost four minutes on stage three, before a cobblestone stretch that resembled the Passage du Gois that had undone Alex Zülle in 1999. On stage six, Tyler Hamilton catapulted into the air and came to earth spine-first. Later, he complained: 'This isn't an injury. This is damage. I'm going to feel this the rest of my life.'

> 'This isn't an injury. This is damage. I'm going to feel this the rest of my life.'
> Tyler Hamilton, after his fall on stage three

As in 2002, the first uphill finish of the Tour took the riders over the Col d'Aspin and halfway up the Tourmalet to La Mongie. Hamilton dropped away from the leading group on the Col d'Aspin. He'd step off the following day. They don't come harder than Hamilton, a man used to shrugging off the pain of broken bones (after the 2002 Tour of Italy, where he finished second, despite breaking his shoulder in a fall, he had to have eleven teeth recapped

Bad blood: Lance Armstrong spikes Filippo Simeoni's breakaway.

after grinding them down in pain). But even Hamilton had a soft centre, and when his dog Tugboat died, he abandoned, heartbroken.

By then, everyone but Armstrong had given up all hope. As Armstrong's teammate José Azevedo worked the pace, Ullrich was the next to peel off, undone by the speed, five and a half kilometres from La Mongie. By the time Azevedo had finished, Armstrong and Ivan Basso were riding fast, but not frantically, at the front. With no discernible attack, those behind them – Santos González, Mayo, Oscar Pereiro, Ullrich's teammate Klöden, Carlos Sastre – quietly ran out of oomph. Basso took the stage. Armstrong followed him in. Barring spontaneous combustion, the Tour was his – and he hadn't even attacked.

On stage seventeen, Armstrong encouraged his mountain domestique, Floyd Landis, to try for the stage win. But when Ullrich's teammate Andreas Klöden got away, Armstrong chased in Merckxian style – no gifts – and took a stage win he didn't need.

Armstrong's only other decisive attack of the Tour had nothing to do with winning it. After decisive wins in stages fifteen, sixteen and seventeen, Armstrong was prepared to allow a breakaway to form in stage eighteen. The one condition was that it shouldn't include Filippo Simeoni, a not-very-good Italian rider who'd testified against Armstrong's former training advisor, Dr Michele Ferrari, and sued Armstrong for defamation when Armstrong called him a liar. When Simeoni attacked, Armstrong was on his wheel in an instant. He even led him up to the breakaway, where he said something like, 'If he stays, I stay.' That, of course, guaranteed the breakaway would be chased down. Simeoni was forced to desist. In Simeoni's version, on the way back to the peloton, Armstrong told him: 'You made a mistake to speak against Ferrari, and you made a mistake to take legal action against me. I have money, time, and lawyers. I can destroy you.'

In the final time-trial the next day, he did – and, more to the point, he destroyed Ullrich, Klöden, and Basso, to win Tour number six.

> **'You made a mistake to speak against Ferrari, and you made a mistake to take legal action against me. I have money, time, and lawyers. I can destroy you.'**
>
> Lance Armstrong tackles Filippo Simeoni

2004				3,390.8 km
	Podium	Nationality	Time	Av speed (kph)
1st	Lance Armstrong	USA	83h 36m 2s	40.56
2nd	Andreas Klöden	Germany	+6m 38s	
3rd	Ivan Basso	Italy	+6m 59s	
Mountains: Richard Virenque		France		
Green jersey: Robbie McEwen		Australia		

2005
Magnificent Seven

The prickly, powder-keg Armstrong came after
LeMond and Induráin, but he took after Bernard
Hinault. The killer glance Armstrong flashed at
Ullrich on Alpe d'Huez in 2001 was the one Hinault
had flashed on the climb up to Le Pleynet in 1981.
Hinault once said: 'I race to win, not to please people.
I'm the one who rides. If someone thinks he can do
it better, let him get a bike.' Armstrong's version was:
'I'm here to win, not to enter a popularity competition.'
The difference between them was this: seven minus five.

Before Armstrong, four men had won five Tours, and only one of
them five in a row. Six had been unthinkable: seven was beyond the
threshold of thinkability. Seven in a row was unthinkably
unthinkable. Seven was for wonders of the world, or cardinal
virtues. Or deadly sins – speaking of which, by the summer of 2005,
Tyler Hamilton had disappeared from professional cycling in yet
another drugs scandal, but not without expanding the conceptual
range of excuse making. No doped up mothers-in-law or pets for
Tyler: he claimed he had a 'vanishing twin' who had deposited
incriminating, third-party red cells in his blood while he was still in
the womb, and then disappeared in the first trimester of pregnancy.
In other words, he was a human chimera. The aura of science fiction
dissipated the following summer, when Spanish police found
documents that proved Hamilton had been using blood
transfusions, EPO, growth hormone, insulin, anabolic steroids, and

**Lance Armstrong bears down on Jan Ullrich in stage one's time-trial.
Bar 3,000-odd kilometres left to ride, the Tour was already over.**

masking agents. It'll be quite an autobiography. Shame Peter Cook got to the obvious title first: 'Tragically, I was an only twin.'

Reality, once described by Armstrong's close friend Robin Williams as 'just a crutch for people who can't cope with drugs', was quickly unbearable for Jan Ullrich. Stage one of the 2005 Tour was a twenty-kilometre time-trial. Ullrich started a minute before Armstrong – and saw the American fly past him, and finish six seconds before him. Armstrong didn't win the stage: that honour went to Dave Zabriskie, a Salt Lake City Mormon. At least we can be sure he wasn't blood-doping.

Zabriskie held the yellow jersey for three days, then Armstrong took over. He was one year older, of course, and oddly, his team had never been weaker. Time was no kinder to Ullrich, of course, but he had one of the strongest teams ever to start the Tour, with Klöden (second the previous year) and Vinokourov (third in 2003) on the same side – or, if not on the same side, in the same colours, because instead of combining with his teammates to attack Armstrong, Ullrich, defeated by the Texan before the race had even started, rode against Vinokourov the moment there was the suggestion of a hill.

In fact, the strongest climbers, Ivan Basso and a Dane named Michael Rasmussen, rode at exactly the pace Armstrong liked, but no faster. That meant he could use them as his mountain domestiques.

> '**I wanted to go out on top. That was the only incentive and that was the only pressure.**'
> Lance Armstrong

Armstrong duly sent his real domestiques off to win stages. George Hincapie did so at Saint-Lary Soulan, and Paolo Savoldelli celebrated three days later at Revel. And, since Basso was a poor time-triallist, and Rasmussen a positively abysmal one, they presented no threat to the reigning champion. On the final time-trial, the Dane had two human cannon-style falls, changed bikes three times, maybe four, and conceded seven minutes forty-seven seconds to Armstrong. It cost him his place on the podium: he finished the Tour back in seventh place.

The remarkable Lance Armstrong, the greatest Tour champion in history, retired the day he won his seventh Tour. 'If you ever get a second chance in life for something, you've got to go all the way,' he used to say. But how far was 'all the way'? On 23 August 2005, *L'Équipe* alleged that analysis of samples frozen during the 1999

Tour indicated EPO use by Lance Armstrong. The test was unofficial, the science was experimental, and the news breached every canon of confidentiality. There was no mechanism for corroborating the analysis, or for defending the rights of the defendant. Armstrong lost nothing, but part of his reputation. The Tour de France, wedged into a claustrophobic no man's land between unproven suspicions and unconvincing denials, carried on regardless, under the impetus of history.

In September 2005, yet another of Armstrong's former teammates, Roberto Heras, had problems with the anti-doping movement. He'd won his fourth Tour of Spain, a new record, before testing positive for EPO. Fourteen months later, Heras was complaining that his lawyer never received important procedural information about the counter analysis – 'I feel defenceless.'

Some said the anti-doping system was a closed, quasi-judicial system with too few checks and balances. They said authorities were acting as prosecutor, judge and jury, enforcing rules they had written for their own benefit, punishing violations based on sometimes questionable scientific tests that they had developed and certified, and barring virtually all outside appeals or challenges. Imagine a world in which any accusation can be made and any defence proffered, no matter how crackpot and unsubstantiated. Welcome to the world of sport.

2005 — 3,607 km

	Podium	Nationality	Time	Av speed (kph)
1st	Lance Armstrong	USA	86h 15m 2s	41.82
2nd	Ivan Basso	Italy	+4m 40s	
3rd	Jan Ullrich	Germany	+6m 21s	
Mountains: M. Rasmussen		Denmark		
Green jersey: Thor Hushovd		Norway		

2006 Meltdown

Robin Williams used to call Armstrong the 'Uniballer', but after seven years of testicular deficiency, the 2006 Tour was to suffer an over-abundance, not of testicles as such, but of the hormone they produce. The result was a debacle, although, seen through its own contentious history, it was a classic, with all the elements that the Tour has always been about, magnified to grotesque proportions.

Even before it was underway, it was mired in scandal. On 23 May, Spanish police searched two Madrid apartments, finding two fridges and a two-hundred litre refrigerated chest containing ninety-six bags of frozen concentrates of blood solids, and twenty bags of frozen plasma – a small hospital, in short, run by Eufemiano Fuentes, a Madrid doctor whose clients include athletes in every sport, with code names that looked easy to decipher.

The raid, part of a long-running Spanish investigation called Operation Puerto, also found transfusion equipment and a mobile pharmacy of performance enhancing drugs. Whatever Fuentes was charging, it wasn't for top-quality gear. The EPO he stocked wasn't the good stuff: it came from clandestine laboratories in China, selling through the internet. Police even found a blood dialysis preparation that had been withdrawn from the market because it was linked with cases of CJD.

Two days after the police submitted their report, Germany's Jan Ullrich and Ivan Basso of Italy reached the Tour start at Strasbourg for their pre-race medicals, but on the morning of Friday 30 June, the report outlining the case reached Strasbourg. First to go, under pressure from his sponsor T-mobile, was the 1997 winner.

By lunchtime Ivan Basso was gone too. Like Ullrich, innocent until proven guilty – but sufficiently implicated by the Spanish police report to be unwelcome at the Tour. They were quickly joined by Francisco Mancebo, leader of the AG2R team, and no fewer than five of the Astana-Würth squad including Australia's Allan Davis and Spain's Joseba Beloki. That effectively disqualified the whole team, something the Tour had been hoping to do ever since Manolo Sáiz, the man who owned it and ran it, was arrested as part of the original police raid. With Astana-Würth went another Tour favourite: Alexander Vinokourov, implicated nowhere, but caught in the crossfire.

So, thirteen riders out – four of the top five in the previous Tour, and the winners of the latest tours of Spain and Italy – plus the entire Communidad Valenciana team who had their invitation withdrawn on June the thirteenth. Sure enough, after their exclusion, the entire Communidad Valenciana team was given official notification by the Spanish police that none of their riders were under investigation. By then, however, they'd lost their place on the Tour, their sponsor, and their livelihood. It was suddenly clear as mud.

The race, therefore, inherited a new favourite: Floyd Landis, Armstrong's former mountain lieutenant – a role once filled by another client of Dr Fuentes, the now disgraced Tyler Hamilton. Landis's stock rose on the first rest day when he embraced the time-honored convention among U.S. contenders by revealing a debilitating illness to be overcome if he was to win the Tour: in his case, avascular necrosis, a degenerative bone condition caused by an injury three and a half years before. He would be undergoing a hip replacement after the Tour, but until then, he would continue to battle grinding arthritic pain.

It didn't stop him taking the yellow jersey on stage eleven. However, it wasn't avascular necrosis, but something resembling early-onset dementia that led him to give the jersey away two days

**Floyd Landis carries off one of the great attacks in Tour history
– believe it or not...**

later. Six riders, among them the Spaniard Oscar Pereiro, tenth in the 2005 Tour, were allowed to ride away for 207 kilometres and build up a lead of more than half an hour. It was Walkowiak squared – cubed – and presented Pereiro with the race lead.

Landis took it back on Alpe d'Huez, but only by ten seconds, and then, disaster! At La Toussuire, on stage sixteen, he ran out of juice and lost eight minutes, ten seconds to Pereiro. From first, Landis dropped to eleventh overall. The Tour had gone. The bookmakers agreed: Landis was now 75 to one to win the Tour, odds no one would take on – except Eddy Merckx, whose son Axel was a member of Landis's team. Eddy thought it was worth 100 euros.

In Landis's version of events, he spent the night on the lash, knocking back enough whisky and beer to devastate his hormonal balance. Then, next day, presumably with the mother of all hangovers, he attacked alone, five cols from the finish, and held off the peloton for seventy-five miles. It was an astonishing display, a monumental fightback. Admittedly, he was assisted by Bjarne Riis's Team CSC and Olaf Ludwig's T-Mobile, who started the chase too late. But Landis still won the stage by five minutes, forty-two seconds. It

> **'I don't expect to win the Tour at this point, it's not easy to get back eight minutes. But I'll keep fighting – it's not over yet.'**
> Floyd Landis after his stage sixteen disaster.

recalled Merckx's 1969 ride to Mourenx-Ville Nouvelle, and it moved him to within half a minute of Pereiro. In the final time trial, he made up those thirty seconds and added another minute. Eddy Merckx was quids in – and Landis had become the third American to win the Tour.

The Wednesday after he celebrated victory on the Champs Élysées, his team was informed that Landis had failed the first part of an anti-doping test.

The weeks passed, and the case took on bizarre, sometimes macabre overtones. In mid-August, Landis's friend and father-in-law David Witt committed suicide. Witt had been a keen amateur cyclist, and he had helped Landis, a former mountain biker, convert to road racing. In mid-October, Landis published hundreds of pages of complex analytical documents on the internet, in an apparent public appeal for assistance.

A month later, hackers broke into the computers at the French laboratory where Landis's sample had been analysed, and sent emails to the International Olympic Committee and the World Anti-Doping Agency, claiming to blow the whistle on systematic analytical blunders.

> **'Floyd went off like a motorbike, unbelievable! He was doing forty kilometres an hour uphill! That he's able to rebound like this is fantastic.'**
> Michael Rogers on Landis's stage seventeen triumph.

'I mean, it was eleven to one! You'd think he'd be violating every virgin within 100 miles. How does he even get on his bicycle?'

World Anti-Doping Agency chief Dick Pound is surprised by Floyd Landis's testosterone levels

The messages were reportedly in poor French, with mistakes typical of an English-speaker. Then, another first: the Floyd Fairness Fund was established to allow his fans to pay Floyd's legal fees. Unbelievable!

While the Landis case descended into farce, Lance Armstrong's old team-mate Frankie Andreu made a David Millar-esque confession that he'd used EPO in 1999, before – but not during – the Tour de France. Jesper Skibby, a stage winner in 1993, did the same in his autobiography, published in December 2006. Then, Johan Museeuw, a stage winner in 1990, and Frank Vandenbrouke, another of Belgium's finest riders in the 1990s, 'fessed up.

Was cycling about to implode and disappear as a credible elite sport? There was talk of stripping it of its Olympic status. But if cycling was full of hypocrisy, so too were neighbouring sports. The clients of Eufemiano Fuentes were reported to include footballers and tennis players, as well as track and field athletes. Where was their public shaming? Where were their confessions? Will their names ever be known?

2006				3,607 km
Podium	Nationality	Time		Av speed (kph)
1st Floyd Landis	USA	89h 39m 30s		40.59
2nd Oscar Pereiro	Spain	+57s		
3rd Andreas Klöden	Germany	+1m 29s		
Mountains: M. Rasmussen	Denmark			
Green jersey: Robbie McEwen	Australia			

2007 Chicken Run

446 days after the 2006 Tour de France started
in Strasbourg, Oscar Pereiro finally won it. It was
20 September 2007, the day the United States
Anti-Doping Agency declared Floyd Landis guilty
of doping, and he was stripped of victory in the
2006 Tour. By then, another Tour had ended in
confusion, controversy and suspicion.

The 2007 Tour was unusual in that most of the action happened on
a rest day. It had started in London where, by a miracle, months of
rainstorms gave way to a weekend of glorious sunshine, allowing
Fabien Cancellara to dart past the Houses of Parliament and
through Hyde Park to win the prologue on The Mall, within sight
of Buckingham Palace. Three days later, a stage win helped him
keep the yellow jersey all the way to the mountains over a series of
slow, sluggish stages that suggested the Tour truly had entered an
age when energy was clean, and therefore in limited supply. By the
time the battle for the general classification began, Alexander
Vinokourov was out of it: a fall on stage five meant stitches to both
knees. He soldiered on, eventually consoling himself with two stage
wins, the first in the time trial around Albi on stage thirteen and the
second two days later at the end of a gruelling mountain stage
ending in Loudenvielle-Le Louron. Not for the first time, the
Kazakh seemed to embody the spirit of the Tour.

Meanwhile, on stage eight up to Tignes in the Alps, the Dane
Michael Rasmussen, nicknamed 'Chicken' for his resemblance to a
figure in Danish comic strip, had ridden, Landis-style, away from the
field, opening a three-minute gap on his nearest rival, the Spaniard
Alejandro Valverde. There was every possibility that Rasmussen had

**Even with the jury still out on the 2006 race, many felt it was only
a matter of time before the Tour tripped itself up in 2007...**

already done enough to win the Tour. Only little Alberto Contador,
riding his first Tour, offered any resistance. On the Plateau de Beille,
despite desperate accelerations to shake off Rasmussen, the Spaniard
cut a minute off Armstrong's record for the climb. It beggared belief.

Then, on the final rest day on the final Monday, the Tour
imploded. Four days earlier it had emerged that the Danish Cycling
Union had banned Rasmussen from the national squad just before
the Tour, after two missed anti-doping tests. A press conference was

called for the rest day. Rasmussen, no Armstrong, turned up with a lawyer who questioned the DCU's authority: Rasmussen, it transpired, had held a Mexican racing licence in 2005 and 2006, and a licence from Monaco in 2007. As Rasmussen admitted, neither authority had ever tested him.

It was a mess, and it seemed neither the cycling authorities, nor the other riders, could stop Rasmussen from winning the Tour. Then, as the conference ended, more bad news: tests had found someone else's blood coursing through Alexander Vinokourov's veins. The spirit of the Tour slipped away before the press reached his hotel.

While all this was going on, Davide Cassani, the ex-rider who now provided RAI's race analysis and colour commentary, inadvertently unjammed the Rasmussen predicament. During RAI's rest day programme, he said he had met Rasmussen training in the Italian Dolomites before the Tour. It had been raining, and Rasmussen had been riding for eight hours, since 6am. What a rider! He remembered the date precisely. It was 13 June. The problem was, Rasmussen had informed the UCI, and his team, that he would be at his wife's family home in Mexico on that date. Untruths had been told. A way out was found. With the Tour won, his team withdrew him from the race, although not before Rasmussen had won on the Aubisque.

The crisis could – should – have been forestalled. The UCI had failed to apply its own anti-doping code: 'In case of a recorded warning or a missed test in a period of forty-five days before the start of a Major Tour, the Rider is not allowed to participate in that Tour.' An independent investigation later found that Rasmussen had submitted incorrect whereabouts information three times between 4 and 29 June 2007, and in an additional instance he had failed to mention a change to his whereabouts altogether. But the UCI combined these four incidents into one single recorded warning. This was in addition to two earlier incidents, making six: if the rules had been applied, three should have meant a suspension. Instead, the Tour was in the world press again, for all the wrong reasons.

> '**The Rasmussen crap is typical. Now it screws us all. It's shit for him, it's shit for the Tour de France, and it's shit for us, the riders and the fans.**'
>
> David Millar

Rasmussen's departure left Alberto Contador, less than two minutes ahead of Australia's Cadel Evans. Evans began the final time trial trying to catch Contador and win the Tour. He ended it trying the keep hold of second place as Levi Leipheimer, Contador's team-mate, won the stage with the time trial of his life. It was the closest Tour of all time, with the podium finishers within 31 seconds of each other.

The shadow of Operation Puerto meant the celebrations were muted. In the notorious files, now gathering dust on a Spanish prosecutor's shelf, Document 31 contained a list of doping products and practices beside the initials of the team riders, included entries for JJ and AC. Jörg Jaksche, Contador's old team-mate-turned-supergrass, admitted: 'I am the JJ in the document 31 and that I doped as stated there.' When asked whether AC could be Contador, Jaksche said: 'That would at least be a reasonable assumption.'

On the other hand, much of the problem lies with us, the sporting public. Dynamic movement induces a physiological and emotional response in us. If the dynamism is supercharged by effective doping products, this emotional contagion produces even greater euphoria. The athlete is doped, we are doped at one remove – and it feels fantastic! Like any drug-induced thrill, we don't want to kick it; we want another fix. Ask Juventus fans if they are ashamed of evidence of doping in their team in the late 1990s, when they were winning right, left and centre. 'Course not!

In this sense, doping is great news for the viewing public: the racing is more vigorous, there are fewer dead moments. A good spectacle means high viewing figures, which means sponsorship and the whole sporting machine working like a dream. The demand for products like EPO from highly-paid sports stars might even reduce their cost to hard-pressed health services. It just gets better.

Anti-doping is treated as a killjoy's attempt to spoil other people's fun, despite the fact that doping empowers organised crime, kills and maims sportsmen, and habituates youngsters to heavy pharmaceuticals. If the Tour took a body blow in 2006, it isn't clear whether it's because of the doping or because the race organisers had decided to fight back. Depending on who's judging, the Tour de France is damned if it resists doping, and damned if it doesn't.

Anyone who regarded the presumption of innocence as the cornerstone of civilized society must have found the exclusions before the 2006 Tour and during the 2007 Tour abominable. But how can event organisers wait for categorical proof before taking action? Doping, like terrorism, or rape, or under-aged crime, falls into a legal category in which normal safeguards simply don't work. A degree of surrender of medical secrecy is needed; further, legal standards have to be tweaked to admit clinical evidence that meets clinical, not legal, standards of proof. Sounds like the lawyers will be happy in coming years.

The question is, when the legal eagles have done their work, will the rest of us be any the wiser? Will we be able to call the Tour de France the supreme sporting event, or will it be the stuff of cheats? A hundred and four years on from its origins, it's clear that the Tour has always been both – and probably always will be.

2007 — 3,570 km

	Podium	Nationality	Time	Av speed (kph)
1st	Alberto Contador	Spain	91h 00m 26s	39.04
2nd	Cadel Evans	Australia	+23s	
3rd	Levi Leipheimer	USA	+31s	
Mountains: Mauricio Soler		Colombia		
Green jersey: Tom Boonen		Belgium		

A Word about the Statistics

The Tour de France takes a certain pride in filling its statistics sections with inexplicable eccentricities. The *Guide Historique* published each year by the Tour de France organisers is full of error and contradiction. So is the statistics section of the official Tour de France website, but its errors and contradictions are its own. In the high-pressure weeks of the Tour, journalists of all nations are driven insane.

I have taken three alternative publications as the most authoritative source for Tour statistics: *L'Équipe*'s own *Tour de France 100 Ans 1903-2003*, compiled by a committee of the best-known cycling writers in France (the English version is *The Official Tour De France Centennial 1903-2003*, edited by Nic Cheetham and myself); the *Tour Encyclopédie*, a compendium of statistics and nothing else which should be as accurate as you could hope for, and is endorsed by the Tour de France; and the reference section of Pierre Chany's *La Fabuleuse Histoire du Tour de France*, now continued by Thierry Cazeneuve. Chany covered every Tour from 1947 to 1995, most of that time for *L'Équipe*, the organ of the race organisers. Authoritative and punctilious, how could he get the statistics wrong?

There is a broad consensus over the lengths of twenty-seven of the ninety-three Tours to date. In order to avoid an unnecessary fight, I've gone along with the general consensus for those years. Elsewhere, *Tour de France 100 Ans* and the *Tour Encyclopédie* are frequently guilty of the same sin: they give the total distance of each Tour, but it disagrees with the sum total of the individual stage lengths. With wisdom and cowardice, Chany and Cazeneuve give stage lengths, but don't give any figure at all for total distance covered.

To make matters worse, these three sources often give different lengths for the same stage. *Tour de France 100 Ans* appears sometimes (but not always) to round up or down, at random, figures with fractions attached, for reasons of space. With others, the reasons behind these discrepancies are less obvious. Was stage six of the 1904 Tour 471, 460 or 462 kilometres? Our sources disagree. Chany attempts an explanation: 'Until 1927,' he writes, 'the distance announced rarely corresponded with the distances covered by the riders. From 1928, distances, timings and average speeds became more rigorous.' Er, not much more rigorous, they don't. The errors continue to the present: was stage thirteen of the 1998 Tour 206, 205.5 or 222 kilometres long? More disagreement.

A definitive solution is unlikely to exist. The Tour's pre-Second World War archives were destroyed during the conflict, and for the rest, there probably are no reliable statistics: if the Tour organisation itself has any, it would surely have published them by now.

For the period 1903 to 1985, I have correlated the stage lengths given by each source, and, allowing for deliberate typographic changes, where two out of the three figures agree, I have adopted that figure. In other cases, I have sought a fourth opinion from the *Almanacco del Ciclismo* by the Italian statistician Lamberto Righi, and a fifth opinion from *Velo Plus 1879-2003*, compiled by Harry Van Den Bremt and Paul De Keyser. If this hasn't resolved the issue, I've manufactured my own criteria, case by case: for instance, a distance that ends with a fraction of a kilometre is more likely to be accurate than a less precise distance, on the basis that I can't think of any reason to make up a fraction, and you're not likely to copy one in by mistake.

For later years, I have relied on Herman Harens's excellent *Wieler Jaarboek*, although even he isn't infallible. For some stages, one distance is given in the stage map and another in the results sheet. Even for the Armstrong Tours, there's no agreement over the total distance covered.

Anyway, armed with my new, painstakingly messed-about-with set of stage lengths – compiled with the help of my wife (tampering with Tour statistics is a game the family can play, and the results will still be as good as or better than the official collection) – and a database program devised by the collaborators of Mr Gates (run on a machine created by the colleagues of Mr Jobs), I have calculated the total length of each Tour, and then divided it by the time taken by the winner to produce the average speed. Which is why my statistics may disagree with other people's statistics. They're undoubtedly wrong (although not as wrong as theirs!), but that's the way the Tour works.

CREDITS

Special thanks to the following: Nic Cheetham, editor extraordinaire, Category 1 racer, and co-conspirator on many publishing adventures, past and future. My wife, Viviana, for help with the statistics section, and putting up with cycling and me. Anna Rendell-Knights and Bryans Knights, for a temporary roof, again, and so much else. Hugh Tisdale, for lending me a shelfload of books when mine were in storage. Edgar Medellín, Patricia Rivera, and their children Manuela and Pablo, for friendship.

1830 55th Street
Boulder, Colorado 80301-2700 USA
303/440-0601 · Fax 303/444-6788 ·
E-mail *velopress@competitorgroup.com*

Distributed in the United States and Canada by
Ingram Publisher Services.

Library of Congress Cataloging-in-Publication Data
Rendell, Matt.
    Blazing saddles : the cruel & unusual history of the Tour de France / Matt Rendell.
    p. cm.
    Includes bibliographical references.
ISBN 978-1-934030-25-7 (hardcover: alk. paper)
1. Tour de France (Bicycle race)—History. 2. Bicycle racing—Social aspects—France—History. I. Title.
GV1049.2.T68R46 2008
796.6'20944—dc22   2008002123

For information on purchasing VeloPress books, please call
800/234-8356 or visit www.velopress.com.

10 11 12 / 10 9 8 7 6 5 4